THE FABER BOOK OF IRISH VERSE

The Faber Book of
IRISH VERSE

edited by
JOHN MONTAGUE

FABER AND FABER
3 Queen Square
London

First published in 1974
by Faber and Faber Limited
3 Queen Square London WC1
Printed in Great Britain by
Robert MacLehose & Co Ltd Glasgow

ISBN 0 571 08393 5

Icham of Irlaunde
Ant of the holy londe of irlande
Gode sir pray ich ye
for of saynte charite
come ant daunce wyt me
in irlaunde.

14th century

Contents

*

In the Irish Grain

I

Gaelic is my national language but it is not my mother tongue.
W. B. YEATS

Every poet must dream of an ideal anthology of the poetry of his country, all the major objects declared and arranged. And no literature stands more in need of such a spring-cleaning than Irish: we have a tendency to applaud work for its local or national interest which has hampered any consistent attempt to apply poetic standards. There are good historical reasons for our uncertainty. After living abroad for over a decade, I came to the conclusion that, unlike prose writers, it is almost impossible for a poet to change languages. And yet this is what happened to Irish poetry in the nineteenth century, after the native tradition seemed to peter out in the doggerel of Raftery. So what we find in the work of Mangan, Walsh, Ferguson, Callinan is a racial sensibility striving to be reborn; is it strange that it comes through with a mournful sound, like a medium's wail? The true condition of Irish poetry in the nineteenth century is not silence, as Thomas Kinsella has argued, but mutilation. Loss is Mangan's only real theme, and in Ferguson's most original ballad (unfortunately too prolix to include here) the choice proposed to the Lynnot Clan, between castration and blindness, might be a symbol of the plight of a subject people; many of the later poets in Irish, from Carolan to Raftery, were physically blind, like the great blues-singers of the American South.

Since then it has been a natural practice for our poets to translate from the Irish. Even Yeats, who knew little, gave his early blessing to Hyde's *Lovesongs of Connacht* and Kuno Meyer's version of *The Vision of MacConglinne*, and forty years later corrected, then borrowed from, the early translations of O'Connor. After the foundation of the Republic, the majority of Irish poets (including those brought up in Ulster Catholic schools like myself and Seamus Heaney) became to some extent bilingual. But the anomaly remains: Irish literature in English is in the uneasy position that the larger part of its past lies in another language. That this could be a strength, I hope to show later, but in order to appreciate the dilemma properly, one must take up the story at the beginning, over a thousand years ago. The first thing that strikes one in early Irish literature is the importance attached to poetry. In an oral culture, the *scop* or *file* is a blend of historian and priest, a repository of information and magic. So we find Amergin, the official poet of the Milesians, apostrophizing Eire on behalf of his patrons; official Irish poetry may be said to have begun on that day. But devotion to Ireland is only part of a religious vision of the universe, an aspect of nature worship. Even if one hesitates before Robert Graves's imaginative reconstruction of 'The Song of Amergin' we have that prospect of a prelapsarian, almost Mohammedan paradise which is one of the recurrent themes of Irish poetry, from *The Wooing of Etain* through *The Vision of MacConglinne* to the Middle English *Land of Cockaigne*.

> *Steadily may Bran row !*
> *It is not far to the Land of Women ...*
> *(Version: Kuno Meyer)*

And here we should remark another aspect of early Irish poetry: it is the only literature in Europe, and perhaps in the world, where one finds a succession of women poets. Psychologically, a female poet has always seemed an absurdity, because of the necessarily intense relationship between the poet and the Muse. Why then did poetry always seem a natural mode of expression for gifted Irish women? I think this was because there was no discrimination against them: the first woman poet of whom we hear, Liadan of Corcaguiney, was a fully-qualified member of the poets' guild, which could mean as much as twelve years of study. It was as an equal that the poet Curithir wooed her, and though she drove him off, for religious reasons, her lament rings in our ears to this day.

There is a long line of such poems, culminating in the majestic 'Keen for Art O'Leary', composed by Dark Eileen, his wife, as late as the end of the eighteenth century. But the greatest of all the early Irish poems supposedly written by women is not a lament for one love, but for many. It might be more accurate to say that it is a lament for mankind in general, a piercing outcry against age which anticipates Villon by several centuries. Behind 'The Hag of Beare' lies the struggle between paganism and Christianity, between bodily pleasure and the doctrine of salvation through repentance. It is the ebb and flow of her misery, with sudden crests of remembered pride, which gives this dramatic lyric its structure; note how it ends as it begins, following the circular aesthetic of Irish art. A thousand years later, the same lonely note is heard, in Maurya's monologue, in 'Riders to the Sea'.

In suggesting that the quarrel between natural and organized religion, between instinct and restraint, is one of the major themes of Irish literature, I am not forgetting that the early Church, the civilization of 'the little monasteries' as Frank O'Connor called it, had the task of transcribing that oral culture:

'Now until the coming of Patrick speech was not suffered to be given in Ireland but to three; to a historian for narration and the relating of tales: to a poet for eulogy and satire; to a brehon lawyer for giving judgement according to the old tradition and precedent. But after the coming of Patrick every speech of these men is under the yoke of the white language, that is, the scriptures.'[1]

This historical irony is part of the fascination of the period, for while these monks might be ardent Christians, they were also increasingly conscious of being Irishmen. There are three kinds of manuscript which contain what might be called 'the Matter of Ireland'. The first are compilations by monks who often left Ireland to suffer 'the white martyrdom of exile'. On the margin of those portable libraries which they used to combat the ignorance of the Dark Ages a vernacular poem as delicate as a *haiku* will suddenly flower:

> *Ah, blackbird, it's well for you*
> *whatever bush holds your nest:*
> *little hermit who clinks no bell,*
> *your clear, sweet song brings rest.*
> (*Version: John Montague*)

But the majority of the manuscripts, like the Book of the Dun Cow and the Book of Leinster, were compiled in monastic settlements,

[1] *Ancient Laws*, i. 18.

like Clonmacnoise on the banks of the Shannon, or Terryglass on Lough Derg. In both of these manuscripts one finds versions of the Great Tain, the Cattle Raid of Cooley which is the nearest thing that Irish literature has to an epic. It makes a curious picture: a monk bending his head (tonsured across the front, in the Irish fashion) to copy the scandalous deeds of some Iron Age chariot-driven head-hunter like Cúchulain. Sometimes this backward look produced even stranger results: what is one to make of a rag-bag of history and myth like *The Book of Invasions* which records with dead-pan seriousness the first orgy in Ireland, the first adultery . . . ? Whatever about their Victorianized descendants, the original Irish were not puritans.

The third group of manuscripts is medieval, historically speaking. After the Norman invasion, and the collapse of the monastic schools, the duty of preserving Irish tradition returned again to the descendants of the *fili* who had held such an important place in pre-Christian society. The Speckled Book, the Yellow Book of Lecan and the Book of Ballymote were great compendia of Irish learning compiled for the use of the leading families by their poet scholars. During the long years when their powers had been reduced by the graphic skills of the monks, the poets must often have thought of revenge. The hero of *The Vision of MacConglinne* is a rogue cleric, and both it and *The Land of Cockaigne* might be regarded as satires on the fish and watercress austerity of Irish monastic life, while in that other medieval masterpiece, *The Frenzy of Sweeny* (which Robert Graves regards as the prime parable of the poetic nature), the poet-king takes to the trees after being cursed by a cleric.

To represent early Irish literature properly would require an anthology in itself; I have only been able to suggest leading themes, and outline a tradition. One constant, certainly, is an almost mystical feeling for nature: it is Columcille, not Patrick, who is the typical figure among the Irish saints, because he is a poet physically in love with his country, like Mad Sweeny, or the Fenians. Patrick is seen as old Tallcrook, a Romanizing bishop; the confrontation between him and Oisin, the last representative of the pagan world, is the dramatic centre of another medieval masterwork, *The Dialogue of the Old Men*, and of the Ossianic lays:

Stop, stop and listen for the bough top
Is whistling and the sun is brighter
Than God's own shadow in the cup now!
Forget the hour-bell. Mournful matins
Will sound, Patric, as well at nightfall.
(Version: Austin Clarke)

II

. . . were our fount of knowledge dry,
Who could to men of rank supply
The branches of their pedigree,
And Gaelic genealogy?
Version: LORD LONGFORD

Perhaps the most difficult form of Irish poetry for us to appreciate is the strict bardic, which extends from the thirteenth to the seventeenth century. A bard was a member of the now rigid professional literary caste; he did not even speak his poems in public but designated that duty to a *reacaire*, or reciter. His aim was to serve his prince, and his training in metrics was lengthy and strenuous. Seven winters in a dark room would be one way of describing it:

'Concerning the poetical Seminary or School . . . it was open only to such as were descended of Poets and reputed within their Tribes. . . . The Structure was a snug, low Hut, and beds in it at convenient Distances, each within a small Apartment. . . . No Windows to let in the Day, nor any Light at all us'd but that of Candles, and these brought in at a proper Season only . . . The reason of laying the Study aforesaid in the Dark was doubtless to avoid the Distraction which Light and the variety of Objects represented thereby commonly occasions.'[1]

But feeling can shine through the chainmail of technique, and in one of the most famous of the bardic poems, we find this training supporting a classic metaphor for human existence; that of Plato's cave. According to one of the leading scholars of the period, Gofraidh Fionn O'Dalaigh's poem on the child born in prison

---

[1] *Clanricarde Memoirs*, London, 1722

'appears to have been for centuries the most popular religious composition in Ireland', and its stately sententiousness represents a constant aspect of the Irish mind, to be found later in the work of the poet-priest, Geoffrey Keating. But we respond more to the few private poems the bards allowed themselves, though when Giolla Brighde MacNamee prays for a son, he is also hoping for an intellectual heir; one of the great poetic families is called Mac An Bhaird, the son of the bard (now Ward).

From a court to a courtly poetry is one graceful step. With what has been called the Norman-Gaelic love-lyric a more cosmopolitan note, ultimately traceable to the *amour courtois* of the Provençal, enters Irish poetry. It is interesting to compare poets like Gerald Fitzgerald and Pierce Ferriter (both Normans who had adopted the bardic tradition) with their English contemporaries, from Surrey to Suckling—especially when one reflects that so many of the best Elizabethan poets, like Raleigh and Sir John Davies, assisted at the destruction of a society which produced a poetry so akin to their own! But one is comparing a mature growth with a blighted: as the best modern translator of the period, the late Lord Longford (and how revealing that he, and the Englishman Robin Flower, should have felt drawn to the period) says:

'If we remember that the systematic annihilation of Irish culture was in full swing before Shakespeare and Spenser began to write, there is no reason to believe that Ireland, had circumstances been favourable, might not have achieved as much in literature as the larger island . . . a unique culture, as interesting in its potentialities as in its achievements, goes down without reaching its fulfilment; and the last of the bards sing of its ruin . . .'

It is this long-drawn-out death song of an order, monotonous in its intensity, like a dog howling after its master, which one finds in later bardic poetry. A detail may suggest the background—not until well into the seventeenth century have we firm dates for most of the poets: we know when Pierce Ferriter was hanged, but not when he was born. And yet through all this strife and confusion—Spenser's great cantos of Mutability were written in Ireland—there never seems to have been any doubt as to who were the master poets, despite the uniformity of their training:

> *Yon spark's a poet, by my troth!*
> *Sprat and whale are fishes both;*
> *All birds build nests; so, like the rest,*
> *We call the tit's wee lodge a nest.*
>   *Version: Robin Flower*

Thus Tadgh Dall O'Huiginn, himself a Muse poet, in the Graves' sense; like Thomas the Rhymer, he had met the Queen of Fairyland:

> *Twice had she come. The maid with longing sore*
> *Wasted my cheek and scarred my brow with care.*
> *Twice hath she come and she will come once more*
> *And still I wait, for she is wondrous fair.*
>   *Version: Lord Longford*

By the end of the century, however, the maid of the *aisling* or vision poems is a captive who is concerned with only one thing, her freedom. But her mournful cries have to compete with a new literature, in the language of her conqueror.

III

> *Irishness is not primarily a question of birth or blood or language; it is the condition of being involved in the Irish situation, and usually of being mauled by it.*
>   CONOR CRUISE O'BRIEN

The growth of an Irish literature in English parallels the spread of the language. From Spenser to Hopkins, a succession of English poets have suffered in Ireland, but we have only an oblique claim on them, although I thought of including the passage on the rivers from *The Faerie Queene* to challenge any narrow definitions of Irish poetry. The sensuous vision of *The Land of Cockaigne*, however, is clearly related to early Irish literature; I am thinking not just of loan words, like *capall*, but of the goliardic spirit of the poem, so close to MacConglinne. The same manuscript contains 'A Satire on the people of Kildare':

> *Hail be ʒe brewsters wiþ ʒur galuns,*
> *Potels and quartes ouer al þe tounes.*

which like 'The Maid of the Moor' may have been one of those 'base, worldly and theatrical songs' the bishop of Ossory rebuked his clerics for singing in the fourteenth century? And did a girl from Munster not get a line in one of Shakespeare's plays?[1]

But until the Ulster Plantation and the Cromwellian Wars, the English language kept shrinking back to the Pale, the first significant literary product of which is Richard Stanihurst's hexameter translation of Virgil. Like a later Dubliner, James Joyce, Stanihurst suffered from logomania, and delightfully so; *bedgle* for making love, *skitop* for the roof of the sky among his compound words, *sloa* and *fats* for fates among his peculiar spellings, *petit degree* a satiric version of pedigree (one thinks of Myles's 'Paddy grees'), and a whole host of onomatopoeic words, like *chuff*, *clush* and *stutting* for stammering. An Elizabethan gone wrong, his alliterated and agglutinated words make him the ancestor of that verbal pedantry which dances through Irish literature.

But Stanihurst is a sport, a special case, and it is ludicrous to claim the odd writer of Irish background who strays into English like Shirley, MacFlecknoe, or Wentworth Dillon, Earl of Roscommon. Anglo-Irish literature proper does not begin until the eighteenth century. The question has often been raised by crusading nationalists, and as often dismissed, whether Swift and Goldsmith can be regarded as Irish writers. It seems to me that the claim has validity whenever a writer shows the pressure of local experience, and is regarded as a seminal influence by later writers.

Take Jonathan Swift. Born in Dublin, educated at Kilkenny and Trinity College, he kept being returned to Ireland by his ecclesiastical superiors; this confirmed him in that outsider's view of English society which may explain why so many Anglo-Irish writers have excelled in comedy and satire. There is also his powerful sense of physical disgust which some critics, thinking of Joyce, have seen as an Irish trait. But it is the rage of the unwilling patriot which makes him our first great voice in English:

> *Remove me from this land of slaves,*
> *Where all are fools, and all are knaves . . .*

I cannot think of any modern Irish writer of quality who has not been influenced by Swift. Yeats claims him as part of his racial

[1] Pistol's 'Calen o custure me' is probably the opening line of an Irish song, 'I am a girl from beside the Suir.'

heritage, Clarke pays homage to him in 'A Sermon for Swift' while Joyce and Kavanagh adapt his technique of self dramatization within a Dublin context for their own satirical verse:

> *He gave the little Wealth he had*
> *To build a House for Fools and Mad:*
> *And show'd by one satiric touch,*
> *No Nation wanted it so much . . .*

is echoed centuries later in 'Gas from a Burner':

> *This lovely land that always sent*
> *Her writers and artists to banishment*
> *And in a spirit of Irish fun*
> *Betrayed her own leaders, one by one.*

and 'The Paddiad':

> *Chestertonian Paddy Frog*
> *Croaking nightly in the bog.*
> *All the Paddies having fun*
> *Since Yeats handed in his gun.*

Goldsmith's case is less clear, although Yeats places him on his 'ancestral stair'. According to Robert Graves 'he was offering, disguised as an essay on the break-up of English village society, a lament for the ills of Ireland, modelled on contemporary minstrel songs.' Brian Merriman was not a minstrel (he was a teacher of mathematics) but if we compare his *Midnight Court* with *The Deserted Village* we discover both that he was more Augustan than is generally allowed, and Goldsmith more Irish. It has never been pointed out, I think, that the four best long poems—I am thinking of *Laurence Bloomfield*, as well as *The Great Hunger*—by Irishmen since the late eighteenth century are all variations on the same rural theme. So while the technique of *The Deserted Village* is late Augustan, its message still applies to Ireland (the ending seems especially relevant, now that we are part of the European Economic Community). And in the opening of *The Traveller*, Goldsmith analyses another of the great Hibernian themes, from Colmcille to Joyce, the intellectual exile's longing for home:

> *Where'er I roam, whatever realms to see,*
> *My heart untravell'd fondly turns to thee . . .*

So in the eighteenth century, the two traditions co-exist, with occasional courteous exchanges; I am thinking of Swift's translation of 'O'Rourke's Feast' and Goldsmith's essay on Carolan. And they illuminate each other; as well as the probable influence of Goldsmith on Merriman, I find it salutary to consider that Swift is contemporary with O'Rahilly and comes after O'Bruadair—three angry men, concerned in their different ways about the state of the country, and vituperating against those in power. Already at the end of the seventeenth century O'Bruadair is deploring the taste for 'gutter poetry' but before the Gaelic tradition goes underground, we hear a voice raised in aristocratic lamentation:

> *So stop your weeping now*
> *Women of the soft, wet eyes*
> *And drink to Art O'Leary*
> *Before he enters the grave school*
> *Not to study wisdom and song*
> *But to carry earth and stone.*
> *(Version: John Montague)*

IV

The Poet launched a stately fleet: it sank.
His fame was rescued by a single plank.
WILLIAM ALLINGHAM

It is only in the nineteenth century that the idea of a specifically Irish literature in English began to emerge. London was still the literary capital for writers in English but there was a subtle, historical change. Whereas Swift and Goldsmith were leading figures within the Augustan tradition, the Act of Union had the psychological effect of placing our poets in a subordinate or satellite position; as Aubrey De Vere was to Wordsworth, Moore to Byron, and Allingham to Tennyson. If one might risk a summary: our Anglicized writers did not exist in their own right and our Anglo-Irish had yet to learn how to speak for themselves.

And yet the older material began to find its way back. At first within the context of the Romantic revival; after MacPherson's garbling of the Ossianic stories, came the more spinsterly approach of Charlotte Brooke's *Reliques of Ancient Poetry* (1789):

'The British Muse is not yet informed that she has an elder sister in this isle; let us introduce them to each other! . . . It is really astonishing of what various and comprehensive powers this neglected language is possessed. In the pathetic it breathes the most beautiful and affecting simplicity . . .'

So the stage was set for Tom Moore, whose light charm covered a multitude of artistic sins. He appropriated the airs so strenuously gathered by Edward Bunting, without giving him the least credit, although he was being paid a hundred pounds for each of his Irish Melodies, folktunes wrought to drawing-room sweetness. He was a *petit bourgeois* snob who dearly loved a lord, but allowed the Memoirs that Byron entrusted to him to be destroyed. And yet he was the first writer of Irish Catholic background to achieve international fame, translated by Lermontov, imitated by Gérard de Nerval, adored by Goethe. He may not have the strength to sustain a theme but his plangent opening lines are as musical as Auden, who admired him:

>*Silent, Oh Moyle, be the roar of thy water . . .*

or

>*Light sounds the harp when the combat is over*

One might blame his artistic shortcomings on the company he kept, but Burns, although subject to similar pressures, remained closer to tradition. The truth is that Moore is a late Augustan, veering between the sentimental and the satiric, 'the tear and the smile'.

With Mangan we are in the presence of a real poetic temperament, as helplessly Irish as O'Rahilly. And also of that strange phenomenon I have already noted in nineteenth-century Irish poetry: like a medium, he rarely speaks in his own voice, but lets the past speak through him. I have transferred these 'melancholy perversions', as he called them, to their chronological place in the anthology: while they are less translations than acts of homage, they are the first real attempt to render Irish poetry in English. Flashes of exultation and desolation succeed each other, like lightning over a desert; Brian's palace is overthrown, the princes of the line of Conn die in unmourned exile, the chief of the Maguires flees through the storm, his face 'strawberry bright'. Did he influence Poe (the editor of 'The Southern Literary Messenger' would have had access to the magazines where Mangan published) or vice versa? In one poem, 'Siberia', he found a metaphor for the stricken psyche, worthy of Baudelaire and, despite its rhetoric, 'The Nameless One' has real intensity.

Samuel Ferguson was a much less haunted man, but he probably knew more Irish than Mangan, and certainly more about Irish music. So while his adaptations of the saga material are dated and literary, his versions of Irish folksong ring true:

> I'd wed you without herds, without money, or rich array,
> And I'd wed you on a dewy morning at day-dawn grey;
> My bitter woe it is, love, that we are not far away
> In Cashel town, though the bare deal board were our
>   marriage-bed this day!

But soon 'my locks are turn'd to grey' and we have 'girl' rhyming with 'churl': one is reminded of 'thy mother's knee' which nearly ruins the tone of his most free striding poem, 'Lament for the Death of Thomas Davis'. Ferguson was full of the contradictions of his period: an Ulster Unionist who married a Guinness heiress and was made a knight, he invented the Celtic Twilight:

> They're glancing through the glimmer of the quiet eve,
> Away in milky wavings of neck and ankle bare;
> The heavy-sliding stream in its sleepy song they leave,
> And the crags in the ghostly air ...

'The Fairy Thorn' is also labelled 'an Ulster ballad'; it was as if his Scots blood and Irish interests led him naturally to the form.

Among the other nineteenth-century poets Darley is consumed by a melancholy which is only incidentally Irish. And I have a fondness for Thomas Caulfield Irwin who bypassed the problem by writing exactly, and often sensuously, about nature:

> Around the stalk of the hollyhock
> The yellow, long, thin-waisted wasp,
> Emitting sounds, now like a lisp
> In the dry glare, now like a rasp ...

The most professional poet of the second half of the century was certainly Allingham, and his verse novel, *Laurence Bloomfield*, a study of Irish landlordism, deserves reprinting for both literary and historical reasons. While admitting the prolixity of nineteenth-century Irish poetry, one has to recognize that it still exercises a potent influence: Kinsella acknowledges a temperamental affinity with Mangan, the solid craftsmanship of Samuel Ferguson is continued by Richard Murphy, while John Hewitt sees himself as an inheritor of Allingham.

V

A tune is more lasting than the voice of the birds,
A word is more lasting than the riches of the world.
DOUGLAS HYDE: Love Songs of Connacht

In any consideration of Irish poetry between Carolan and Yeats one comes up against the importance of folksong. As Irish declined, the poets, like Owen Roe or Raftery, moved closer to song to reach their last audience in the cabins. Almost simultaneously, Irish songs began to filter into English: in 1792, the Belfast Society—remember the motto of the United Irishmen: 'It is new strung and shall be heard'—sponsored the last gathering of harpers, where Bunting got the idea for his first *Collection of Ancient Irish Music* which Moore plundered. Callanan, Walsh, Ferguson all try to match the 'sweet, wild twist' of Irish versification.

At the same time, this begins to have its effect on a new growth, the ballad in English. John Holloway has argued very persuasively that these anonymous songs are the true achievement of Anglo-Irish poetry in the nineteenth century, and with their hedge-schoolmaster diction and strenuous simplicity of emotion they can be very touching. If there is nothing like the great Gaelic lovesongs, the last vestige of the courtly tradition, there is a greater variety of subject, drinking songs, enlisting songs, sporting songs, political songs, springing directly from the lives of the people. 'When the Irish language was fading,' says the leading authority on the subject, Colm O'Lochlainn, 'the Irish street ballad in English was the half-way-house between the Irish culture and the new English way.' Nearly every Anglo-Irish poet, from Goldsmith onwards, has tried to add to this store, sometimes 'improving' an existing ballad, like

Padraic Colum with 'She moved through the Fair', or writing a new one, like Donagh MacDonagh. Their influence on our two greatest modern writers, Yeats and Joyce, shows that they can be a taproot for the most gifted.

VI

Every man everywhere is more of his age than of his nation
W. B. YEATS

Enfin, Yeats vint. His long, marvellous career illustrates how the apparent disadvantages of being Irish could all be turned into gains. He began writing during one of the worst periods of English poetry but he was saved from the aestheticism of his English contemporaries by his nationalism, and vice versa. The success of his early work led to a whole school of Irish poetry but the main achievement of A.E.'s anthology *New Songs* (1904) may have been to provoke him to a change of style. Of those who persisted as poets, Padraic Colum practised the pastoral lyric (a mode more consistently developed by Joseph Campbell, the Ulster imagist) while Seamus O'Sullivan turned to vignettes of Georgian Dublin. Those who reacted against him did better; one thinks of Synge, of Joyce's ballads and satires, his few very personal lyrics.

But again how quickly Yeats got the point, absorbing their savagery into his own style! He escapes the stereotypes of Irish poetry, from Celtic melancholy to rapscallion masculinity, because he is at all times a professional poet, whose primary concern is the human imagination in all its complexity. So Ireland was only one of several symbols, to be defined as the need struck him, in folk or patriotic or Anglo-Irish terms; her principal value was as a backdrop. 'Behind all Irish history hangs a great tapestry, even Christianity had to accept, and be itself pictured there.'

Robert Graves follows Yeats in regarding himself as an Anglo-Irish poet, though only an occasional ballad cadence betrays the influence of his father, a minor Victorian poet and song writer, in the tradition of Father Prout. His allegiance shows itself rather in his inherited interest in Celtic literature, as documented in *The White Goddess* and elsewhere (he has written a long essay on *The Frenzy of Sweeny*) and above all, in his belief in the poet as a magician, under the rule of the Muse, a role that Yeats alone, among contemporary poets, would have recognized.

Austin Clarke's lifework can be seen as a deliberate attempt to reconcile the two traditions; he is our first completely Irish poet in English. A student of Thomas MacDonagh at University College, Dublin, he developed the idea of a distinctive Irish mode with an almost exclusive integrity. He also revived the role of the poet as satirist; his favourite *persona* is that of the straying cleric, a modern version of MacConglinne. He can be very intense, as in the closely-knit religious lyrics, and also beautifully relaxed, when he praises the city he loves so much, as in 'A Sermon for Swift'. While he may finally be seen as an autobiographical poet, his immediate historical importance is that, like MacDiarmid in Scotland, he dedicated himself to the idea of a separate Irish poetry in English, so that his work is both a rallying point and a focus for fierce reaction.

It was not surprising, therefore, that the most original poet to appear after Clarke should decide he wanted nothing to do with Irishry whatsoever. Patrick Kavanagh's magnificent but melodramatic outcry against the frustrations of rural life, *The Great Hunger* (1942), is one of the better long poems of our time, and its releasing influence on other writers, from R. S. Thomas to Seamus Heaney, has still to be estimated. And twice during his lifetime he produced lyric poetry of a high order, in simple, sensuous memories like 'Spraying the Potatoes' and in the sonnets written after his operation for lung cancer. 'I feel I have the permanent stuff in me and only need to be stirred' he wrote once to his brother, and perhaps all the flailing anger, and the famous lawcase, were only his way of stirring the sediment; his braggadocio sheltered a talent as lonely as John Clare's.

The one thing that all these writers shared was a contempt for contemporary literature; one thinks of the jingoistic finale of 'Under Ben Bulben' and Clarke's long war against what he called 'modernism'. A poet who might have extended our view of poetry was Denis Devlin but his unwillingness to publish means that his work is still little known, and lacks a kind of primary readability. He was profoundly influenced by Spanish and French literature (even collaborating in a hare-brained scheme to translate modern

French poetry into Irish) and his sequence of longer poems from 'Lough Derg' through 'The Heavenly Foreigner' to 'The Colours of Love' shows a capacity for intellectual passion as elaborate as Claudel's. Though it would be wrong to restrict his view of the world even to the European tradition: one of his best poems is about the Cambodian temple of Ank'hor Vat. The most dedicated poet of the lost generation of the Irish thirties, his work shows how an awareness of Irish literary and religious tradition can be a spring-board to the widest possible vision.

After the Irish mode of Clarke, and the comedy of Kavanagh, we have the gravity of Kinsella. His great achievement was to have restored the sense of poetry as craft; from the elegance of *Another September* to the sombre density of *Nightwalker* and *Notes from the Land of the Dead*, his strenuous dedication makes a striking contrast with Kavanagh's jauntiness. He can write with an exact fluency as in 'Chrysalides' but that is only a simple, preparatory statement compared to the pained complexity of his analysis of mutability in poems like 'Ballydavid Pier'. His work so far presents a central paradox: modern in its reliance on the integrity of the individual sensibility, it is still haunted by the mournfulness of an Irish Catholic upbringing, and despite his years in America and his overwhelming awareness of contemporary evil, he can still lapse into Parnassian metre and diction.

So, in the late fifties, Irish poets began to write, without strain, a poetry that was indisputably Irish (in the sense that it was in-fluenced by the country they came from, its climate, history and linguistic peculiarities) but also modern. Kinsella's spearheading success encouraged others, and by the middle of the following decade, Irish poets began to filter into modern anthologies, especially American, so that the critic M. L. Rosenthal could dedicate a section of his study *The New Poets* to Irish poetry. This wider audience did not mean any abjuring of older allegiances; Kinsella's translation of *The Tain* is a landmark in Anglo-Irish poetry's repossession of its past, while Pearse Hutchinson writes in both languages. Even in the detached music of *The Battle of Aughrim*, where Richard Murphy probes the relationship between history and the self, as it presents itself to a Southern Protestant, one savours the half and internal rhymes of the older tradition:

> *There was ice on the axe*
> *When it hacked the king's head.*

The next generation of poets sprang from that forgotten and history-burdened area, the North. There has been some criticism in the Republic of the way Ulster writers tend to look to London as their literary capital, and it is true that the poems of Longley, Mahon, Heaney and Simmons share an epigrammatic neatness which shows the influence of a limited British mode. But in other ways they are very different; Heaney is a naturally sensuous writer, very close to early Frost, while the others are more in the tradition of melancholy wit, inherited from MacNeice, who is very much a father figure for the poets of the province. What is striking in all the Northern writers is how well they write, though I would hope for a more experimental approach, if they are to confront the changes in their society.

But Heaney's brooding devotion to the earth goddess, and Mahon's lithe metaphysical intelligence already place them among the most gifted Irish poets. There is not such a clearly-defined generation in the South, although Michael Hartnett is the most dedicated English poet to come so far from Munster, where the tradition of Gaelic poetry was strongest. A fine translator, he extends the Irish mode, arguing that an Anglo-Irish writer should be as familiar with Gaelic metres as English. One's general impression of the younger poets is of a competing multiplicity of styles, from which only a few names separate themselves, like Richard Ryan in the South, and above all, Paul Muldoon, again from the North. Not since early Kinsella has such an elegant and intelligent talent appeared. But since it is notoriously difficult to judge the work of an emerging generation, I have hopefully included more names than from nearly any other period.

I have tried to create an anthology which leads up to the present, with the Irish tradition as it has been glimpsed by English-speaking writers. An Irish poet seems to me in a richly ambiguous position, with the pressure of an incompletely discovered past behind him, and the whole modern world around. We might find parallels in the way contemporary English poets, from Auden to Geoffrey Hill, have contacted the Anglo-Saxon world, but our literature is both closer to us, and more varied. A tradition, however, should not be an anachronistic defence against experience, and through our change of languages we have access to the English-speaking world—without that protective attitude an English poet might naturally feel towards his language. Stephen Spender[1] has compared the present subordinate position of the English writer to his powerful American contemporary with that of the Anglo-Irish, who were compelled to straddle 'two different civilizations which shared a common language'. But this has been our problem for a long time, so that the Irish writer, at his best, is a natural cosmopolitan; Yeats may echo O'Rahilly in 'The Curse of Cromwell' but 'The Second Coming' is as central to his vision. And that is our best example for the future, balanced between the pastoral and the atomic age; if a poet is someone who, through words, turns psychic defeats into victories, we stand a better chance than most in the storm-driven, demon-crossed last quarter of the century:

> *Growing up, I heard talk of Ulster regionalism,*
> *A literature for our province, a lyric Stormont.*
> *Coming South, I was religiously told*
> *Of our Irish Renaissance, a lyric Sinn Fein.*
> *Now both winds fail: we belong to a world.*

*

A final technical note. Limitations of space, and a desire to emphasize what seemed to me most relevant in both literatures, has led to the exclusion, or streamlining, of many excellent but lengthy poems. This applied particularly to the nineteenth century; as well as 'The Welshmen of Tirawley' I would have liked to include Carleton's splendidly romantic ballad 'Sir Turlough or the Churchyard Bride':

> *The bride she bound her golden hair—*
> *Killeevy, O Killeevy!*

And Ferguson's Browningesque monologue on the Phoenix Park murders, 'At the Polo-Ground', is one of our few good poems on political violence:

[1] In *The Times Literary Supplement* 5 Oct 1967.

Is it worth while—the crime itself apart—
To pull this settled civil state of life
To pieces, for another just the same,
Only with rawer actors for the posts . . .

Exclusions from the Irish were simpler: either there were no good translations or the ones that existed were already well known, like Robin Flower's 'Pangur Ban' and most of Frank O'Connor. In the case of two accepted masterpieces, *The Midnight Court* and 'The Lament for Art O'Leary', I have tried to counterpoint differing translations. Nor could I find any suitable version of the South Armagh poets of the eighteenth century, though Seamus Dall and Peadar O'Doirnin are at least as good as Owen Roe. And to have included modern poetry in Irish would have been unfair, as well as burdening an already heavy contemporary section: I could only hope to include a few names with translations, which, however good, would place them at a disadvantage among their English contemporaries. When I come to revise the anthology, I hope to find many new poems and more fresh translations; this exchange between the two languages seems to me crucial for the future of Irish literature, always allowing that there will be any communication in the future. Samuel Beckett sums up our linguistic problem in *All That Fall*:

MR. ROONEY: . . . Do you know, Maddy, sometimes one would think you were struggling with a dead language.

MRS. ROONEY: Yes, indeed, Dan, I know well what you mean, I often have that feeling, it is unspeakably excruciating.

MR. ROONEY: I confess I have it sometimes myself, when I happen to overhear what I am saying.

MRS. ROONEY: Well, you know, it will be dead in time, just like our own poor dear Gaelic, there is that to be said.

Urgent baa

JOHN MONTAGUE

Old Mythologies

THE FIRST INVASION OF IRELAND

According to Leabhar Gabhála, The Book of Invasions, *the first invasion of Ireland was by relatives of Noah, just before the Flood. Refused entry into the Ark, they consulted an idol which told them to flee to Ireland. There were three men and fifty-one women in the party and they may have landed where the Barrow, Nore and Suir meet.*

Fleeing from threatened flood, they sailed,
Seeking the fair island, without serpent or claw;
From the deck of their hasty barque watched
The soft edge of Ireland nearward draw.

A sweet confluence of waters, a trinity of rivers,
Was their first resting place:
They unloaded the women and the sensual idol,
Guiding image of their disgrace.

Division of damsels they did there,
The slender, the tender, the dimpled, the round,
It was the last just bargain in Ireland,
There was enough to go round.

Lightly they lay and pleasured
In the green grass of that guileless place.
Ladhra was the first to die;
He perished of an embrace.

Bith was buried in a stone heap,
Riot of mind, all passion spent.
Fintan fled from the ferocious women
Lest he, too, by love be rent.

Great primitive princes of our line
They were the first, with stately freedom,
To sleep with women in Ireland;
Soft the eternal bed they lie upon.

On a lonely headland the women assembled,
Chill as worshippers in a nave,
And watched the eastern waters gather
Into a great virile flooding wave.

THE FIRST LAWCASE

According to Leabhar Gabhála, *the second invasion of Ireland, after the Flood, was by Partholan, whose wife's behaviour anticipates the freedom of the Brehon Laws.*

Partholan went out one day
To tour his wide spread lands;
Leaving his wife and servant,
Both bound by his commands.

Long they waited in his house,
Until the lady, feeling desperate—
A state before unheard of—
Propositioned the pure servant.

Rightly he ignored her,
Stubborn against temptation,
Until she removed her clothes:
Strange work for a decent woman!

Then, so frail is humanity,
Topa rose, long limbed,
And joined the lovely Delgnat,
Lonely upon her couch.

Wise Partholan possessed
A vat of ale, cool and sweet,
From which none might drink
Save through a golden spigot.

Thirsty after their actions,
Topa and Delgnat, truth to tell,
Leaped from bed so urgently
Their mouths met on the barrel.

When Partholan returned
From wandering his wide fields
A surly black demon revealed
The stains on the golden tube.

'Look, the track of the mouth
Of Topa, as low down as this,
And beside it, the smear left
By married Delgnat's kiss!'

Whereupon his wife replied:
'Surely the right to complain
Is mine, innocently left
To confront another man.

Honey with a woman, milk with a cat,
A sharp tool with a craftsman,
Goods with a child or spendthrift:
Never couple things like that.

The woman will eat the honey,
The cat lap the new milk,
While the child destroys the things
Not bestowed by the spendthrift.

The craftsman will use the tool,
Because one and one make two:
So never leave your belongings
Long unguarded, without you.'

That is the first adultery
To be heard of in Ireland;
Likewise the first lawcase:
The right of his wife against Partholan.

THE FIRST POET

Also in The Book of Invasions *we find the incantations of Amergin,
the chief bard of the Milesians, and supposedly the first poet of Ireland.
The first uses chain alliteration, the second is a* rosc, *a form of rhetoric
with a freer metre. In his reconstruction, Robert Graves has incorporated
a similar poem by Taliesen, the earliest of the Welsh bards; the
argument can be followed in Chapter XII of* The White Goddess.

THE MUSE OF AMERGIN

I speak for Erin,
Sailed and fertile sea,
Fertile fruitful mountains,
Fruitful moist woods,
Moist overflowing lochs,
Flowing hillside springs,
Springs of men assembling,
Assembling men at Tara,
Tara, hill of tribes,
Tribes of the sons of Mil,
Mil of boats and ships,
The high ship of Éire,
Eire of high recital,
Recital skilfully done,
The skill of the women
Of Breisi, of Buagnai;
That haughty lady, Éire,
By Eremon conquered,
Ir and Eber bespoken:
I speak for Erin.
            Versions: John Montague

I am a stag : *of seven tines*
I am a flood : *across a plain*
I am a wind : *on a deep lake*
I am a tear : *the Sun lets fall,*
I am a hawk : *above the cliff*
I am a thorn : *beneath the nail*
I am a wonder : *among flowers,*
I am a wizard : *who but I*
Sets the cool head aflame with smoke?

I am a spear : *that rears for blood,*
I am a salmon : *in a pool,*
I am a lure : *from paradise,*
I am a hill : *where poets walk,*
I am a boar : *ruthless and red,*
I am a breaker : *threatening doom,*
I am a tide : *that drags to death,*
I am an infant : *who but I*
Peeps from the unhewn dolmen arch?

I am the womb : *of every holt,*
I am the blaze : *on every hill,*
I am the queen : *of every hive,*
I am the shield : *for every head,*
I am the grave : *of every hope.*
                    Version: Robert Graves

THE DOUBLE VISION OF MANANNAN
8th century

The clear ocean seems
A marvel of beauty to Bran
In his currach; but mine
Rides a flowering plain.

Those bright waves
Under the prow of Bran
To my double-rimmed chariot
Are blossoms of the Honey Plain.

On the bright ocean Bran
Sees endless waves breaking.
I see the flawless red-headed
Flowers of the Brave Plain.

Sea-horses glisten in summer
Far as the glance of Bran
But streams of honey pour
Through the land of Manannan.

The sealight where you float,
The glint from lifting oars,
Are also solid earth,
Moulded yellow and blue.

You see speckled salmon
Flash from the white sea's womb:
They are calves, fleecy lambs
Living in peace, not war.

Though you see a single chariot
On the many blossomed Honey Plain
You cannot see alongside
A great host riding.

The vast plain, its radiant host,
A stream of white silver,
Stairs of gold to bring
Delight to every feast.

While under shady branches
Men and gentle women contest
Their guileless, pleasing game
Without sin, without blame.

Across ridges, the crest of
A wood, your curragh sails:
A forest, heavy with mast,
Sleeps under your keel.

A wood of flowers and fruit,
The true fragrance of the vine,
A wood without decay or fault,
Gold leaves that shine.

Since the beginning of creation,
Without age or corruption:
We fear no loss of strength,
Exempt from mortal sin.

THE WOOING OF ETAIN

Fair lady, will you travel
To the marvellous land of stars?
Pale as snow the body there,
Under a primrose crown of hair.

No one speaks of property
In that glittering community:
White teeth shining, eyebrows black,
The foxglove hue on every cheek.

The landscape bright and speckled
As a wild bird's eggs—
However fair Ireland's Plain,
It is sad after the Great Plain!

Warm, sweet streams water the earth,
And after the choicest of wine and mead,
Those fine and flawless people
Without sin, without guilt, couple.

We can see everyone
Without being seen ourselves:
It is the cloud of Adam's transgression
Conceals us from mortal reckoning.

O woman if you join my strong clan,
Your head will hold a golden crown.
Fresh killed pork, new milk and beer,
We shall share, O Lady Fair!

THE PLAIN OF ADORATION

Here was raised
a high idol of cruel fights:
the Cromm Cruaich—
the King Idol of Ireland.

He was their Moloch,
this withered hump of mists,
dominating every harbour,
denying the eternal kingdom.

In a circle stood
four times three idols of stone:
to bitterly enslave his people,
the pivot figure was of gold.

In dark November
when the two worlds near each other,
he glittered among his subjects,
blood-crusted, insatiable.

To him, without glory,
would they sacrifice their firstborn;
with wailing and danger
pouring new blood for the Stooped One.

Under his shadow
they cried and mutilated their bodies;
from this worship of dolour
it is called the Plain of Adoration.

From the rule of Eremon
well bred and graceful Goidels
worshipped such stones until
the coming of good Patrick to Armagh.
Versions: John Montague

ADZE-HEAD

Across the sea will come Adze-head,
crazed in the head,
his cloak with hole for the head,
his stick bent in the head.

He will chant impiety
from a table in the front of his house;
all his people will answer:
'Be it thus. Be it thus.'
Version: James Carney

A Way of Life

CORMAC MAC AIRT PRESIDING AT TARA

Beautiful was the appearance of Cormac in that assembly, flowing and slightly curling was his golden hair. A red buckler with stars and animals of gold and fastenings of silver upon him. A crimson cloak in wide descending folds around him, fastened at his neck with precious stones. A torque of gold around his neck. A white shirt with a full collar, and intertwined with red gold thread upon him. A girdle of gold, inlaid with precious stones, was around him. Two wonderful shoes of gold, with golden loops upon his feet. Two spears with golden sockets in his hands, with many rivets of red bronze. And he was himself, besides, symmetrical and beautiful of form, without blemish or reproach.

Version: Douglas Hyde

from THE INSTRUCTIONS OF KING CORMAC
early 9th century

'O Cormac, grandson of Conn,' said Carbery,
'what were your habits when you were a lad?'
'Not hard to tell,' said Cormac.
'I was a listener in woods,
I was a gazer at stars,
I was blind where secrets were concerned,
I was silent in a wilderness,
I was talkative among many,
I was mild in the mead-hall,
I was stern in battle,
I was gentle towards allies,
I was a physician of the sick,
I was weak towards the feeble,

I was strong towards the powerful,
I was not close lest I should be burdensome,
I was not arrogant though I was wise,
I was not given to promising though I was strong,
I was not venturesome though I was swift,
I did not deride the old though I was young,
I was not boastful though I was a good fighter,
I would not speak about anyone in his absence,
I would not reproach, but I would give praise,
I would not ask, but I would give,—
for it is through these habits that the young
become old and kingly warriors.'

'O Cormac, grandson of Conn,' said Carbery,
'what is the worst thing you have seen?'

'Not hard to tell,' said Cormac. 'Faces of
foes in the rout of battle.'

'O Cormac, grandson of Conn,' said Carbery,
'what is the sweetest thing you have heard?'

'Not hard to tell,' said Cormac.

'The shout of triumph after victory,
Praise after wages,
A lady's invitation to her pillow.'

Version: Kuno Meyer

PLEASANT THE HOUSE

Pleasant the house where
men, women, and children
are swayed by the fair
and yellow haired Creide;

with a swift moving groom,
a door-keeper and butler to
carve when the druid sits
among the musicians . . .

Berries drip into the bowl
to dye her black shawl.
She has a crystal vat,
pale goblets and glasses.

Lime white, her skin;
quilts line her rushy floor,
silk, her blue cloak,
red gold, her drinking horn.

Her sun room glitters with
yellow gold and silver,
under warm ridged thatch
tufted brown and scarlet.

Two door posts of green
you pass, a shapely hinge,
and the beam of her lintel
far famed for its silver.

More lovely still, her chair,
On the left as you enter,
with a filigree of Alpine gold
round the foot of her bed.

To the right, another bed,
wrought from precious metals,
a hyacinthine canopy,
bronze curtain rods . . .

A hundred foot from front
to back is the span
of the house of Creide;
twenty, her noble doorway.

THE POET'S REQUEST
7th century

I demand a thatched house,
swept spick and span;
not a hut for dogs or cattle
but dignified in welcome:
I demand a high chair
cushioned with down.
Versions: John Montague

TRIADS
9th century

Three excellent qualities in narration: a good flow, depth of thought, conciseness.

Three dislikeable qualities in the same: stiffness, obscurity, bad delivery.

Three things that are always ready in a decent man's house: beer, a bath, a good fire.

Three accomplishments well regarded in Ireland: a clever verse, music on the harp, the art of shaving faces.

Three signs of concupiscence: sighing, gamey tricks, going to hooleys.

Three smiles that are worse than griefs: the smile of snow melting, the smile of your wife when another man has been with her, the smile of a mastiff about to spring.

The three with the lightest hearts: a student after reading his psalms, a young lad who has left off his boy's clothes for good, a maid who has been made a woman.

The three doors by which falsehood enters: anger in stating the case, shaky information, evidence from a bad memory.

Three times when speech is better than silence: when urging a king to battle, when reciting a well turned line of poetry, when giving due praise.

Three scarcities that are better than abundance: a scarcity of fancy talk, a scarcity of cows in a small pasture, a scarcity of friends around the beer.

Versions: Thomas Kinsella

from PRINCE ALFRID'S ITINERARY

I found in Munster, unfettered of any,
Kings and queens, and poets a many—
Poets well skilled in music and measure,
Prosperous doings, mirth and pleasure.

I found in Connaught the just, redundance
Of riches, milk in lavish abundance;
Hospitality, vigour, fame,
In Cruachan's land of heroic name.

I found in Ulster, from hill to glen,
Hardy warriors, resolute men;
Beauty that bloomed when youth was gone,
And strength transmitted from sire to son.

I found in Leinster the smooth and sleek,
From Dublin to Slewmargy's peak;
Flourishing pastures, valour, health,
Long-living worthies, commerce, wealth.

Version: James Clarence Mangan

CATHLEEN

Lovely whore though,
Lovely, lovely whore
And choosy—
Slept with Conn,
Slept with Niall,
Slept with Brian,
Slept with Rory.

Slide then,
The long slide.

Of course it shows.
  Version: Thomas MacIntyre

A Monastic Church

THE MONASTIC SCRIBE

(I)
early 9th century

A hedge before me, one behind,
a blackbird sings from that,
above my small book many-lined
I apprehend his chat.

Up trees, in costumes buff,
mild accurate cuckoos bleat,
Lord love me, good the stuff
I write in a shady seat.

(II)
11–12th century

My hand has a pain from writing,
Not steady the sharp tool of my craft.
Its slender beak spews bright ink—
A beetle-dark shining draught.

Streams of wisdom of white God
from my fair-brown, fine hand sally,
On the page they splash their flood
In ink of the green-skinned holly.

My little dribbly pen stretches
Across the great white paper plain,
Insatiable for splendid riches—
That is why my hand has pain!

Versions: Flann O'Brien

MARBAN, A HERMIT SPEAKS

For I inhabit a wood
   unknown but to my God
my house of hazel and ash
   as an old hut in a rath.

And my house small, not too small,
   is always accessible:
women disguised as blackbirds
   talk their words from its gable.

The stags erupt from rivers,
   brown mountains tell the distance:
I am glad as poor as this
   even in men's absence.

Death-green of yew,
huge green of oak
   sanctify,
and apples grow
close by new nuts:
   water hides.

      Young of all things,
      bring faith to me,
         guard my door:
      the rough, unloved
      wild dogs, tall deer,
         quiet does.

In small tame bands
the badgers are,
   grey outside:
and foxes dance
before my door
   all the night.

      All at evening
      the day's first meal
         since dawn's bread:

                        trapped trout, sweet sloes
                        and honey, haws,
                            beer and herbs.

Moans, movements of
silver-breasted
    birds rouse me:
pigeons perhaps.
And a thrush sings
    constantly.

                        Black-winged beetles
                        boom, and small bees:
                            November
                        through the lone geese
                        a wild winter
                            music stirs.

Come fine white gulls
all sea-singing,
    and less sad,
lost in heather,
the grouse's song,
    little sad.

                        For music I
                        have pines, my tall
                            music-pines
                        so who can I
                        envy here, my
                            gentle Christ?
                            Version: Michael Hartnett

BELFAST LOUGH

        The whistle
        of the bright
        yellow billed
            little bird:

Over the loch
upon a golden
whin, a blackbird
      stirred.
Version: John Montague

A HERMIT'S SONG

My heart stirs quietly now to think
of a small hut that no one visits
in which I will travel to death in silence.

Nothing will draw my eyes away,
there, from repentance for evil done,
or hinder my view of Heaven and Earth.

Feeble and properly tearful, I'll pray
as the body decays, always treating it firmly
to serve only my soul there.

Passions, grown weak, will not divide me:
where they die the soul steps forward
eager to serve and seek for pardon.

I will have no ease nor long lying,
but short sleep, out on the edge of life,
and early waking for penance and long prayer.

Hardly a mile from this pleasant clearing
is a bright spring to drink from and use
for moistening measured pieces of bread.

For all my renouncing and sparse diet
and regular tasks of reading and penance
I forsee only delight in my days there.

The thinness of face and fading of skin,
the pain given by damp and a hard bed
to a frail body, will hardly distress me,

for I look to have frequent visits from birds
and sunlight and Jesus the King who made me,
and my mind will be calling on Him each morning.

When I and the things I used are faded,
some men will remember and respect the place
where a man all day prepared his dying.

Version: James Simmons

THE VIKINGS

Bitter the wind tonight,
combing the sea's hair white:
from the North, no need to fear
the proud sea-coursing warrior.

Version: John Montague

Leaving, Returning

GAZE NORTH-EAST

Gaze north-east
over heaving crest
with sea press
    ceaseless:

seals' road
for sleek sport
the tide run to
    fulness.

Version: John Montague

THE FISH AT MASS

St. Peter's Day was celebrated by St. Brendan at sea, and the water was so clear that the monks could see every movement of life beneath the boat; so clear, indeed, that the animals on the ocean bed seemed near enough to touch. If the monks looked down into the deep, they could see many different kinds of creature lying on the sandy bottom like flocks at pasture, so numerous that, lying head to tail, and moving gently with the swell, they looked like a city on the march.

The monks urged their master to say mass silently lest the fish, hearing his voice, might rise up and attack them. Brendan chaffed them: 'I am surprised at your foolishness. What—are you afraid of these creatures? Have you not several times landed on the monarch of the deep, the beast who eats all other sea creatures? Why, you have sat down on his back and sung psalms, have even gathered sticks, lighted a fire and cooked food—and all this without showing fear. Then how can you be afraid of these? Is not Our Lord Jesus

Christ the Lord of Creation? Can he not make all creatures docile?' Brendan sang at the top of his voice, causing the brethren to cast an anxious eye in the direction of the fish, but at the sound of singing the fish rose up from the sea bed and swam round and round the coracle. There was nothing to be seen but crowds of swimming forms. They did not come close but, keeping their distance, swam back and forth till mass was over.

Version: J. F. Webb from 9th-century Latin

Colmcille

6th century (?)

(I)

On some island I long to be,
a rocky promontory, looking on
the coiling surface of the sea.

To see the waves, crest on crest
of the great shining ocean, composing
a hymn to the creator, without rest.

To see without sadness the strand
lined with bright shells, and birds
lamenting overhead, a lonely sound.

To hear the whisper of small waves
against the rocks, that endless sea-
sound, like keening over graves.

To watch the sea-birds sailing
in flocks, and most marvellous
of monsters, the turning whale.

To see the shift from ebbtide
to flood and tell my secret name:
'He who set his back on Ireland.'

(II)

Clamour of the wind making music
    in the elms:
Gurgle of the startled blackbird
    clapping its wings.

I have lost the three settled places
    I loved best:

63

Durrow, Derry's ledge of angels,
   my native parish.

I have loved the land of Ireland
   almost beyond speech;
to sleep at Comgall's, to visit Canice,
   it would be pleasant!
            Versions: John Montague

Sedulius Scottus

9th century

NUNC VIRIDANT SEGETES

The standing corn is green, the wild in flower,
   The vines are swelling, 'tis the sweet o' the year,
Bright-winged the birds, and heavens shrill with song,
   And laughing sea and earth and every star.

But with it all, there's never a drink for me,
   No wine, nor mead, nor even a drop of beer.
Ah, how hath failed that substance manifold,
   Born of the kind earth and the dewy air!

I am a writer, I, a musician, Orpheus the second,
   And the ox that treads out the corn, and your well-wisher I,
I am your champion armed with the weapons of wisdom and logic,
   Muse, tell my lord bishop and father his servant is dry.

APOLOGIA PRO VITA SUA

I read or write, I teach or wonder what is truth,
   I call upon my God by night and day.
I eat and freely drink, I make my rhymes,
   And snoring sleep, or vigil keep and pray.
And very 'ware of all my shames I am;
   O Mary, Christ, have mercy on your man.

Colman (?)

TO COLMAN RETURNING

So, since your heart is set on those sweet fields
    And you must leave me here,
Swift be your going, heed not any prayers,
    Although the voice be dear.

Vanquished art thou by love of thine own land,
    And who shall hinder love?
Why should I blame thee for thy weariness,
    And try thy heart to move?

Since, if but Christ would give me back the past,
    And that first strength of days,
And this white head of mine were dark again,
    I too might go your ways.

Do but indulge an idle fond old man
    Whose years deny his heart.
The years take all away, the blood runs slow,
    No leaping pulses start.

All those far seas and shores that must be crossed,
    They terrify me: yet
Go thou, my son, swift be thy cleaving prow,
    And do not quite forget.

Hear me, my son; little have I to say
    Let the world's pomp go by.
Swift is it as a wind, an idle dream,
    Smoke in an empty sky.

Go to the land whose love gives thee no rest,
    And may almighty God,

Hope of our life, Lord of the sounding sea,
  Of wind and waters Lord,

Give thee safe passage on the wrinkled sea,
  Himself thy pilot stand,
Bring thee through mist and foam to thy desire,
  Again to Irish land.

Live, and be famed and happy: all the praise
  Of honoured life to thee.
Yea, all this world can give thee of delight,
  And then eternity.
      Versions: Helen Waddell from medieval Latin

Women and Love

LOVE

My love is no short year's sentence.
It is a grief lodged under the skin,
Strength pushed beyond its bounds;
The four quarters of the world,
The highest point of heaven.
    It is
A heart breaking or
Battle with a ghost,
Striving under water,
Outrunning the sky or
Courting an echo.

So is is my love, my passion
   & my devotion
To him to whom I give them.

LÍADAN LAMENTS CUIRITHIR
9th century

Joyless
what I have done;
to torment my darling one.

But for fear
of the Lord of Heaven
he would lie with me here.

Not vain,
it seemed, our choice,
to seek Paradise through pain.

I am Líadan,
I loved Cuirithir
as truly as they say.

The short time
I passed with him
how sweet his company!

The forest trees
sighed music for us;
and the flaring blue of seas.

What folly
to turn him against me
whom I had treated most gently!

No whim
or scruple of mine
should have come between

Us, for above
all others, without shame
I declare him my heart's love.

A roaring flame
has consumed my heart:
I will not live without him.
                    Versions: John Montague

THE SONG OF CREDE

*(In the battle of Aidne, Crede, the daughter of King Guare of Aidne,
beheld Dinertach of the HyFidgenti, who had come to the help of Guare,
with seventeen wounds upon his breast. Then she fell in love with him.
He died and was buried in the cemetery of Colman's Church.)*

These are the arrows that murder sleep
At every hour in the night's black deep;
Pangs of Love through the long day ache,
All for the dead Dinertach's sake.

Great love of a hero from Roiny's plain
Has pierced me through with immortal pain,
Blasted my beauty and left me to blanch
A riven bloom on a restless branch.

Never was song like Dinertach's speech
But holy strains that to Heaven's gate reach;
A front of flame without boast or pride,
Yet a firm, fond mate for a fair maid's side.

A growing girl—I was timid of tongue,
And never trysted with gallants young,
But since I have won into passionate age,
Fierce love-longings my heart engage.

I have every bounty that life could hold,
With Guare, arch-monarch of Aidne cold,
But, fallen away from my haughty folk,
In Irluachair's field my heart lies broke.

There is chanting in glorious Aidne's meadow,
Under St. Colman's Church's shadow;
A hero flame sinks into the tomb—
Dinertach, alas my love and my doom!

Chaste Christ! that now at my life's last breath
I should tryst with Sorrow and mate with Death!
At every hour of the night's black deep,
These are the arrows that murder sleep.

Version: Alfred Perceval Graves

EVE

I am Eve, great Adam's wife,
I that wrought my children's loss,
I that wronged Jesus of life,
Mine by right had been the cross.

I a kingly house forsook,
Ill my choice and my disgrace,
Ill the counsel that I took
Withering me and all my race . . .

I that brought winter in
And the windy glistening sky,
I that brought sorrow and sin,
Hell and pain and terror, I.
Version: Thomas MacDonagh

THE HAG OF BEARE
9th century

Ebb tide has come for me:
My life drifts downwards
Like a retreating sea
With no tidal turn.

I am the Hag of Beare,
Fine petticoats I used to wear,
Today, gaunt with poverty,
I hunt for rags to cover me.

Girls nowadays
Dream only of money—
When we were young
We cared more for our men.

Riding over their lands
We remember how, like nobles,
They treated us well;
Courted, but didn't tell.

Today every upstart
Is a master of graft;
Skinflint, yet sure to boast
Of being a lavish host.

But I bless my King who gave—
Balanced briefly on time's wave—
Largesse of speedy chariots
And champion thoroughbreds.

These arms, now bony, thin
And useless to younger men,
Once caressed with skill
The limbs of princes!

Sadly my body seeks to join
Them soon in their dark home—
When God wishes to claim it,
He can have back his deposit.

No more gamy teasing
For me, no wedding feast:
Scant grey hair is best
Shadowed by a veil.

Why should I care?
Many's the bright scarf
Adorned my hair in the days
When I drank with the gentry.

So God be praised
That I mis-spent my days!
Whether the plunge be bold
Or timid, the blood runs cold.

After spring and autumn
Come age's frost and body's chill:
Even in bright sunlight
I carry my shawl.

Lovely the mantle of green
Our Lord spreads on the hillside!
Every spring the divine craftsman
Plumps its worn fleece.

But my cloak is mottled with age—
No, I'm beginning to dote—
It's only grey hair straggling
Over my skin like a lichened oak.

And my right eye has been taken away
As down-payment on heaven's estate;
Likewise the ray in the left
That I may grope to heaven's gate.

No storm has overthrown
The royal standing stone.
Every year the fertile plain
Bears its crop of yellow grain.

But I, who feasted royally
By candlelight, now pray
In this darkened oratory.
Instead of heady mead

And wine, high on the bench
With kings, I sup whey
In a nest of hags:
God pity me!

Yet may this cup of whey
O! Lord, serve as my ale-feast—
Fathoming its bitterness
I'll learn that you know best.

Alas, I cannot
Again sail youth's sea;
The days of my beauty
Are departed, and desire spent.

I hear the fierce cry of the wave
Whipped by the wintry wind.
No one will visit me today
Neither nobleman nor slave.

I hear their phantom oars
As ceaselessly they row
And row to the chill ford,
Or fall asleep by its side.

Flood tide
And the ebb dwindling on the sand!
What the flood rides ashore
The ebb snatches from your hand.

Flood tide
And the sucking ebb to follow!
Both I have come to know
Pouring down my body.

Flood tide
Has not yet rifled my pantry
But a chill hand has been laid
On many who in darkness visited me.

Well might the Son of Mary
Take their place under my roof-tree
For if I lack other hospitality
I never say 'No' to anybody—

Man being of all
Creatures the most miserable—
His flooding pride always seen
But never his tidal turn.

Happy the island in mid-ocean
Washed by the returning flood
But my ageing blood
Slows to final ebb.

I have hardly a dwelling
Today, upon this earth.
Where once was life's flood
All is ebb.

THE ONLY JEALOUSY OF EMER

CÚCHULAIN
(*to his charioteer*): Look, Loig, behind—
civil, sensible women are listening,
grey daggers in their right hands,
gold plate on their breasts.
A fine figure they cut,
fierce as warriors in their chariots:
clearly, my wife has changed!

(*to his mistress*): Show no fear and she will not approach
Come, sit beside me
in the sun-warmed prow
of my great chariot
and I will protect you from
all the female hordes of Ulster.
Though the daughter of Forgall come
storming with her company of women
she will not dare lay a hand on me.

(*to Emer,
his wife*): I shun you, woman,
as all creatures shun the yoke.
That stiff spear in your trembling hand,
your thin, lean knife,
cannot harm my majesty,
far above a woman's strength.

EMER:

A question, fickle though you are,
Cúchulain. Why did you shame me
before all the women of Ulster,
the women of Ireland, and
all mannerly people?
I came, under your care,
the full strength of your bond,
and though success makes you vain,
it may be a while, little hound,
before you get rid of me.

CÚCHULAIN:

A question, Emer,
Why would you not let
me linger with a woman?
To begin with, this girl
is chaste, sincere, and clever
fit to be the consort of a king,
conquering across heavy seas.
Style, grace and breeding,
embroidery, husbandry and weaving,
thrift, commonsense and character,
all these she has, as well as herds
of horses and cattle.
There is little she would
not do for her lover's wife
if it were agreed between them.
Ah, Emer, you will never find
a good-looking, death-dealing,
triumphant champion like I am!

EMER:

And maybe the woman you follow is no better.
But everything glittering is beautiful,
everything new is bright, everything far is fair,
everything lacking is lovely, everything
    customary is sour,
everything familiar is neglected,
until all knowledge be known.

Versions: John Montague

from THE TAIN

Now it was that the Morrígan settled in bird shape
on a standing stone in Temair Chuailnge, and said
to the Brown Bull:

> 'Dark one are you restless
> > do you guess they gather
> to certain slaughter
> > the wise raven
> groans aloud
> > that enemies infest
> the fair fields
> > ravaging in packs
> learn I discern
> > rich plains
> softly wavelike
> > baring their necks
> greenness of grass
> > beauty of blossoms
> on the plains war
> > grinding heroic
> hosts to dust
> > cattle groans the Badb
> the raven ravenous
> > among corpses of men
> affliction and outcry
> > and war everlasting
> raging over Cuailnge
> > death of sons
> death of kinsmen
> > death   death!'

77

The first warp-spasm seized Cúchulain, and made him into a monstrous thing, hideous and shapeless, unheard of. His shanks and his joints, every knuckle and angle and organ from head to foot, shook like a tree in the flood or a reed in the stream. His body made a furious twist inside his skin, so that his feet and shins and knees switched to the rear and his heels and calves switched to the front. The balled sinews of his calves switched to the front of his shins, each big knot the size of a warrior's bunched fist. On his head the temple-sinews stretched to the nape of his neck, each mighty, immense, measureless knob as big as the head of a month-old child. His face and features became a red bowl: he sucked one eye so deep into his head that a wild crane couldn't probe it onto his cheek out of the depths of his skull; the other eye fell out along his cheek. His mouth weirdly distorted: his cheek peeled back from his jaws until the gullet appeared, his lungs and liver flapped in his mouth and throat, his lower jaw struck the upper a lion-killing blow, and fiery flakes large as a ram's fleece reached his mouth from his throat. His heart boomed loud in his breast like the baying of a watch-dog at its feed or the sound of a lion among bears. Malignant mists and spurts of fire—the torches of the Badb—flickered red in the vaporous clouds that rose boiling above his head, so fierce was his fury. The hair of his head twisted like the tangle of a red thornbush stuck in a gap; if a royal apple tree with all its kingly fruit were shaken above him, scarce an apple would reach the ground but each would be spiked on a bristle of his hair as it stood up on his scalp with rage. The hero-halo rose out of his brow, long and broad as a warrior's whetstone, long as a snout, and he went mad rattling his shields, urging on his charioteer and harassing the hosts. Then, tall and thick, steady and strong, high as the mast of a noble ship, rose up from the dead centre of his skull a straight spout of black blood darkly and magically smoking like the smoke from a royal hostel when a king is coming to be cared for at the close of a winter day.

Versions: Thomas Kinsella

from THE FENIAN CYCLE

SCEL LEM DUIB
9th century

Here's a song—
stags give tongue
winter snows
summer goes.

High cold blow
sun is low
brief his day
seas give spray.

Fern clumps redden
shapes are hidden
wildgeese raise
wonted cries.

Cold now girds
wings of birds
icy time—
that's my rime.
                    Version: Flann O'Brien

THE FINEST MUSIC

Once, as they rested on a chase, a debate arose among the Fianna-Finn as to what was the finest music in the world.

'Tell us that,' said Fionn, turning to Oisin.

'The cuckoo calling from the tree that is highest in the hedge,' cried his merry son.

'A good sound,' said Fionn. 'And you, Oscar,' he asked, 'what is to your mind the finest of music?'

'The top of music is the ring of a spear on a shield,' cried the stout lad.

'It is a good sound,' said Fionn.

And the other champions told their delight: the belling of a stag across water, the baying of a tuneful pack heard in the distance, the song of a lark, the laughter of a gleeful girl, or the whisper of a moved one.

'They are good sounds all,' said Fionn.

'Tell us, chief,' one ventured, 'what do you think?'

'The music of what happens,' said great Fionn, 'that is the finest music in the world.'

James Stephens, Irish Fairy Stories

THE BLACKBIRD OF DERRYCAIRN

Stop, stop and listen for the bough top
Is whistling and the sun is brighter
Than God's own shadow in the cup now!
Forget the hour-bell. Mournful matins
Will sound, Patric, as well at nightfall.

Faintly through mist of broken water
Fionn heard my melody in Norway.
He found the forest track, he brought back
This beak to gild the branch and tell, there,
Why men must welcome in the daylight.

He loved the breeze that warns the black grouse,
The shout of gillies in the morning
When packs are counted and the swans cloud
Loch Erne, but more than all those voices
My throat rejoicing from the hawthorn.

In little cells behind a cashel,
Patric, no handbell gives a glad sound.
But knowledge is found among the branches.

Listen! That song that shakes my feathers
Will thong the leather of your satchels.
                              Version: Austin Clarke

THE DESERTED MOUNTAIN
14th century (?)

A gloomy thought, Ben Bulben,
shapely crested mountain;
before old Tall Crook came
how lovely shone your peak.

Many hounds and gillies
strayed on your slopes;
many strong warriors heard
the hoarse hunting horn.

The pack's cry in the glens
on the wild boar's track:
every Fenian was followed
by lovely, leashed hounds.

Many a sweet-strung harp
was struck on your green sward,
the well made tale or poem
with gold was always matched.

The heron's lament by night,
the moorhen in the heather—
how sweet it was to hear
their melodies twine together.

It would lift your heart
to hear the eagle's cry,
the sweet chant of the otters,
the yelp of jack foxes.

At that time, Ben Bulben,
no one shunned your lofty sides.
Tonight, I have few companions,
of my kindred none survives.

Your blackbirds and thrushes,
an amulet against loneliness:
doves clusters in your branches
comforted sorrowing women.

Many's the time these same
fair Fenian women gathered
fragrant tasting blackberries
from your tangled brambles.

Bogberries, brightly scarlet,
brookline, cuckoo spit and cress:
the daughters of the King of Ulster
hummed sweetly at their harvest.

Honeysuckle and black sloes,
hazel, pignut and woodbine;
those were marching rations
when the Fianna roamed Erin.

Lovely inlets of water,
sweet free running streams;
though tonight a spent veteran,
I lived in pleasant times.
             Version: John Montague

from THE FRENZY OF SWEENY
12th century

Sweeny, King of Dalriada in North Antrim, is driven mad by a cleric's curse, and wanders the woods of Ireland lamenting his lot.

WOLVES FOR COMPANY

Terrible is my plight this night
the pure air has pierced my body,
lacerated feet, my cheek is green—
O Mighty God, it is my due.

It is bad living without a house,
Peerless Christ, it is a piteous life!
a filling of green-tufted fine cresses
a drink of cold water from a clear rill.

Stumbling out of the withered tree-tops
walking the furze—it is truth—
wolves for company, man-shunning,
running with the red stag through fields.

SWEENY AND THE HAG

. . . they entrusted the mad one to the care of Linchehaun till he would take him away to a quiet place for a fortnight and a month, to the quiet of a certain room where his senses returned to him, the one after the other, with no one near him but the old mill-hag.

'O hag,' said Sweeny, 'searing are the tribulations I have suffered; many a terrible leap have I leaped from hill to hill, from fort to fort, from land to land, from valley to valley.'

'For the sake of God,' said the hag, 'leap for us now a leap such as you leaped in the days of your madness.'

And thereupon Sweeny gave a bound over the top of the bedrail till he reached the extremity of the bench.

'My conscience indeed,' said the hag, 'I could leap the same leap myself.'

And the hag gave a like jump.

Sweeny then gathered himself together in the extremity of his jealousy and threw a leap right out through the skylight of the hostel.

'I could vault that vault too,' said the hag and straightway she vaulted the same vault. And the short of it is this, that Sweeny travelled the length of five cantreds of leaps until he had penetrated to Glenn na nEachtach in Fiodh Gaibhle with the hag at her hag's leaps behind him; and when Sweeny rested there in a huddle at the top of a tall ivy-branch, the hag was perched there on another tree beside him. He heard there the voice of a stag and he thereupon made a lay eulogizing aloud the trees and the stags of Erin, and he did not cease or sleep until he had achieved these staves.

Flann O'Brien, *At Swim-Two-Birds*

HE PRAISES THE TREES

Huge-headed oak,
you are tall, tall.
Small hazel, pick
me your secret nuts.

Alder, friendly one,
gleam, shine;
you bar no gap
with a toothed thorn.

Blackthorn, dark one,
provide sloes;
watercress, brim
the blackbirds' pools.

Small one, pathway
loiterer, green
leaved berry, give me
your speckled crimson.

Apple tree, let me
shake you strongly.
Rowan, drop me
your bright blossom.

Briar, relent.
Your hooks have fed
content till you
are filled with holy blood.

Church Yew, calm
me with grave talk.
Ivy, bring dream
through the dark wood.

Hollybush, bar me
from winter winds.
Ash, be a spear
in my fearful hand.

Birch, oh blessed
birchtree, sing
proudly the tangle
of the wind.
Version: Robin Skelton

*But Sweeny flew on until he reached the church of Swim Two Birds,
opposite Clommacnoise. He landed on a Friday, to be exact; the clerics
were chanting Nones while women beat flax and one was giving birth.
As he watched from his tree, Sweeny heard the Vesper bell ring:*

SWEETNESS

Although my claws weaken
Sweeter across water
The cuckoo's soft call
Than girn of church-bell.

Woman, don't give birth,
Nevertheless, on a Friday,
When even Mad Sweeny
Fasts for the King of Truth.

As the women scutch flax—
Though I say it myself—
So were our folk scutched
At the battle of Mag Rath.

From Loch Diolar of the cliffs
To Derry Colm Cille
It wasn't war I heard
From melodious, proud swans.

And the belling of the stag
In Siodhmhuine's steep glen;
No music on earth soothes
My soul like its sweetness.

O hear me, Christ
Without stain, never
Let me be severed
O Christ, from your sweetness!
                    Version: John Montague

from THE VISION OF MACCONGLINNE
12th century

The vision that appeared
Splendidly to me, I now
    Relate to all;
Carved from lard, a coracle
In a port of New Milk Lake
    On the world's calm sea.

We climbed that handsome boat,
Over ocean's heaving way
    Set out bravely;
Our oars as we leaned
Raised the sea's harvest
    Of honeyed algae.

The fort we reached was beautiful—
Thick breastworks of custard
    Above the lake
Fresh butter for a drawbridge
A moat of wheaten bread
    A bacon palisade.

Stately and firmly placed
On strong foundations, it seemed
    As I entered
Through a door of dried beef
A threshold of well-baked bread
    Walls of cheese-curd.

Sleek pillars of ripe cheese
And fleshed bacon posts
    In alternate rows;

Fine beams of yellow cream
Thin rafters of white spice
    Held up the house.

Spurting behind, a spring of wine
Beer and ale flowing in streams
    And tasty pools;
From a well-head of nectar
A crest of creamy malt ran
    Over the floor.

An estuary of juicy pottage,
Winking with oozy fat, lay
    Next the sea:
A hedge of butter to guard,
Under blossoms of mantling lard,
    The wall outside.

A row of flowering apple-trees,
An orchard in pink-topped bloom
    Before the nearest hill:
A forest of lanky leeks,
Of scallions and carrot clumps
    Under the back sill.

Within, a welcoming household
Of ruddy, well-fleshed men
    About the fire;
Seven necklaces of tangy cheese
Seven strings of tripe, dangling
    About each neck.

Swathed in a mantle of beefy fat
Beside his well proportioned wife
    I glimpsed the Chief:
Before the mighty cauldron's mouth
Crouched the Dispenser, his flesh fork
    Upon his back.

            Version: John Montague, after Kuno Meyer

EPIGRAMS

I know him;
He'll give no horse for a poem;
He'll give you what his kind allows,
Cows.
Version: Vivian Mercier

He is my love
    my sweet nutgrove:
a boy he is—
    for him a kiss.
Version: Michael Hartnett

The son of the King of the Moy
met a girl in green woods on midsummer's day:
she gave him black fruit from thorns
and the full of his arms
of strawberries, where they lay.
Version: John Montague

Cú Chuimne in youth
Read his way through half the truth.
He let the other half lie
While he gave women a try.

Well for him in old age.
He became a holy sage.
He gave women the laugh.
He read the other half.
Version: John V. Kelleher

Ah! light lovely lady with delicate lips aglow
With breast more white than a branch heavy-laden with snow,

When my hand was uplifted at Mass to salute the Host
I looked at you once, and the half of my soul was lost.

Version: Robin Flower

Though riders be thrown in black disgrace,
    Yet I mount for the race of my life with pride,
May I keep to the track, may I fall not back,
    And judge me, O Christ, as I ride my ride.

Version: Douglas Hyde

Peace is made with a warlike man—
An old saying, but a true one!
People parley only with a bully
In Ireland of the white hedges.

Version: John Montague

O King of the Friday
Whose limbs were stretched on the cross,
O Lord who didst suffer
The bruises, the wounds, the loss,

We stretch ourselves
Beneath the shield of thy might.
May some fruit from the tree of thy passion
Fall on us this night!

Version: Douglas Hyde

Muireadach O'Dalaigh

early 13th century

ON THE DEATH OF HIS WIFE

I parted from my life last night,
　　A woman's body sunk in clay:
The tender bosom that I loved
　　Wrapped in a sheet they took away.

The heavy blossom that had lit
　　The ancient boughs is tossed and blown;
Hers was the burden of delight
　　That long had weighed the old tree down.

And I am left alone tonight
　　And desolate is the world I see
For lovely was that woman's weight
　　That even last night had lain on me.

Weeping I look upon the place
　　Where she used to rest her head—
For yesterday her body's length
　　Reposed upon you too, my bed.

Yesterday that smiling face
　　Upon one side of you was laid
That could match the hazel bloom
　　In its dark delicate sweet shade.

Maelva of the shadowy brows
　　Was the mead-cask at my side;

Fairest of all flowers that grow
  Was the beauty that has died.

My body's self deserts me now,
  The half of me that was her own,
Since all I knew of brightness died
  Half of me lingers, half is gone.

The face that was like hawthorn bloom
  Was my right foot and my right side;
And my right hand and my right eye
  Were no more mine than hers who died.

Poor is the share of me that's left
  Since half of me died with my wife;
I shudder at the words I speak;
  Dear God, that girl was half my life.

And our first look was her first love;
  No man had fondled ere I came
The little breasts so small and firm
  And the long body like a flame.

For twenty years we shared a home,
  Our converse milder with each year;
Eleven children in its time
  Did that tall stately body bear.

It was the King of hosts and roads
  Who snatched her from me in her prime:
Little she wished to leave alone
  The man she loved before her time.

Now King of churches and of bells,
  Though never raised to pledge a lie
That woman's hand—can it be true?—
  No more beneath my head will lie.
                Version: Frank O'Connor

Giolla Brighde MacNamee

late 13th century

CHILDLESS

Blessed Trinity have pity!
    You can give the blind man sight,
Fill the rocks with waving grasses—
    Give my house a child tonight.

You can bend the woods with blossom,
    What is there you cannot do?
All the branches burst with leafage,
    What's a little child to you?

Trout out of a spawning bubble,
    Bird from shell and yolk of an egg,
Hazel from a hazel berry—
    Jesus, for a son I beg!

Corn from shoot and oak from acorn
    Miracles of life awake,
Harvest from a fist of seedlings—
    Is a child so hard to make?

Childless men although they prosper
    Are praised only when they are up,
Sterile grace however lovely
    Is a seed that yields no crop.

There is no hell, no lasting torment
    But to be childless at the end,

A naked stone in grassy places,
 A man who leaves no love behind.

God I ask for two things only,
 Heaven when my life is done,
Payment as befits a poet—
 For my poem pay a son.

Plead with Him, O Mother Mary,
 Let Him grant the child I crave,
Womb that spun God's human tissue,
 I no human issue leave.

Brigid after whom they named me,
 Beg a son for my reward,
Let no poet empty-handed
 Leave the dwelling of his lord.
                    Version: Frank O'Connor

Gofraidh Fionn O'Dalaigh

d. 1387

UNDER SORROW'S SIGN

A pregnant girl, under sorrow's sign,
Condemned to a cell of pain,
Bore, by leave of Creation's Lord,
Her small child in prison.

Swiftly the young lad flourished,
Eager as a bardic novice,
For those first years in prison,
Clear as if we were looking on.

Who would not be moved, alas,
As he darts playful little runs
Within the limit of his walls
While his mother falls into sadness!

For all daylight brought to them—
O sharp plight—was the glimpse
A single augurhole might yield
Of the bright backbone of a field.

Seeing one day on her pale face
A shining tear, the child cried:
'Unfold to me your sorrow
Since I follow its trace.

Does there exist another world
Brighter than where we are:

A home lovelier than this
Source of your heavy weariness?'

'Seeing the narrow track we tread
Between the living and the dead
It would be small wonder if I
Were not sad, heedless boy.

But had you shared my life
Before joining this dark tribe
Then on the tender hobbyhorse
Of your soul, sorrow would ride.

The flame of the wide world
Warmed my days at first;
To be closed in a dark cell
Afterwards: that's the curse.'

Realising this life's distress
Beyond all balm or sweetness,
The boy's brow did not darken
Before his cold and lonely prison.

This image—this poem's dungeon:
Of those closed in a stern prison
These two stand for the host of living,
Their sentence, life imprisonment.

Against the gaiety of God's son,
Whose kingdom holds eternal sway
Sad every dungeon where earth's hosts
Lie hidden from the light of day.
                    Version: John Montague

THE LAND OF COCKAIGNE

Far to sea, west from Spain
Is a land called Cockaigne.
No land as wealthy lies,
Or kind, under heaven's skies.
Though Paradise be merrily bright,
Cockaigne is a fairer sight.
What is there in Paradise
But flowers and green leaves?
Though there is joyous delight,
There is no meat, but fruit;
Neither hall, bower, nor bench,
Only water our thirst to quench.
There are no people, but two;
Sadly one wanders through a place,
Deserted by the human race.

Meat and drink are in Cockaigne,
Without care, or anxious pain,
The clearest drink, the choicest meat,
From noon to supper you eat . . .
There is a fine fair abbey
Of white monks and of grey,
All of pasties are the walls,
Of flesh, fish and rich meat,
The juiciest man may eat.
Flower cakes are the shingles all
Of church, cloister, bower and hall
Underpinned with fat puddings,
Rich meat for princes and kings.
Man may eat enough thereof,
It is right to stuff oneself,

All is shared by young and old,
By stout and stern, meek and bold.
There is a cloister, fair and light,
All its pillars are of crystal
Wrought, with base and capital
Of green jasper and red coral.

On the lawn there is a tree
Ginger and galingale its roots,
Aromatic zedoary its shoots,
Choice nutmeg as the flower,
With cinnamon rind of sweet odour
And fruit, good tasting gillyflower.
There are roses of reddest hue,
Jujubes, arum lilies too;
Never fading day or night
A most pleasing, sweet sight.
In the abbey spring four wells
Of treacle, and of mineral,
Of balm and spiced wine,
Ever erring in straight line.
Precious stones inlay the mould
Of these streams, with gold,
Sapphire and large pearl,
Astiune and carbuncle,
Emerald, ligure and topaz,
Beryl, onyx, chrysoprase,
Amethyst and chrysolite,
Chalcedony and red epitite.

Throstle, thrush and nightingale,
Woodlark and golden oriole,
Never stint their might,
Singing merrily day and night.
Fat geese roasted on the spit
Fly, God knows, to that abbey
And 'geese, all hot' they cry,
Carrying garlic in great plenty,
The best garnished man might see.

The larks, plump and couth,
Settle into man's mouth,
Stewed until they taste well,
Stuffed with gillyflower, caramel.
No one speaks of lacking liquor
But fills up without a care. . . .

The young monks each day
After meat, go out to play:
Despite their sleeves and cowl
There is no hawk or swift fowl
Faster flying through the sky
Than these monks when feeling high.
When the abbot sees them flee,
He follows them with glee,
But nevertheless bids the throng
To alight for evensong.
When the monks don't come down,
But further flee, at random,
He takes a maiden, from the mass,
And turning up her plump white ass,
Beats the tabours with his hand,
To make his monks alight to land.
The monks, all seeing that,
Drop from the sky, upon the dot,
And ring the wench all about
To thwack her white toute,
And after this pleasant work
Wend meekly home to drink
Going to their collation
In a goodly fair procession.

Another abbey is thereby—
Forsooth, a great fair nunnery,
Up a river of sweet milk,
Where there is surplus of silk.
When the summer sun is hot,
The young nuns take a boat

And sail upon that river,
Both with oars and rudder.
When they are far from the abbey
They strip themselves naked to play,
And leaping down into the brim
Set themselves skilfully to swim.
The monks, when they this espy,
Rise up, and forthwith fly
And coming to the nuns anon
Each monk grabs him one
And quickly bears forth his prey
To the great, grey abbey,
And teaches the nuns an orison
With jigging up and down.

He that would be a stallion good
And can set straight his hood,
That monk shall have, without fear,
Twelve new wives each year,
While the monk who sleeps the best
And above all, likes his rest,
There is hope for him, God wot,
Soon to be a father abbot.

Whoever to that land will go,
Full great penance he must do,
Seven years he must wade
In swine's dung, I'm afraid,
All the way up to the chin;
If he shall to that land win.
Lords, courteous and trained,
May ye never from this world wend
Until you have had your chance
To fulfill that penance, and
That you may to that land gain
Nevermore to return again.
We pray God, so may it be,
Amen, *pur seint charite.*
    Version: John Montague, from Middle English

Courtly Love

AGAINST BLAME OF WOMAN

Gerald Fitzgerald, Earl of Desmond (d. 1398)

Speak not ill of womankind,
  'Tis no wisdom if you do.
You that fault in women find,
  I would not be praised of you.

Sweetly speaking, witty, clear,
  Tribe most lovely to my mind,
Blame of such I hate to hear.
  Speak not ill of womankind.

Bloody treason, murderous act,
  Not by women were designed,
Bells o'erthrown nor churches sacked.
  Speak not ill of womankind.

Bishop, King upon his throne,
  Primate skilled to loose and bind,
Sprung of women every one!
  Speak not ill of womankind.

For a brave young fellow long
  Hearts of women oft have pined.
Who would dare their love to wrong?
  Speak not ill of womankind.

Paunchy greybeards never more
  Hope to please a woman's mind.
Poor young chieftains they adore!
  Speak not ill of womankind.
                    Version: Earl of Longford

THE DISPRAISE OF ABSALOM

Veiled in that light amazing,
Lady, your hair soft wavèd
Has cast into dispraising
Absalom son of David.

Your golden locks close clinging,
Like birdflocks of strange seeming,
Silent with no sweet singing
Draw all men into dreaming.

That bright hair idly flowing
Over the keen eyes' brightness,
Like gold rings set with glowing
Jewels of crystal lightness.

Strange loveliness that lingers
From lands that hear the Siren:
No ring enclasps your fingers,
Gold rings your neck environ,

Gold chains of hair that cluster
Round the neck straight and slender,
Which to that shining muster
Yields in a sweet surrender.
                    Version: Robin Flower

MY LOVE I GAVE FOR HATE

My love I gave for hate,
not long my days will be.
My curses lie on him
that loves her after me.

Calm eye and golden head,
speech sweet as cuckoo's stave;
to brows drawn fine as thread
my love for hate I gave.

White tongue and lips of red,
kind tongue and gentle gait,
'tis sad it should be said—
my love I gave for hate.
        Version: George Campbell Hay

SORAIDH SLÁN DON OIDHCHE ARÉIR

Niall Mór Mac Muireadach

'Tis goodbye then to last night,
Swift its flight and long our pain,
'Tho the morrow saw me hang
Would it ran its course again.

Two within tonight there chance
Whom a glance must give away,
Mouth to mouth they may not set,
But once met their eyes betray.

Keep we counsel—have a care
To that roving pair of eyes,
All our silence is small gain
When so plain they court surmise.

See these liars gathered here,
For their fear I ask no whit,
But my thoughts, which way they tend,
My eyes send you where you sit—

This night only keep for us
To be thus and then no more—
Here shall morning not make way;
Rise and turn day from the door!

Stand to me, Mother of God,
At your nod the wise obey—
Pity and redeem my plight:
Speed last night upon its way.

TAISIGH AGAT FÉIN DO PHÓG

Keep to yourself your kisses,
    Bright teeth and parted lip,
Keep your mouth away from me,
    I have no mind for your kiss.

A kiss more sweet than honey
    From the wife of another man
Has left without taste all kisses
    That were since the world began.

Till, and please God I may—
    I see that woman again—
Her kiss being as it was—
    I ask no other till then.
            Versions: Máire Cruise O'Brien

SECOND HONEYMOON

Don't drive me out of my mind;
our minds should be one
as the bed bartered for the banns
in Ireland.

Mellow your mouth as a spray
of berries, your skin is cream,
your arms about me blossom
full and fragile.

Light of my generous love,
don't hesitate but come
able and agile for my love's
full knowledge.

Idle the eyes of our men.
Don't bother them with notice!
The milk-white tooth of passion
is between us.

Version: Augustus Young

O WOMAN, SHAPELY AS THE SWAN

O woman, shapely as the swan,
On your account I shall not die:
The men you've slain—a trivial clan—
Were less than I.

I ask me shall I die for these—
For blossom teeth and scarlet lips—
And shall that delicate swan-shape
Bring me eclipse?

Well-shaped the breasts and smooth the skin,
The cheeks are fair, the tresses free—
And yet I shall not suffer death,
God over me!

Those even brows, that hair like gold,
Those languorous tones, that virgin way,
The flowing limbs, the rounded heel
Slight men betray!

Thy spirit keen through radiant mien,
Thy shining throat and smiling eye,
Thy little palm, thy side like foam—
I cannot die!

O woman, shapely as the swan,
In a cunning house hard-reared was I:
O bosom white, O well-shaped palm,
I shall not die!

Version: Padraic Colum

AOIBHINN, A LEABHRÁIN, DO THRIALL

Delightful, book, your trip
to her of the ringlet head,
a pity it's not you
that's pining, I that sped.

To go, book, where she is
delightful trip in sooth!
the bright mouth red as blood
you'll see, and the white tooth.

You'll see that eye that's grey
the docile palm as well,
with all that beauty you
(not I, alas) will dwell.

You'll see the eyebrow fine
the perfect throat's smooth gleam,
and the sparkling cheek I saw
latterly in a dream.

The lithe good snow-white waist
that won mad love from me—
the handwhite swift neat foot—
these in their grace you'll see.

The soft enchanting voice
that made me each day pine
you'll hear, and well for you—
would that your lot were mine.
                Version: Flann O'Brien

THE SNORING BEDMATE

You thunder at my side,
Lad of ceaseless hum;
There's not a saint would chide
My prayer that you were dumb.

The dead start from the tomb
With each blare from your nose.
I suffer, with less room,
Under these bedclothes.

Which could I better bide
Since my head's already broke—
Your pipe-drone at my side,
Woodpecker's drill on oak?

Brass scraped with knicky knives,
A cowbell's tinny clank,
Or the yells of tinkers' wives
Giving birth behind a bank?

A drunken, braying clown
Slapping cards down on a board
Were less easy to disown
Than the softest snore you've snored.

Sweeter the grunts of swine
Than yours that win release.
Sweeter, bedmate mine,
The screech of grieving geese.

A sick calf's moan for aid,
A broken mill's mad clatter,
The snarl of flood cascade . . .
Christ! now what's the matter?

That was a ghastly growl!
What signified that twist?—
An old wolf's famished howl,
Wave-boom at some cliff's breast?

Storm screaming round a crag,
Bellow of raging bull,
Hoarse bell of rutting stag,
Compared with this were lull!

Ah, now a gentler fall—
Bark of a crazy hound?
Brats squabbling for a ball?
Ducks squawking on a pond?

No, rough weather's back again.
Some great ship's about to sink
And roaring bursts the main
Over the bulwark's brink!

Farewell, tonight, to sleep.
Every gust across the bed
Makes hair rise and poor flesh creep.
Would that one of us were dead!
                Version: John V. Kelleher

Tadhg Dall O'Huiginn
d. 1591

from THE FIRST VISION

A Vision of a Queen of Fairyland
My soul to ravish came to me last night,
And never lady at my side did stand
To my undoing so unearthly bright.

Last night she came, a bright and lovely ghost,
And rose before me, while I seemed to sleep,
And of that slumber where my soul was lost
My tongue shall tell while I my memory keep.

Fair was her face, her cheeks outblushed the rose;
There might you see the floods of crimson rise,
And dark unfaltering brows above disclose
The hyacinthine petals of her eyes.

Her pretty mouth more sweet than honeycomb
Would with red lips the budding rose excel,
And each soft whisper that from thence did come
Would charm the sick and make the dying well.

Between her lips like fallen rain of pearl
On scarlet cushions twain her teeth reposed;
How bright they shone, how sweetly spoke the girl;
Each languid word new loveliness disclosed.

Between her arms that taper to the hand
Are set twin glories, beautiful to see.

Two snowy mountains in her bosom stand,
Mid golden thickets of embroidery.

Gold-bordered slippers on her gentle feet
Do guard her steps wherever she may move;
You'd swear that maid so radiantly sweet
Had them a present from the God of Love.

Her purple mantle fringed with satin round,
Her golden shift with scarlet borders gay,
Her gilded bodice o'er her bosom bound
Did all her fairy loveliness display . . .

'I came to seek you: come away with me!'
Thus spake the lady, and her voice was low,
And in my ear she murmured secretly,
As softest notes from sweetest organs flow.

'I will not go.' I answered like a fool,
For love had brought me to distraction,
And as I spake that vision beautiful
Had vanished in the darkness and was gone.

And now my soul and body part in pain.
The queen with blushing cheek and brown-lashed eyes
Leaves me to pine and cometh not again,
Tho' she was kind and beautiful and wise . . .

The mound of Midhir with its rampart fair,
The fort of Sanbh, Abhartach's magic hill,
No lady in their castles can compare
With this sweet maid for whom I languish still.

Not in Emania of the apple-trees,
Nor halls of Aonghus of the golden sword,
The fairy dwells that hath such charms as these,
So soft a beauty or so kind a word.

But she is gone, and I would follow fast
To lands unknown, who languish in despair.
Would it were possible to find at last
That country and to dwell for ever there!

A little hour I loved her rosy cheek—
The ebb must follow ever on the flow—
The vision fled, the joy of love grew weak,
My spirit sank and I was left to woe.

A PRESENT OF BUTTER

A woman gave me butter now,
    Good butter too it claimed to be.
I don't think it was from a cow,
    And if it was it finished me.

A beard was growing on the stuff,
    A beastly beard without a doubt,
The taste was sickly, sour and rough,
    With poison juices seeping out.

The stuff had spots, the stuff was grey,
    I doubt if any goat produced it.
I had to face it every day,
    And how I wish I had refused it!

This splendid butter had a mane,
    The glory of my humble home.
No knife could cut it down again,
    It made me sick for weeks to come.

This nasty grease a wrapping had
    Like a discarded winding sheet.
Its very aspect was so bad,
    I scarcely had the nerve to eat.

This horror had a heavy stink
    That left one fuddled, stunned and dead.
'Twas rainbow-hued, with what you'd think
    A crest of plumes above its head.

The salt's a thing it hardly knew,
    In fact I think they'd barely met.
It was not white, but rather blue.
    I am not quite recovered yet.

'Twas made of grease and wax and fat,
    O thoughts too horrible to utter!
You may be sure that after that,
    I rather lost my taste for butter.
                Versions: Earl of Longford

THE DIFFERENCE

Yon spark's a poet, by my troth!
Sprat and whale are fishes both;
All birds build nests; so, like the rest,
We call the tit's wee lodge a nest.
          Version: Robin Flower

Pierce Ferriter

d. 1653

LAY YOUR ARMS ASIDE

Gentlest of women, put your weapons by,
Unless you want to ruin all mankind;
Leave the assault or I must make reply,
Proclaiming that you are murderously inclined.
Put by your armour, lay your darts to rest,
Hide your soft hair and all its devious ways:
To see it lie in coils upon your breast
Poisons all hope and mercilessly slays.

Protest you never murdered in your life;
You lie: your hand's smooth touch, your well-shaped knee
Destroy as easily as axe or knife.
Your breasts like new spring flowers, your naked side
—I cry for aid to heaven—conceal from me;
Let shame for the destruction you have made
Hide your bright eyes, your shining teeth, away;
If all our sighs and trembling and dismay
Can touch your heart or satisfy your pride,
Gentlest of women, lay your arms aside.

Version: Eiléan Ní Chuilleanáin

Richard Stanihurst

1536–1618

from VIRGIL HIS ÆNEIS

Now manhood and garbroyls I chaunt, and martial horror.
I blaze thee captayne first from Troy cittye repairing,
Lyke wandring pilgrim too famosed Italie trudging,
And coast of Lauyn: soust wyth tempestuus hurlwynd,
On land and sayling, bi Gods predestinat order:
But chiefe through Iunoes long fostred deadlye reuengment.
Martyred in battayls, ere towne could statelye be buylded,
Or Gods theare setled: thence flitted thee Latin ofspring,
Thee roote of old Alban: thence was Rome peereles inhaunced.
My muse shew the reason, what grudge or what furye kendled
Of Gods thee Princesse, through so cursd mischeuus hatred,
Wyth sharp sundrye perils too tugge so famus a captayne.
Such festred rancoure doo Sayncts celestial harbour?
    A long buylt city theare stood, Carthago so named,
From the mouth of Tybris, from land eke of Italye seauerd,
Possest wyth Tyrians, in streingh and ritches abounding.
Theare Iuno, thee Princes her Empyre wholye reposed,
Her Samos owtcasting, heere shee dyd her armonye settle,
And warlick chariots, heere chiefly her ioylitye raigned.
This towne shee labored too make thee gorgeus empresse,
Of towns and regions, her drift yf destenye furthred.
But this her hole meaning a southsayd mysterie letted
That from thee Troians should branch a lineal ofspring,
Which would thee Tyrian turrets quite batter a sunder,
And Libye land likewise wyth warlick victorye conquoure.

*

114

Wee leaue Creete Country; and our sayls vnwrapped vphoysing,
With woodden vessel thee rough seas deepelye we furrowe.
When we fro land harbours too mayne seas gyddye dyd enter
Voyded of al coast sight with wild fluds roundly bebayed,
A watrye clowd gloomming, ful aboue mee clampred, apeered,
A sharp storme menacing, from sight beams soonye reiecting:
Thee flaws with rumbling, thee wroght fluds angrye doe iumble:
Vp swel thee surges, in chauffe sea plasshye we tumble:
With the rayn, is daylight through darcknesse mostye bewrapped,
And thundring lightbolts from torneclowds fyrye be flasshing.
Wee doe mis oure passadge through fel fluds boysterus erring,
Oure pilot eke, Palinure, through dymnesse clowdye bedusked
In poinccts of coompasse dooth stray with palpabil erroure.
Three dayes in darcknesse from bright beams soony repealed,
And three nigths parted from lightning starrye we wandered,
The fourth day foloing thee shoare, neere setled, apeered
And hils vppeaking; and smoak swift steamed to the skyward.
Oure sayls are strucken, we roa furth with speedines hastye,
And the sea by our mariners with the oars cleene canted is harrowd
On shoars of strophades from storme escaped I landed,
For those plats Strophades in languadge Greekish ar highted,
With the sea coucht Islands. Where foule bird foggye Celaeno
And Harpy is nestled: sence franckling Phines his housroume
From theym was sunderd, and fragments plentye remooued.
No plage more perilous, no monster grislye more ouglye,
No stigian vengaunce lyke too theese carmoran haggards.
Theese fouls lyke maydens are pynde with phisnomye palish;
With ramd cramd garbadge, thire gorges draftye be gulled,
With tallants prowling, theire face wan withred in hunger,
With famin vpsoaken.

OF TYNDARVS, THAT FRVM-
ped a gentlewoman for hauing a long nose,
deliuered by the former author *in Latin.*

Tyndarus attempting too kis a fayre lasse with a long nose,
Would needs bee finish, with bitter frumperye taunting.

In vayn I doo coouet my lips too linck toe thye sweete lips,
Thy nose, as a stickler, toe toe long vs parteth a sunder.
Heere the mayd al bashful, the vnsau'ry saucines heeding:
With choler oppressed, thus shrewdlye toe Tyndarus aunswerd,
Syth mye nose owtpeaking, good syr, your liplabor hindreth,
Hardlye ye may kisse mee, where no such gnomon apeereth.

Geoffrey Keating

b. 1570

MOURN FOR YOURSELF

Mourn for yourself, poor wretched thing,
Cease mourning all those other ones;
Mourn no daughter, mourn no son
Laid under graveyard covering.

Mourn first of all for your own sin
Before your body sinks in clay;
Mourn, since you shall pay that score,
The pain that Christ bore for your sake.

Mourn his wounds defending you,
Mourn his two hands and his two feet,
Christ on the cross who paid for all,
And mourn his heart the blind man split.

Everyone must go in turn:
Mourn for none already gone,
Saddest for you is your own fate,
Grimmer your grave than anyones.

Of all those the Shaper made,
All those children, women, men,
None among us weak or strong
But is extinguished in the end.

If you could see the ranks of dead
Gone down ahead to crowd below,

More than for any buried deep
You'd weep for your own turn to go.

Unless you mourn your present state,
However graceful now your form,
Blacker than coal your face shall be
On Sion Hill, the Day of Doom.

Since death is messenger of God,
If you should find this hard to bear,
You would bring trouble on yourself,
Trouble on him who went before.

Pity it is, wretch without sense,
If once you knew just what you were,
You would cease mourning other men,
Yet you would mourn for evermore.

Version: Seán Lucy

The Bards Mourn

Eochaidh O'Hussey

d. 1612

ODE TO THE MAGUIRE

Where is my Chief, my master, this bleak night, *mavrone*!
O, cold, cold, miserably cold is this bleak night for Hugh,
Its showery, arrowy, speary sleet pierceth one through and through—
Pierceth one to the very bone!

Rolls real thunder? Or was that red, livid light
Only a meteor? I scarce know; but through the midnight dim
The pitiless ice-wind streams. Except the hate that persecutes *him*
Nothing hath crueller venomy might.

An awful, a tremendous night is this, meseems!
The flood-gates of the rivers of heaven, I think, have been burst
    wide—
Down from the overcharged clouds, like unto headlong ocean's tide,
Descends grey rain in roaring streams.

Though he were even a wolf ranging the round green woods,
Though he were even a pleasant salmon in the unchainable sea,
Though he were a wild mountain eagle, he could scarce bear, he,
This sharp, sore sleet, these howling floods.

O mournful is my soul this night for Hugh Maguire!
Darkly, as in a dream he strays! Before him and behind
Triumphs the tyrannous anger of the wounding wind,
The wounding wind, that burns as fire!

It is my bitter grief—it cuts me to the heart—
That in the country of Clan Darry this should be his fate!
O, woe is me, where is he? Wandering, houseless, desolate,
Alone, without or guide or chart!

Medreams I see just now his face, the strawberry bright,
Uplifted to the blackened heavens, while the tempestuous winds
Blow fiercely over and round him, and the smiting sleet-shower
    blinds
The hero of Galang tonight!

Large, large affliction unto me and mine it is,
That one of his majestic bearing, his fair, stately form,
Should thus be tortured and o'erborne—that this unsparing storm
Should wreak its wrath on head like this!

That his great hand, so often the avenger of the oppressed,
Should this chill, churlish night, perchance, be paralysed by frost—
While through some icicle-hung thicket—as one lorn and lost—
He walks and wanders without rest.

The tempest-driven torrent deluges the mead,
It overflows the low banks of the rivulets and ponds—
The lawns and pasture-grounds lie locked in icy bonds
So that the cattle cannot feed.

The pale bright margins of the streams are seen by none,
Rushes and sweeps along the untameable flood on every side—
It penetrates and fills the cottagers' dwellings far and wide—
Water and land are blent in one.

Through some dark wood, 'mid bones of monsters, Hugh now strays,
As he confronts the storm with anguished heart, but manly brow—
O, what a sword-wound to that tender heart of his were now
A backward glance at peaceful days.

But other thoughts are his—thoughts that can still inspire
With joy and onward-bounding hope the bosom of MacNee—
Thoughts of his warriors charging like bright billows of the sea,
Borne on the wind's wings, flashing fire!

And though frost glaze tonight the clear dew of his eyes,
And white ice-gauntlets glove his noble fine fair fingers o'er,
A warm dress is to him that lightning-garb he ever wore,
The lightning of the soul, not skies.

Avran[1]

Hugh marched forth to the fight—I grieved to see him so depart;
And lo! tonight he wanders frozen, rain-drenched, sad, betrayed—
But the memory of the limewhite mansions his right hand hath laid
In ashes, warms the hero's heart.

Version: James Clarence Mangan

[1] *Avran*: Envoi

Aindrais MacMarcuis

THIS NIGHT SEES IRELAND DESOLATE

This night sees Éire desolate,
Her chiefs are cast out of their state;
Her men, her maidens weep to see
Her desolate that should peopled be.

How desolate is Connla's Plain,
Though aliens swarm in her domain;
Her rich bright soil had joy in these
That now are scattered overseas.

Man after man, day after day
Her noblest princes pass away
And leave to all the rabble rest
A land dispeopled of her best.

O'Donnell goes. In that stern strait
Sore-stricken Ulster mourns her fate,
And all the northern shore makes moan
To hear that Aodh of Annagh's gone.

Men smile at childhood's play no more,
Music and song, their day is o'er;
At wine, at Mass the kingdom's heirs
Are seen no more; changed hearts are theirs.

They feast no more, they gamble not,
All goodly pastime is forgot,
They barter not, they race no steeds,
They take no joy in stirring deeds.

No praise in builded song expressed
They hear, no tales before they rest;
None care for books and none take glee
To hear the long-traced pedigree.

The packs are silent, there's no sound
Of the old strain on Bregian ground.
A foreign flood holds all the shore,
And the great wolf-dog barks no more.

Woe to the Gael in this sore plight!
Henceforth they shall not know delight.
No tidings now their woe relieves,
Too close the gnawing sorrow cleaves.

These the examples of their woe:
Israel in Egypt long ago,
Troy that the Greek hosts set on flame,
And Babylon that to ruin came.

Sundered from hope, what friendly hand
Can save the sea-surrounded land?
The clan of Conn no Moses see
To lead them from captivity.

Her chiefs are gone. There's none to bear
Her cross or lift her from despair;
The grieving lords take ship. With these
Our very souls pass overseas.

Version: Robin Flower

Fearghal Óg MacWard

from THE FLIGHT OF THE EARLS, 1607

All Ireland's now one vessel's company,
And riding west by cliffs of Beare to sea.
Upon the snowy foam of the ebbing tide
Away in one frail bark goes all our pride.
Now stolen is the soul from Éire's breast,
And all her coasts and islands mourn oppressed.
The great twin eagles of the flock of Conn
In perilous flight are in one vessel gone.
For they whose pinions shaded Ulster's plain
In their high bark have gone nor come again;
Two last and yet most royal birds of all
Fly westward to the sea beyond recall . . .
Rory our darling, and our most gracious Hugh!
And tho' we named no names beyond the two,
Yet in this sailing have we lost a host
Of men that fainting Ireland needed most . . .

Now let the hearts of all rejoice again,
For our great Earls have safely come to Spain;
And yet their going o'er the sea must fill
With bitter wailing Éire's every hill.
Comparing their good fortune, being away,
With their sad impotence if they should stay,
Let Uisneach's land lament and yet rejoice,
And gloom and glory mingle now their voice.
And yet to know that they are gone from me,
And sail with good success beyond the sea,
Has left me lying in affliction sore.
Alas, for them, for me, for evermore!

Version: Earl of Longford

Owen Roe MacWard (?)

DARK ROSALEEN

O my Dark Rosaleen,
   Do not sigh, do not weep!
The priests are on the ocean green,
   They march along the Deep.
There's wine ... from the royal Pope
   Upon the ocean green;
And Spanish ale shall give you hope,
   My Dark Rosaleen!
   My own Rosaleen!
Shall glad your heart, shall give you hope,
Shall give you health, and help, and hope,
   My Dark Rosaleen.

Over hills and through dales
   Have I roamed for your sake;
All yesterday I sailed with sails
   On river and on lake.
The Erne ... at its highest flood
   I dashed across unseen,
For there was lightning in my blood,
   My Dark Rosaleen!
   My own Rosaleen!
Oh! there was lightning in my blood,
Red lightning lightened through my blood,
   My Dark Rosaleen!

All day long in unrest
   To and fro do I move
The very soul within my breast
   Is wasted for you, love!
The heart ... in my bosom faints
   To think of you, my Queen,

My life of life, my saint of saints,
My Dark Rosaleen!
My own Rosaleen!
To hear your sweet and sad complaints,
My life, my love, my saint of saints,
My Dark Rosaleen!

Woe and pain, pain and woe,
Are my lot night and noon,
To see your bright face clouded so,
Like to the mournful moon.
But yet . . . will I rear your throne
Again in golden sheen;
'Tis you shall reign, shall reign alone,
My Dark Rosaleen!
My own Rosaleen!
'Tis you shall have the golden throne,
'Tis you shall reign, and reign alone,
My Dark Rosaleen!

Over dews, over sands
Will I fly for your weal;
Your holy delicate white hands
Shall girdle me with steel.
At home . . . in your emerald bowers,
From morning's dawn till e'en,
You'll pray for me, my flower of flowers,
My Dark Rosaleen!
My fond Rosaleen!
You'll think of me through daylight's hours,
My virgin flower, my flower of flowers,
My Dark Rosaleen!

I could scale the blue air,
I could plough the high hills,
Oh, I could kneel all night in prayer,
To heal your many ills!
And one . . . beamy smile from you
Would float like light between

My toils and me, my own, my true,
    My Dark Rosaleen!
    My fond Rosaleen!
Would give me life and soul anew,
A second life, a soul anew,
    My Dark Rosaleen!

O! the Erne shall run red
    With redundance of blood,
The earth shall rock beneath our tread,
    And flames wrap hill and wood,
And gun-peal, and slogan cry,
    Wake many a glen serene,
Ere you shall fade, ere you shall die,
    My Dark Rosaleen!
    My own Rosaleen!
The Judgement Hour must first be nigh,
Ere you can fade, ere you can die,
    My Dark Rosaleen!
                Version: James Clarence Mangan

Mahon O'Heffernan

MY SON, FORSAKE YOUR ART

My son, forsake your art,
In that which was your fathers' own no part—
Though from the start she had borne pride of place,
Poetry now leads to disgrace.

Serve it not then, this leavings of a trade,
Nor by you be an Irish measure made,
Polished and perfect, whole in sound and sense—
Ape the new fashion, modish, cheap and dense.

Spin spineless verses of the commonplace,
Suffice it that they hold an even pace
And show not too nice taste within their span—
Preferment waits upon you if you can.

Give no man meed of censure nor just praise,
But if needs must your voice discreetly raise,
Not where there's only hatred to be earned,
Praising the Gael and for your labour spurned.

Break with them! Reckon not their histories
Nor chronicle them in men's memories,
Make it no study to enrich their fame,
Let all be named before an Irish name.

Thus you may purge your speech of bitterness,
Thus your addresses may command success—
What good repute has granted, do you hide,
Asperse their breeding, be their blood denied.

The good that has been, see you leave alone,
That which now goes for good dilate upon;
Polish the praises of a foreign rout,
Allies more likely as has come about.

The race of Miled and the sons of Conn,
Who now maintains it, that their sway goes on?
A lying prophet in men's eyes to stand,
Proclaiming alien dynasts in the land!

The tribe of Lorc, proud Carthach's company,
Be these your strangers come from oversea,
Over Flann's ground girt with the smooth sea-ring,
Let none who bore their name bear it as king.

Conn of the Hundred Battles be forgot,
The son of Eochaidh hold you now as naught:
The stock of Conn, modest and generous,
Who had deserved a better fate from us.

Drive out of mind thought of their excellence,
Gerald's king-blood, our store of recompense,
Whom might no man for love of pelf condemn—
No poem ponder thou in praise of them.

For, since none now care,
For knowledge and the comely things that were,
And were not then like fencing in a plot,
The making of a poem shall profit not.

                    Version: Máire Cruise O'Brien

David O'Bruadair

c. 1625–1698

THE CHANGE

Sad for those without sweet Anglo-Saxon
Now that Ormonde has come to Erin;
For the rest of my life in the land of Conn
I'll do better with English than a poem.

Version: John Montague

ÉIRE

Lady of the bright coils and curlings,
　Intricate turns of your body
Have pleased the foreign churls
　Who kept a bodyguard.
Though middle-aged and long a matron,
　The wife of Nial the fearless,
You played the harlot with men you hated
　And those who loved you dearly.

You smiled at them, calm stately woman,
　Unsmocked your noble limbs,
Conferred with the Saxon, old in statecraft.
　The wife of Eiver—robed as
A young queen in lime-white mansions—
　Cast modesty in a corner,
Betraying the heroes who were vanquished
　By clatter of hide, war-horn.

You were the wife of Lewy the courageous,
 And never lacked a husband.
Cairbre, Cúchulain, the sage Fionn,
 Felim, no bagman in lust,
Had known the bride of Laery the King
 And Conn the Hundred Fighter.
Too late the gleam of coil and of ringlet,
 Is changed into a sigh.

The Normans went under your mantle,
 Whenever a stronghold burned,
And you pushed back their basinets,
 Cathedral mail, spurning
The meadows inching with dew, the thickets
 At dawn, the river harbours,
Hill-bounding of the hunted prickets,
 For wanton snirt and farding.

The Binding

God soon will humble your pride, pucker your cheeks,
And bring the wife of Fintan and Diarmuid—flaxed
With hair-dye—the church door, ragged, meekly,
Her placket no longer open to the Saxon.
         Version: Austin Clarke

O'BRUADAIR

I will sing no more songs! The pride of
 my country I sang
Through forty long years of good rhyme,
 without any avail;
And no one cared even the half of the half of
 a hang
For the song or the singer—so, here is an
 end to the tale!

If you say, if you think, I complain, and have
  not got a cause,
Let you come to me here, let you look at
  the state of my hand!
Let you say if a goose-quill has calloused
  these horny old paws,
Or the spade that I grip on, and dig with,
  out there in the land?

When our nobles were safe and renowned
  and were rooted and tough,
Though my thought went to them and had
  joy in the fortune of those,
And pride that was proud of their pride—
  they gave little enough!
Not as much as two boots for my feet, or
  an old suit of clothes!

I ask of the Craftsman that fashioned the fly
  and the bird;
Of the Champion whose passion will lift
  me from death in a time;
Of the Spirit that melts icy hearts with the
  wind of a word,
That my people be worthy, and get, better
  singing than mine.

I had hoped to live decent, when Ireland was
  quit of her care,
As a poet or steward, perhaps, in a house of
  degree,
But my end of the tale is—old brogues and
  old breeches to wear!
So I'll sing no more songs for the men
  that care nothing for me.

                    Version: James Stephens

THE NEW STYLE

How strange the pride of many Irishmen!
Stuffed with pride and ostentation;
They try to master the foreigner's laws
But their tongue gets caught in his 'Hms' and 'Haws'.

Version: John Montague

Jonathan Swift

1667-1745

HOLYHEAD. SEPT. 25TH, 1727

Lo here I sit at holy head
With muddy ale and mouldy bread
All Christian vittals stink of fish
I'm where my enemyes would wish
Convict of lyes is every sign,
The Inn has not one drop of wine
I'm fasnd both by wind and tide
I see the ship at anchor ride
The Captain swears the sea's too rough
He has not passengers enough.
And thus the Dean is forc't to stay
Till others come to help the pay.
In Dublin they'll be glad to see
A packet though it brings in me.
They cannot say the winds are cross
Your Politicians at a loss
For want of matter swears and fretts,
Are forced to read the old gazettes.
I never was in hast before
To reach that slavish hateful shore
Before, I always found the wind
To me was most malicious kind
But now, the danger of a friend
On whom my fears and hopes depend
Absent from whom all Clymes are curst
With whom I'm happy in the worst
With rage impatient makes me wait
A passenger to the land I hate.
Else, rather on this bleaky shore
Where loadest winds incessant roar
Where neither herb nor tree will thrive,

Where nature hardly seems alive,
I'd go in freedom to my grave,
Than Rule yon Isle and be a Slave.

from STELLA AT WOOD-PARK

The Winter-Sky began to frown,
Poor Stella must pack off to Town.
From purling Streams and Fountains bubbling,
To Liffy's stinking tide in Dublin:
From wholesome Exercise and Air
To sossing in an easy Chair;
From Stomach sharp and hearty feeding,
To piddle like a Lady breeding:
From ruling there the Household singly,
To be directed here by Dingly:
From ev'ry Day a lordly Banquet,
To half a Joint, and God be thank it:
From ev'ry Meal Pontack in Plenty,
To half a Pint one Day in Twenty.
From Ford attending at her Call,
To Visits of Archdeacon Wall.
From Ford, who thinks of nothing mean,
To the poor Doings of the Dean.
From growing Richer with good Chear,
To running out by starving here.

But now arrives the dismal Day:
She must return to Ormond Key:
The Coachman stopt, she lookt, and swore
The Rascal had mistook the Door:
At coming in you saw her stoop;
The Entry brushed against her Hoop:
Each Moment rising in her Airs,
She curst the narrow winding Stairs:
Began a Thousand Faults to spy;

The Ceiling hardly six Foot high;
The smutty Wainscot full of Cracks,
And half the Chairs with broken Backs:
Her Quarter's out at Lady-Day,
She vows she will no longer stay,
In Lodgings, like a poor Grizette,
While there are Lodgings to be lett.

Howe'er, to keep her Spirits up,
She sent for Company to sup;
When all the while you might remark,
She strove in vain to ape Wood-Park.
Two Bottles call'd for, (half her Store;
The Cupboard could contain but four;)
A Supper worthy of her self,
Five Nothings in five Plates of Delph.

Thus, for a Week the Farce went on;
When all her Country-Savings gone:
She fell into her former Scene,
Small Beer, a Herring, and the Dean.

Thus far in jest. Though, now I fear,
You think my Jesting too severe:
But Poets when a Hint is new
Regard not whether false or true:
Yet Raillery gives no Offence,
Where Truth has not the least Pretence;
Nor can be more securly plac't
Than on a Nymph of Stella's Taste.
I must confess, your Wine and Vittle
I was too hard upon a little;
Your Table neat, your Linnen fine;
And, though in Miniature, you shine.
Yet, when you sigh to leave Wood-Park,
The Scene, the Welcome, and the Spark,
To languish in this odious Town,
And pull your haughty Stomach down;

We think you quite mistake the Case;
The Virtue lies not in the Place:
For though my Raillery were true,
A Cottage is Wood-Park with you.

from THE LEGION CLUB
Written in the Year, 1736

As I strole the City, oft I
Spy a Building large and lofty,
Not a Bow-shot from the College,
Half the Globe from Sense and Knowledge.
By the prudent Architect
Plac'd against the Church direct;
Making good my Grandames Jest,
Near the Church—you know the rest.

Tell us, what this Pile contains?
Many a Head that holds no Brains.
These Demoniacs let me dub
With the Name of *Legion Club*.
Such Assemblies, you might swear,
Meet when Butchers bait a Bear;
Such a noise, and such haranguing,
When a Brother Thief is hanging.
Such a Rout and such a Rabble
Run to hear Jackpudding gabble;
Such a Croud their Ordure throws
On a far less Villain's Nose.

Could I from the Building's Top
Hear the rattling Thunder drop,
While the Devil upon the Roof,
If the Devil be Thunder proof,
Should with Poker fiery-red
Crack the Stones, and melt the Lead;

Drive them down on every Scull,
While the den of Thieves is full,
Quite destroy that Harpies Nest,
How might then our Isle be blest?
For Divines allow, that God
Sometimes makes the Devil his Rod:
And the Gospel will inform us
He can punish Sins enormous.

Yet should *Swift* endow the Schools
For his Lunatics and Fools,
With a Rood or two of Land,
I allow the Pile may stand.
You perhaps will ask me, why so?
But it is with this Proviso,
Since the House is like to last,
Let a Royal Grant be pass'd,
That the Club have Right to dwell
Each within his proper Cell;
With a Passage left to creep in,
And a Hole above for peeping.

Let them, when they once get in
Sell the Nation for a Pin;
While they sit a picking Straws
Let them rave of making Laws;
While they never hold their Tongue,
Let them dabble in their Dung;
Let them form a grand Committee,
How to plague and starve the City;
Let them stare and storm and frown,
When they see a Clergy-Gown.

Let them, 'ere they crack a Louse,
Call for th' Orders of the House;
Let them with their gosling Quills,
Scribble senseless Heads of Bills;
We may, while they strain their Throats,
Wipe our Arses with their Votes. . . .

ON DREAMS
An Imitation of Petronius

Those Dreams that on the silent Night intrude,
And with false flitting Shades our Minds delude,
Jove never sends us downward from the Skies,
Nor can they from infernal Mansions rise;
But all are meer Productions of the Brain,
And Fools consult Interpreters in vain.

For, when in Bed we rest our weary Limbs,
The Mind unburthen'd sports in various Whims,
The busy Head with mimick Art runs o'er
The Scenes and Actions of the Day before.

The drowsy Tyrant, by his Minions led,
To regal Rage devotes some Patriot's Head.
With equal Terrors, not with equal Guilt,
The Murd'rer dreams of all the Blood he spilt.

The Soldier smiling hears the Widow's Cries,
And stabs the Son before the Mother's Eyes.
With like Remorse his Brother of the Trade,
The Butcher, feels the Lamb beneath his blade.

The Statesman rakes the Town to find a Plot,
And dream of Forfeitures by Treason got.
Nor less Tom Turd-Man of true Statesman mold,
Collects the City Filth in search of Gold.

Orphans around his Bed the Lawyer sees,
And takes the Plaintiff's and Defendant's Fees.
His Fellow Pick-Purse, watching for a Job,
Fancies his Fingers in the Cully's Fob.

The kind Physician grants the Husband's Prayers,
Or gives Relief to long-expecting Heirs.
The sleeping Hangman ties the fatal Noose,
Nor unsuccessful waits for dead Men's Shoes.

The grave Divine with knotty Points perplext,
As if he were awake, nods o'er his Text:
While the sly Mountebank attends his Trade,
Harangues the Rabble, and is better paid.

The hireling Senator of modern Days,
Bedaubs the guilty Great with nauseous Praise:
And *Dick* the Scavenger with equal Grace,
Flirts from his Cart the Mud in *Walpole's* Face.

ONYONS

Come, follow me by the Smell,
Here's delicate Onyons to sell,
I promise to use you well.
They make the Blood warmer,
You'll feed like a Farmer:
For this is ev'ry Cook's Oponion,
No sav'ry Dish without an Onyon;
But lest your Kissing should be spoyl'd,
Your Onyons must be th'roughly boyl'd;
Or else you may spare
Your Mistress a Share,
The Secret will never be known;
She cannot discover
The Breath of her Lover,
But think it as sweet as her own.

THE DAY OF JUDGEMENT

With a Whirl of Thought oppress'd
I sink from Reverie to Rest.
An horrid Vision seiz'd my Head,
I saw the Graves give up their Dead.

Jove, arm'd with Terrors, burst the Skies,
And Thunder roars, and Light'ning flies!
Amaz'd, confus'd, its Fate unknown,
The World stands trembling at his Throne.
While each pale Sinner hangs his Head,
Jove, nodding, shook the Heav'ns, and said,
'Offending Race of Human Kind,
By Nature, Reason, Learning, blind;
You who thro' Frailty step'd aside,
And you who never fell—*thro' Pride*;
You who in different Sects have shamm'd,
And come to see each other damn'd;
(So some Folks told you, but they knew
No more of Jove's Designs than you)
The World's mad Business now is o'er,
And I resent these Pranks no more.
I to such Blockheads set my Wit!
I damn such Fools! Go, go, you're bit.'

ON HIS OWN DEAFNESS

Deaf, giddy, helpless, left alone,
To all my Friends a Burthen grown,
No more I hear my Church's Bell,
Than if it rang out for my Knell:
At Thunder now no more I start,
Than at the Rumbling of a Cart:
Nay, what's incredible, alack!
I hardly hear a Woman's Clack.

Egan O'Rahilly

1670–1726

THE BRIGHTEST OF THE BRIGHT

The Brightest of the Bright met me on my path so lonely;
  The Crystal of all Crystals was her flashing dark-blue eye;
Melodious more than music was her spoken language only;
  And glorious were her cheeks, of a brilliant crimson dye.

With ringlets above ringlets her hair in many a cluster
  Descended to the earth, and swept the dewy flowers;
Her bosom shone as bright as a mirror in its lustre;
  She seemed like some fair daughter of the Celestial Powers.

She chanted me a chant, a beautiful and grand hymn,
  Of him who should be shortly Éire's reigning King—
She prophesied the fall of the wretches who had banned him;
  And somewhat else she told me which I dare not sing.

Trembling with many fears I called on Holy Mary,
  As I drew nigh this Fair, to shield me from all harm,
When, wonderful to tell! she fled far to the Fairy
  Green mansions of Sliabh Luachra in terror and alarm.

O'er mountain, moor and marsh, by greenwood, lough and hollow,
  I tracked her distant footsteps with a throbbing heart;
Through many an hour and day did I follow on and follow,
  Till I reached the magic palace reared of old by Druid art.

There a wild and wizard band with mocking fiendish laughter
  Pointed out me her I sought, who sat low beside a clown;
And I felt as though I never could dream of Pleasure after
  When I saw the maid so fallen whose charms deserved a crown.

Then with burning speech and soul, I looked at her and told her
  That to wed a churl like that was for her the shame of shames

When a bridegroom such as I was longing to enfold her
  To a bosom that her beauty had enkindled into flames.

But answer made she none; she wept with bitter weeping,
  Her tears ran down in rivers, but nothing could she say;
She gave me then a guide for my safe and better keeping,—
  The Brightest of the Bright, whom I met upon my way.
                    Version: James Clarence Mangan

MORE POWER

More power to you, Cromwell,
O King who crowned clodhoppers:
From your visit flowed peace,
The honey and cream of honour.

We pray that neither Kavanagh,
Nolan, nor Kinsella,
Burke, nor Rice, nor Roche,
Ever hold sod of their fathers

And that only Cromwell preside,
That noble King of Clan Lout,
Who gave all to the flail wielders
And left the true heirs—nothing.

And may all in this house
Be even healthier and wealthier
A year from today; together
With all whom we like.
                    Version: John Montague

A TIME OF CHANGE

Without flocks or cattle or the curved horns
Of cattle, in a drenching night without sleep
My five wits on the famous uproar
Of the wave toss like ships
And I cry for boyhood, long before
Winkle and dogfish had defiled my lips.

O if he lived, the prince who sheltered me
And his company who gave me entry
On the river of the Laune,
Whose royalty stood sentry
Over intricate harbours, I and my own
Would not be desolate in Dermot's country.

Fierce McCarthy Mor whose friends were welcome,
McCarthy of the Lee a slave of late,
McCarthy of Kenturk whose blood
Has dried underfoot:
Of all my princes not a single word—
Irrevocable silence ails my heart.

My heart shrinks in me, my heart ails
That every hawk and royal hawk is lost;
From Cashel to the far sea
Their birthright is dispersed
Far and near, night and day, by robbery
And ransack, every town oppressed.

Take warning, wave, take warning, crown of the sea
I, O'Rahilly—witless from your discords—
Were Spanish sails again afloat
And rescue on our tides,
Would force this outcry down your wild throat,
Would make you swallow these Atlantic words.
                    Version: Eavan Boland

INIS FÁL

Now may we turn aside and dry our tears,
And comfort us, and lay aside our fears,
For all is gone—all comely quality,
All gentleness and hospitality,
All courtesy and merriment is gone;
Our virtues all are withered every one,
Our music vanished and our skill to sing:
Now may we quiet us and quit our moan,
Nothing is whole that could be broke; nothing
Remains to us of all that was our own.

Version: James Stephens

Turlough O'Carolan

1670–1738

MABEL KELLY

Lucky the husband
Who puts his hand beneath her head.
   They kiss without scandal
Happiest two near feather-bed.
He sees the tumble of brown hair
Unplait, the breasts, pointed and bare
   When nightdress shows
   From dimple to toe-nail,
All Mabel glowing in it, here, there, everywhere.

Music might listen
   To her least whisper,
Learn every note, for all are true.
   While she is speaking,
   Her voice goes sweetly
To charm the herons in their musing.
Her eyes are modest, blue, their darkness
Small rooms of thought, but when they sparkle
   Upon a feast-day,
   Glasses are meeting,
Each raised to Mabel Kelly, our toast and darling.

Gone now are many Irish ladies
Who kissed and fondled, their very pet-names
Forgotten, their tibia degraded.
She takes their sky. Her smile is famed.
Her praise is scored by quill and pencil.
   Harp and spinet
   Are in her debt
And when she plays or sings, melody is content.

No man who sees her
   Will feel uneasy.
He goes his way, head high, however tired.
   Lamp loses light
   When placed beside her.
She is the pearl and being of all Ireland
Foot, eye, mouth, breast, thigh and instep, all that we desire.
Tresses that pass small curls as if to touch the ground;
   So many prizes
   Are not divided.
Her beauty is her own and she is not proud.

PEGGY BROWNE

The dark-haired girl, who holds my thoughts entirely
Yet keeps me from her arms and what I desire,
Will never take my word for she is proud
And none may have his way with Peggy Browne.

Often I dream that I am in the woods
At Westport House. She strays alone, blue-hooded,
Then lifts her flounces, hurries from a shower,
But sunlight stays all day with Peggy Browne.

Her voice is music, every little echo
My pleasure and O her shapely breasts, I know,
Are white as her own milk, when taffeta gown
Is let out, inch by inch, for Peggy Browne.

A lawless dream comes to me in the night-time,
That we are stretching together side by side,
Nothing I want to do can make her frown.
I wake alone, sighing for Peggy Browne.
                              Versions: Austin Clarke

Oliver Goldsmith

1728 (?)—1774

from THE TRAVELLER

Remote, unfriended, melancholy, slow,
Or by the lazy Scheldt, or wandering Po;
Or onward, where the rude Carinthian boor
Against the houseless stranger shuts the door;
Or where Campania's plain forsaken lies,
A weary waste expanding to the skies:
Where'er I roam, whatever realms to see,
My heart untravell'd fondly turns to thee;
Still to my brother turns, with ceaseless pain,
And drags at each remove a lengthening chain.

Eternal blessings crown my earliest friend,
And round his dwelling guardian saints attend;
Blest be that spot, where chearful guests retire
To pause from toil, and trim their evening fire;
Blest that abode, where want and pain repair,
And every stranger finds a ready chair;
Blest be those feasts with simple plenty crown'd,
Where all the ruddy family around
Laugh at the jests or pranks that never fail,
Or sigh with pity at some mournful tale,
Or press the bashful stranger to his food,
And learn the luxury of doing good.

But me, not destin'd such delights to share,
My prime of life in wand'ring spent and care:
Impell'd, with steps unceasing, to pursue
Some fleeting good, that mocks me with the view;
That, like the circle bounding earth and skies,
Allures from far, yet, as I follow, flies;
My fortune leads to traverse realms alone,
And find no spot of all the world my own.

A DESCRIPTION OF AN AUTHOR'S
BEDCHAMBER

Where the Red Lion flaring o'er the way,
Invites each passing stranger that can pay;
Where Calvert's butt, and Parson's black champaign,
Regale the drabs and bloods of Drury Lane;
There is a lonely room, from bailiffs snug,
The muse found Scroggen stretch'd beneath a rug.
A window patch'd with paper lent a ray,
That dimly shew'd the state in which he lay;
The sanded floor that grits beneath the tread;
The humid wall with paltry pictures spread:
The royal game of goose was there in view,
And the twelve rules the royal martyr drew;
The seasons fram'd with listing found a place,
And brave prince William shew'd his lamp-black face:
The morn was cold, he views with keen desire
The rusty grate unconscious of a fire:
With beer and milk arrears the frieze was scor'd,
And five crack'd tea cups dress'd the chimney board.
A night-cap deck'd his brows instead of bay,
A cap by night—a stocking all the day!

from THE DESERTED VILLAGE

O luxury! Thou curst by Heaven's decree,
How ill exchanged are things like these for thee!
How do thy potions with insidious joy,
Diffuse their pleasures only to destroy!
Kingdoms by thee, to sickly greatness grown,
Boast of a florid vigour not their own.
At every draught more large and large they grow,
A bloated mass of rank unwieldy woe;
Till sapped their strength, and every part unsound,
Down, down they sink, and spread a ruin round.

Even now the devastation is begun,
And half the business of destruction done;
Even now, methinks, as pondering here I stand,
I see the rural virtues leave the land.
Down where yon anchoring vessel spreads the sail,
That idly waiting flaps with every gale,
Downward they move, a melancholy band,
Pass from the shore, and darken all the strand.
Contented toil, and hospitable care,
And kind connubial tenderness, are there;
And piety with wishes placed above,
And steady loyalty, and faithful love.
And thou, sweet Poetry, thou loveliest maid,
Still first to fly where sensual joys invade;
Unfit in these degenerate times of shame,
To catch the heart, or strike for honest fame;
Dear charming nymph, neglected and decried,
My shame in crowds, my solitary pride;
Thou source of all my bliss, and all my woe,
Thou found'st me poor at first, and keep'st me so;
Thou guide by which the nobler arts excell,
Thou nurse of every virtue, fare thee well.
Farewell, and O where'er thy voice be tried,
On Torno's cliffs, or Pambamarca's side,
Whether where equinoctial fervours glow,
Or winter wraps the polar world in snow,
Still let thy voice prevailing over time,
Redress the rigours of the inclement clime;
Aid slighted truth, with thy persuasive strain
Teach erring man to spurn the rage of gain;
Teach him that states of native strength possest,
Tho' very poor, may still be very blest;
That trade's proud empire hastes to swift decay,
As ocean sweeps the labour'd mole away;
While self-dependent power can time defy,
As rocks resist the billows and the sky.

Eibhlin Dubh O'Connell

b. 1743 (?)

LAMENT FOR ART O'LEARY

I

HIS WIFE: My love forever!
The day I first saw you
At the end of the market-house,
My eye observed you,
My heart approved you,
I fled from my father with you,
Far from my home with you.

II

I never repented it:
You whitened a parlour for me,
Painted rooms for me,
Reddened ovens for me,
Baked fine bread for me,
Basted meat for me,
Slaughtered beasts for me;
I slept in ducks' feathers
Till midday milking-time
Or more if it pleased me.

III

My friend forever!
My mind remembers
That fine spring day
How well your hat suited you,
Bright gold-banded,
Sword silver-hilted—
Right hand steady—
Threatening aspect—

Trembling terror
On treacherous enemy—
You poised for a canter
On your slender bay horse.
The Saxons bowed to you,
Down to the ground to you,
Not for love of you
But for deadly fear of you,
Though you lost your life to them,
Oh my soul's darling.

IV

Oh white-handed rider!
How fine your brooch was
Fastened in cambric,
And your hat with laces
When you crossed the sea to us,
They would clear the street for you,
And not for love of you
But for deadly hatred.

V

My friend you were forever!
When they will come home to me,
Gentle little Conor
And Farr O'Leary, the baby,
They will question me so quickly,
Where did I leave their father.
I'll answer in my anguish
That I left him in Killnamartyr.
They will call out to their father:
And he won't be there to answer.

VI

My friend and my love!
Of the blood of Lord Antrim,

And of Barry of Allchoill,
How well your sword suited you,
Hat gold-banded,
Boots of fine leather,
Coat of broadcloth,
Spun overseas for you.

VII

My friend you were forever!
I knew nothing of your murder
Till your horse came to the stable
With the reins beneath her trailing,
And your heart's blood on her shoulders
Staining the tooled saddle
Where you used to sit and stand.
My first leap reached the threshold,
My second reached the gateway,
My third leap reached the saddle.

I struck my hands together
And I made the bay horse gallop
As fast as I was able,
Till I found you dead before me
Beside a little furze-bush.
Without Pope or bishop,
Without priest or cleric
To read the death-psalms for you,
But a spent old woman only
Who spread her cloak to shroud you—
Your heart's blood was still flowing;
I did not stay to wipe it
But filled my hands and drank it.

Version: Eilís Dillon

My love and my delight!
Rise up now, straight,
And come on home with me,
We'll have a beast slaughtered,
Call friends to the feast,
Get the music started.
We'll get ready a bed
With crisp linen sheets
And bright speckled quilts
To bring out a sweat instead
Of the chill that grips you.

HIS SISTER: My friend and my treasure,
There's not a shapely woman
From Cork of the sails
To the bridge of Toime
With her bit of money gathered
And her herd of cattle
Would go to sleep in her room
The night of your wake.

HIS WIFE: My friend everlasting!
You must never believe
The gossip that's flying,
That slanderous story
That I slept at your wake.
It wasn't real slumber
But your children were unhappy
And needed me near them
To lull them asleep.

Neighbours, don't listen
To such lying tales!
Is there a woman in Ireland,
Who, at each day's end,
Stretched at his side,
Who bore his three children,
Would not lose her mind

After Art O'Leary, who
Lies spent here with me
Since yesterday morning.

My long lasting sorrow
That I was not at your side
When the bullet was fired
To take it in my right side
Or the folds of my linen
And you would still be at liberty,
O smooth-handed horseman!

HIS SISTER: My sharp, bitter grief
That I wasn't near you
When the powder blazed
To take it in my right flank
Or the fold of my gown
And you would have gone free,
O grey-eyed horseman!

HIS WIFE: My friend, my true fortune!
It's poor treatment to put down
A soldier, cowled in his coffin;
A stout-hearted chevalier
Who fished in the streams
And drank in the halls
With warm-breasted women.
A thousand laments—
I've lost my companion!

My love and my delight,
When you went out the gate,
You turned back quickly,
You kissed your children,
You kissed my fingers
Saying: 'Eileen, get up
And put your things together
Carefully and quickly,
I'm leaving from home

And it's not sure I'll return'.
I could only mock such talk,
You'd said it so often.

My friend and my choice!
Bright-sworded cavalier,
Put on your courtly suit,
Put on your black beaver,
Pull up your riding gloves,
Lift up your riding crop—
Your mare is waiting
To strike the path east
Where the trees will thin out
The streams narrow to a trickle
The men and women salute you—
If they still have the old ways,
Though I fear they've gone.

My love and my companion
It's not my dead kindred
Nor the death of my three children
Nor Donal Mor O'Connell
Nor Conall whom the tide drowned,
Nor the woman of twenty-six
Who crossed over the sea
To be the friend of kings—
It's none of these I'm calling
But Art who was mown down last night
At the inch of Carriganima
And lies with me here
With no one to wake him
But the dark little women of the mill,
Not a single one weeping.

HIS SISTER: My love and my treasure,
My bright-breasted pigeon!
If I come to mourn you
Without my escort,

156

It's no shame on me,
For they lie locked
In a sleep without waking,
In narrow coffins,
In closed vaults.

But for the smallpox
And the black death
And the spotted fever
That proud hosts of riders
Would be clattering
With bridles ringing
To join the cortège
Of Art of the white breast.

My love and my delight!
Friend of the wild horsemen
Who hunted the glens
Till you turned their heads
Home to your hall where
Knives were sharpening
Long tables being laid
For the roast beef,
The sucking pig and bacon,
The countless ribs of lamb,
With yellow oats pouring
To make the horses snort
And stable boys who
Would never go to bed
But fodder the beasts
If they stayed for a week
With my much loved brother!

My love and my calf!
A vision broke through
My dreams last night
As I lay in bed late
And lonely, in Cork:

That lime-white courtyard,
The fair stronghold
Where we played together
As children was fallen,
The hounds voiceless,
The birds songless,
While you were found
On the bare hillside
Without priest or cleric
But an old, old woman
To spread her cloak
Where the earth held you—
Art O'Leary—
Your life blood pouring
Over your linen shirt.

HIS WIFE: My love and my secret,
How well they became you,
Your five-ply stockings,
Your knee-high boots
And three-cornered Caroline,
With a light whip
For a frisky gelding:
Many's the modest, mannerly girl
Turned to gaze after you.

My steadfast love,
When you rode into town,
Sturdy and strong,
The shopkeepers' wives
Bowed and scraped
Knowing only too well
How good you were in bed,
What a fine cavalier
And sire for children.

If my cries could reach my kindred
In far, famed Derrynane

Or Capling of the yellow apples,
Many's the supple, spirited rider
And women with spotless kerchiefs
Would be here without delay
To weep upon your brow,
Art O'Leary of the smiles!

So part of my heart goes to you
Bright women of the mill
For your skill in lamenting
The brown mare's rider.

Christ himself knows
I'll have no hat on my head
No linen next my skin
No shoes on my feet
No supplies in my house
No harness for the mare
But I'll spend all at law
And I'll cross overseas
To speak to the king
And if no one pays heed
I'll return on my own
To the black-blooded clown
Who stole my precious one.

My love and my treasure,
Your stacks are roped,
Your cows heavy with milk
But sorrow in my heart
All Munster can't cure,
Nor the druids of the past.
Until Art O'Leary comes again
This sorrow won't lift
That lies across my heart
Like a tightly-locked trunk
With rust on the hasps
And the key thrown away.

So stop your weeping now
Women of the soft, wet eyes
And drink to Art O'Leary
Before he enters the grave school
Not to study wisdom and song
But to carry earth and stone.

Version: John Montague

Owen Roe O'Sullivan

1748–1784

HIS REQUEST

Forge me a tool, my Seamus,
Fit for the earth
A well-tempered spade
To work and till
Clean furrows, welded
To shape and hand-set.

No sign of beating mar
The press of silver steel,
Loose and free with flexible
Sweep, the grain
Of the wood-shaft tapered
To regular borders,
My tool will shine in the field.

No buckle or wrinkle
On the edges if possible,
I see its sleek flange
In the spare form of a beak,
The socket without flaw to take
The handle, the whole to have
Harmony like a bell.

Version: Joan Keefe

THE VOLATILE KERRYMAN

OWEN: I travelled the land from Leap to Corbally
From bright Glandore to sweet Roscarbery,
Oh-roh! and to Cashel of sloes.

Fairs twice a week there on Thursday and Saturday,
High and low Masses there sung by the clergy,
Tankards and quarts full of wine and brandy,
Fine young women to keep you handy,
Oh-roh! 'tis Heaven below.

GIRL: That would be the poor day if I ran away with you,
    'Tis a rake of your like that would make me play with
      you,
    Oh-roh! 'Twould be madness to go!
    Oh, my father won't mind if you say you'll marry me,
    But he'll murder us both if to Kerry you carry me,
    Oh-roh! with a terrible blow.
    But if you give your oath that you'll never stray from
      me
    I'll buy you strong drink that will coax you to stay with
      me.
    Make up your mind and say you'll come home with me,
(*Coaxing*) Make up your mind and say you'll come home with me,
    Oh-roh! And my fortune you'll own.

OWEN: Oh, there's no place on earth that I wouldn't go with
      you,
    And I'd fit out a ship if I thought 'twould pleasure you,
    Oh-roh! O'er the ocean we'd go.
    I would carry you with me across to Germany,
    In Venice or Rome we'd have wine and company,
    Come and be brave! Don't be afraid of me!
(*Coaxing*) Come and be nice, and travel away with me.
    Oh-roh! my darling, my own.

GIRL: Oh, I'd travel the world and Newfoundland with you,
    And to see foreign countries would surely be grand with
      you,
    Oh-roh! 'tis happy I'd go.
    But to wed me your promise I must be certain of,
    And to live out our lives in sweet contentment, love,
    Oh-roh! 'tis you I adore.

OWEN: Here is my hand in your hand to hold with you,
To bind us for life so that I'll grow old with you,
Our engagement is made now, and love in my heart for
    you,
There's a half of my soul that will never part from you.
Oh-roh! while the world shall roll.

GIRL: If I follow you close to the slopes of Carbery,
My senses I'll lose if you don't come home with me,
Oh-roh! the teardrops will flow.

OWEN: Bring a purseful of gold for the road along with you,
For money's no load when 'tis golden sovereigns,
Oh-roh! to spend as we roam.

GIRL: Your hands will be soft without trace of work on them
No digging potatoes or cutting turf with them,

OWEN: There'll be dancing all night, and drinking and devilment;

GIRL: Music and whiskey,

OWEN: For money makes merriment,

BOTH: Oh-roh! 'tis the Devil's own sport.

GIRL: But you're telling me lies, you don't mean the half of
    it,
Coaxing me now, and in a while you'll laugh at it,
Oh-roh! 'Twould make me a show.

OWEN: Oh love of my heart, my dear, pay heed to me,
I wouldn't deceive you for Ireland free to me.
For fear it would lead me to Hell's black deanery,
Sweet and dear will you always be to me,
Oh-roh! 'til in the coffin I go.

GIRL: Don't mention the coffin, bad luck to speak of it,
But talk of fine sport for 'tis we'll be seeking it,
Oh-roh! and adventures galore!
Call in the neighbours, there's barrels of porter full
And we'll make a great noise will be heard in Waterford.
Oh-roh! while the world shall roll!
Oh, I'd rather your love than the riches of Solomon,
Acres of cattle or valleys of singing birds,

I've made up my mind, and the Pope couldn't change it
    now,
I'd give you the world if I could arrange it now.
Oh-roh! my darling, my own!

OWEN: A fortnight spent travelling far and wide with her,
Making up songs for her, telling lies to her,
Oh-roh! to keep her aglow,
'Til the last golden sovereign I winkled out of her,
Sweetly and easily, never a shout from her,
Oh-roh! indeed money's no load!
Oh, 'twas smartly I settled my beaver hat on me,
The blackthorn stick and the coat that flattered me,
And over the ditches I fled like a bat from her,
Home to Kerry, like a scalded cat from her,
Oh-roh! while she trotted below.

As nightfall came on, she was most astonished
To see that her darling had totally vanished—
Oh-roh! with a great hullagone!
She tore at her hair like a raving lunatic,
She swore I betrayed her and fairly ruined her,

GIRL: Oh-roh! He's gone with my gold.
Where is he now, oh where is that vagabond?
Make haste and be after him, carry him back to me,
That cursed rogue, that blathering Kerryman,
Breaking my heart with his rakish merriment,
Oh-roh!

OWEN: and it's goodbye to Owen!

Version: Seán O'Riada

Brian Merriman

1747-1805

from THE MIDNIGHT COURT

WALK

I used to walk the morning stream,
The meadows fresh with the dew's wet gleam,
Beside the woods, in the hillside's shade,
No shadow or doubt on the lightsome day.
It'd gladden the heart in a broken man,
Spent without profit, vigour or plan.
Let a withered old ballocks, but rich in gall,
View the trees' arms, raised like ladies' tall,
The ducks smooth-swimming the shining bay,
The swan all proud, to lead the way,
The blue of the lake and lusty wave,
Battering mad, in the gloomy cave.
The fish for energy, leaping high,
To take a bite from the spacious sky....

Version: Brendan Behan

THE COUNTRY'S CRISIS

The Court considered the country's crisis,
And what do you think its main advice is—
That unless there's a spurt in procreation
We can bid goodbye to to the Irish nation;
It's growing smaller year by year—
And don't pretend that's not your affair.
Between death and war and ruin and pillage
The land is like a deserted village;
Our best are banished, but you, you slob,
Have you ever hammered a single job?
What use are you to us, you cissy?
We have thousands of women who'd keep you busy,

With breasts like balloons or small as a bud
Buxom of body and hot in the blood,
Virgins or whores—whatever's your taste—
At least don't let them go to waste;
It's enough to make us broken-hearted—
Legs galore—and none of them parted.
They're ready and willing for any endeavour—
But you can't expect them to wait forever.

Version: David Marcus

THE MAIDEN'S PLIGHT

I fasted three canonical hours
To try and come round the heavenly powers;
I washed my shift where the stream was deep
To hear a lover's voice in sleep;
Often I swept the woodstack bare,
Burned bits of my frock, my nails, my hair,
Up the chimney stuck the flail,
Slept with a spade without avail;
Hid my wool in the limekiln late
And my distaff behind the churchyard gate;
I had flax on the road to halt coach or carriage
And haycocks stuffed with heads of cabbage,
And night and day on the proper occasions
Invoked Old Nick and all his legions;
But 'twas all no good and I'm broken-hearted
For here I'm back at the place I started;
And this is the cause of all my tears
I am fast in the rope of the rushing years,
With age and need in lessening span,
And death beyond, and no hope of a man.

Version: Frank O'Connor

THE OLD MAN'S TALE

The things I'm told, I could raise your hair
By recounting the times she's been stretched out bare,

On the flat of her back upon the ground
And the customers rushing from miles around.
From youth to grandad, all can speak
Of her adaptable technique—
In Ibrickane with big and small,
In Tirmaclane with one and all,
In Kilbrickane with thick and thin,
In Clare, in Ennis, and in Quin,
In Cratlee and Tradree where they're tough
She never seemed to have enough!
But I'd still have allowed her a second chance
And blamed it on youthful extravagance
Were it not that I saw with my own two eyes
On the roadway—naked to the skies—
Herself and a lout from the Durrus bogs
Going hammer and tongs like a couple of dogs.

Version: David Marcus

NOW GOD STAND UP FOR BASTARDS

This bond of the prelates I pray you revoke
For the sake of the necks not yet under the yoke,
'Tis the cause of the dearth and decrease of our nation
And the source of our sickly and sad generation,
But a brave breed of heroes would spring in its place,
If this bar was removed, to replenish the race,
For why call a priest in to bind and to bless
Before candid nature can give one caress?
Why lay the banquet and why pay the band
To blow their bassoons and their cheeks to expand?
Since Mary the Mother of God did conceive
Without calling the clergy or begging their leave,
The love-gotten children are famed as the flower
Of man's procreation and nature's power;
For love is a lustier sire than law
And has made them sound without fault or flaw,
And better and braver in heart and head
Than the puny breed of the bridal bed,

In body and brains and gift and grace
The palm is born by the bastard race.

Version: Arland Ussher

AN IRISH MARRIAGE NIGHT

A starved old gelding, blind and lamed
And a twenty-year-old with her parts untamed.
It wasn't her fault if things went wrong,
She closed her eyes and held her tongue;
She was no ignorant girl from school
To whine for her mother and play the fool
But a competent bedmate smooth and warm
Who cushioned him like a sheaf of corn.
Line by line she bade him linger
With gummy lips and groping finger,
Gripping his thighs in a wild embrace
Rubbing her brush from knee to waist
Stripping him bare to the cold night air,
Everything done with love and care.
But she'd nothing to show for all her labour;
There's wasn't a jump in the old deceiver,
And all I could say would give no notion
Of that poor distracted girl's emotion,
Her knees cocked up and the bedposts shaking,
Chattering teeth and sinews aching,
While she sobbed and tossed through a joyless night
And gave it up with the morning light.

Version: Frank O'Connor

THE SOLUTION

What is the use of the rule insane
That marriage has closed to the clerical clan
In the church of our fathers since first it began.
It's a melancholy sight to a needy maid
Their comely faces and forms displayed,
Their hips and thighs so broad and round,
Their buttocks and breasts that in flesh abound,
Their lustrous looks and their lusty limbs,

Their fair fresh features, their smooth soft skins,
Their strength and stature, their force and fire,
Their craving curbed and uncooled desire.
They eat and drink of the fat of the land,
They've wealth and comfort at their command,
They sleep on beds of the softest down,
They've ease and leisure their lot to crown,
They commence in manhood's prime and flood,
And well we know that they're flesh and blood!
If I thought that sexless saints they were
Or holy angels, I would not care,
But they're lusty lads with a crave unsated
In slothful sleep, and the maids unmated.
We know it is true there are few but hate
The lonely life and the celibate state;
Is it fair to condemn them to mope and moan,
Is it fair to force them to lie alone,
To bereave of issue a sturdy band
The fruit of whose loins might free the land?
Tho' some of them ever were grim and gruff,
Intractable, sullen and stern and tough,
Crabbed and cross, unkind and cold,
Surly and wont to scowl and scold,
Many are made of warmer clay,
Affectionate, ardent, kind and gay;
It's often a woman got land or wealth,
Store or stock from a priest by stealth,
Many's the case I call to mind
Of clergymen who were slyly kind,
I could show you women who were their flames,
And their children reared beneath false names;
And often I must lament in vain
How they waste their strength on the old and plain
While marriageable maids their plight deplore
Waiting unwooed thro' this senseless law;
'Tis a baleful ban to our hapless race
And beneath its sway we decay apace.

                              Version: Arland Ussher

Samuel Thompson

1766–1816

TO A HEDGEHOG

Thou grimmest far o grusome tykes
Grubbin thy food by thorny dykes
Gude faith, thou disna want for pikes
    Baith sharp an rauckle;[1]
Thou looks (Lord save's) arrayed in spikes,
    A creepin heckle.

Sure Nick begat thee, at the first,
On some auld whin or thorn accurst;
An some horn-fingered harpie nurst
    The ugly urchin;
Then Belzie, laughin like to burst,
    First caad thee Hurchin.[2]

Fowk tell how thou, sae far frae daft,
Whan wind-faan fruit be scattered saft,
Will row thysel wi cunning craft
    An bear awa
Upon thy back, what fares thee aft,
    A day or twa.

But whether this account be true
Is mair than I will here avow;
If that thou stribs the outler cow,
    As some assert,
A pretty milkmaid, I allow,
    Forsooth thou art.

Now creep awa the way ye came,
And tend your squeakin pups at hame;

---

[1] *Rauckle*: strong   [2] *Hurchin*: hedgehog

Gin Colly should oerhear the same,
    It might be fatal,
For you, wi aa the pikes ye claim,
    Wi him to battle.

APRIL

Behold the ever-tim'rous hare
Already quits her furzy shade,
And o'er the field, with watchful care,
Unseen will nip the sprouting blade.

Adown the whin-beskirted way,
There thoughtless plods the schoolboy young,
At times in haste, anon he'll stay,
And thinks he hears the cuckoo's song.

Anthony Raftery

1784–1835

THE LASS FROM BALLY-NA-LEE

On my way to Mass
                    to say a prayer,
The wind was high
                    sowing rain,
I met a maid
                    with wind-wild hair
And madly fell
                    in love again.
I spoke with learning,
                    charm and pride
And, as was fitting,
                    answered she:
'My mind is now
                    well satisfied
So walk with me
                    to Bally-na-Lee.'
Given the offer
                    I didn't delay
And blowing a laugh
                    at this willing young lass,
I swung with her over
                    the fields through the day
Till shortly we reached
                    the rump of the house.

A table with glasses
                    and drink was set
And then says the lassie
                    turning to me:
'You are welcome Raftery,
                    so drink a wet

To love's demands
        in Bally-na-Lee.'

I've walked in my time
        across England and France,
From Spain to Greece
        and back by sea;
Met many a maid
        at many a dance,
But none had an airy
        grace like she.
If I had the power
        and the flower of youth,
I'd find her out
        wherever she'd be,
I'd comb all the coasts
        from Cork to Beirut,
To live with this gem
        from Bally-na-Lee.

Mary Egan
        is a bred lass,
With the looks and grace
        of the queen of a tribe;
Looks, two hundred scholars
        en masse,
Or the pick of the poets
        could never describe.
Venus and Deirdre
        were no more grand,
Nor Helen, who launched
        the ships in the sea,
She's the brightest blossom
        of all Ireland,
This fabulous flower
        from Bally-na-Lee.
My star of light,
        my autumn sun,

My curly head,
                my summer sky,
In Sunday's shadow
                    let's rise and run
And arrange the place
                     where we shall lie.
All I ask is to sing
                  to you each Sunday night,
With drink on the table
                    and you on my knee—
Dear God high in Heaven,
                    who gives and takes sight,
Allow me this pleasure
                in Bally-na-Lee.
                Version: Desmond O'Grady

A Wandering Voice:
Songs from the Irish

O'ROURKE'S FEAST
Hugh MacGowran (c. 1720)

O'Rourke's revel rout let no person forget
Who has been, who will be, or never was yet.
See seven-score hogs in the morning we slay,
With bullocks and sheep for the feasting each day.
Hundred pails usquebaugh drunk in madders like wort,
In the morning we rise, and with us was the sport.
My breeches is stole, my pipe it is broke,
My pocket is picked, where the devil's my cloak?
My kercher I've lost and my mantle's not on,
Seven blessings be with them, my friends are all gone.
Come, strike up the harp, your music in haste,
A swill of your liquor, how quiet the feast!

A-shaking their feathers, just roused from their slumber,
By the noise of the harp and of feet without number,
The sons of O'Rourke bounced up in a throng,
Each man with his woman and danced to the song:
Till the ground shaking under partook of their cogues,
Which as they quick-trotted glig-glugged in their brogues.
Long life and good health to you, Loughlin O'Enegan,
By my hand you dance bravely, Margery Grinigan!
Here's to you, dear mother, I thank you, dear Pat,
Pitch this down your throat, I'm the better of that.
Come shake us down rushes, an excellent bed,
And over us next the winnow-cloth spread.

Dear Anna, some snuff, to keep me awake,
And a little to drink as long as I speak.
Good heaven, how strange! What must people think?
After filling their skins thus to fight in their drink!

Such stabbing, such gashing, such tugging and strife,
Half an arm at least the length of each knife!
What whacking and cracking, with cleftings of oak,
What sounding, rebounding, a hundred heads broke!
My father he built the monastery of Lusk,
With Boyle, Sligo, Galway and Carrickdrumrusk.
Betagh of Moynalty and the Earl of Kildare,
I was nursed by their mother—ask that woman there!

'Who raised this alarm?' says one of the clergy,
A-threatening severely, 'Cease fighting, I charge ye!'
A good knotted staff, the full of his hand,
Instead of the spiridis backed his command.
So falling to thresh fast as he was able,
A trip and a box fetched him under the table.
Then rose a big friar to settle them straight,
But the back of the fire was quickly his fate!
From whence he cried out, 'Do ye thus treat your pastors?
Ye, who scarcely were bred to the Seven Wise Masters!
That when with the Pope I was getting my lore,
Ye were roasting potatoes not far from Sheemore!'
Version: Charles Wilson (1758–1808)

THE OUTLAW OF LOCH LENE

Oh, many a day have I made good ale in the glen,
That came not of stream, or malt, like the brewing of men;
My bed was the ground, my roof the greenwood above,
And the wealth that I sought, one far kind glance from my love.

Alas! on that night when the horses I drove from the field,
That I was not near from terror my angel to shield.
She stretched forth her arms—her mantle she flung to the wind,
And swam o'er Loch Lene her outlawed lover to find.

Oh, that a freezing, sleet-wing'd tempest did sweep,
And I and my love were alone, far off on the deep!

I'd ask not a ship, or a bark, or pinnace to save;
With her hand round my waist, I'd fear not the wind or the wave.

'Tis down by the lake where the wild tree fringes its sides
The maid of my heart, the fair one of heaven, resides;
I think as at eve she wanders its mazes along,
The birds go to sleep by the sweet, wild twist of her song.

Version: J. J. Callanan (1795–1829)

DO YOU REMEMBER THAT NIGHT?

Do you remember that night
When you were at the window
With neither hat nor gloves
Nor coat to shelter you?
I reached out my hand to you
And you ardently grasped it,
I remained to converse with you
Until the lark began to sing.

Do you remember that night
That you and I were
At the foot of the rowan tree
And the night drifting snow?
Your head on my breast,
And your pipe sweetly playing?
Little thought I that night
That our love ties would loosen!

Beloved of my inmost heart,
Come some night, and soon,
When my people are at rest,
That we may talk together.
My arms shall encircle you
While I relate my sad tale,
That your soft, pleasant converse
Hath deprived me of heaven.

The fire is unraked,
The light unextinguished,
The key under the door,
Do you softly draw it.
My mother is asleep,
But I am wide awake;
My fortune in my hand,
I am ready to go with you.

Version: Eugene O'Curry (1796–1862)

HAVE YOU BEEN AT CARRICK

Have you been at Carrick, and saw you my true-love there,
And saw you her features, all beautiful, bright and fair?
Saw you the most fragrant, flowering sweet apple tree?
Oh! saw you my loved one, and pines she in grief like me?

'I have been at Carrick, and saw thy own true-love there;
And saw, too, her features, all beautiful, bright and fair;
And saw the most fragrant, flowering, sweet apple tree—
I saw thy loved one—she pines not in grief like thee.'

Five guineas would price every tress of her golden hair—
Then think what a treasure her pillow at night to share!
These tresses thick-clustering and curling around her brow—
O Ringlet of Fairness! I'll drink to thy beauty now!

When, seeking to slumber, my bosom is rent with sighs—
I toss on my pillow till morning's blest beams arise;
No aid, bright beloved! can reach me save God above,
For a blood-lake is formed of the light of my eyes with love!

Until yellow autumn shall usher the paschal day,
And Patrick's gay festival come in its train alway—
Until through my coffin the blossoming boughs shall grow,
My love on another I'll never in life bestow!

Lo! yonder the maiden illustrious, queen-like, high,
With long-flowing tresses adown to her sandal-tie—
Swan, fair as the lily, descended of high degree,
A myriad of welcomes, dear maid of my heart, to thee!

MY HOPE, MY LOVE

My hope, my love, we will go
Into the woods, scattering the dews,
Where we will behold the salmon, and the ousel in its nest,
The deer and the roe-buck calling,
The sweetest bird on the branches warbling,
The cuckoo on the summit of the green hill;
And death shall never approach us
In the bosom of the fragrant wood!

Versions: Edward Walsh (*1805–1850*)

CASHEL OF MUNSTER

I'd wed you without herds, without money, or rich array,
And I'd wed you on a dewy morning at day-dawn grey;
My bitter woe it is, love, that we are not far away
In Cashel town, though the bare deal board were our marriage-bed
    this day!

Oh, fair maid, remember the green hillside
Remember how I hunted about the valleys wide;
Time now has worn me; my locks are turn'd to grey,
The year is scarce and I am poor, but send me not, love, away!

Oh, deem not my blood is of base strain, my girl,
Oh, deem not my birth was as the birth of the churl;
Marry me, and prove me, and say soon you will,
That noble blood is written on my right side still!

My purse holds no red gold, no coin of the silver white,
No herds are mine to drive through the long twilight!
But the pretty girl that would take me, all bare though I be and lone
Oh, I'd take her with me kindly to the county Tyrone.

Oh, my girl, I can see 'tis in trouble you are,
And, oh, my girl, I see 'tis your people's reproach you bear:
'I am a girl in trouble for his sake with whom I fly,
And, oh, may no other maiden know such reproach as I!'

DEAR BLACK HEAD

Put your head, darling, darling, darling,
  Your darling black head my heart above;
Oh, mouth of honey, with the thyme for fragrance,
  Who, with heart in breast, could deny you love?
Oh, many and many a young girl for me is pining,
  Letting her locks of gold to the cold wind free,
For me, the foremost of our gay young fellows;
  But I'd leave a hundred, pure love, for thee!
Then put your head, darling, darling, darling,
  Your darling black head my heart above;
Oh, mouth of honey, with the thyme for fragrance,
  Who, with heart in breast, could deny you love?
                              Versions: Samuel Ferguson

THE COUNTY OF MAYO

On the deck of Patrick Lynch's boat I sat in woeful plight,
Through my sighing all the weary day and weeping all the night.
Were it not that full of sorrow from my people forth I go,
By the blessed sun, 'tis royally I'd sing thy praise, Mayo.

When I dwelt at home in plenty, and my gold did much abound,
In the company of fair young maids the Spanish ale went round.
'Tis a bitter change from those gay days that now I'm forced to go,
And must leave my bones in Santa Cruz, far from my own Mayo.

They're altered girls in Irrul now; 'tis proud they're grown and high,
With their hair-bags and their top-knots—for I pass their buckles by.
But it's little now I heed their airs, for God will have it so,
That I must depart for foreign lands, and leave my sweet Mayo.

'Tis my grief that Patrick Loughlin is not Earl in Irrul still,
And that Brian Duff no longer rules as Lord upon the Hill;
And that Colonel Hugh MacGrady should be lying dead and low,
And I sailing, sailing swiftly from the county of Mayo.

Version: George Fox (1809–1880)

A CURSE

Bruadar and Smith and Glinn
   Amen, dear God, I pray,
May they lie low in waves of woe,
   And tortures slow each day!
              Amen!...

Bruadar and Smith and Glinn
   May flails of sorrow flay!
Cause for lamenting, snares and cares
   Be theirs for night and day!
              Amen!...

For Bruadar gape the grave,
   Up-shovel for Smith the mould,
Amen, O King of the Sunday! Leave
   Glinn in the Devil's hold.
              Amen!...

Glinn in a shaking ague,
   Cancer on Bruadar's tongue,
Amen, O King of the Heavens! and Smith
   Forever stricken dumb.
              Amen!...

Smith like a sieve of holes,
    Bruadar with throat decay,
Amen, O King of the Orders, Glinn
    A buck-show every day.
                          Amen!

Hell-hounds to hunt for Smith,
    Glinn led to hang on high,
Amen, O King of the Judgement Day!
    And Bruadar rotting by.
                          Amen! ...

May none of their race survive,
    May God destroy them all,
Each curse of the psalms in the holy books
    Of the prophets upon them fall.
                          Amen!

Blight skull, and ear, and skin,
    And hearing, and voice, and sight,
Amen! before the year be out,
    Blight, Son of the Virgin, blight.
                          Amen!

May my curses hot and red
    And all I have said this day,
Strike the Black Peeler too,
    Amen! dear God, I pray!
                          Amen!
                    Version: Douglas Hyde

THE POOR GIRL'S MEDITATION

I am sitting here
Since the moon rose in the night,
Kindling a fire
And striving to keep it alight;
The folk of the house are lying

In slumber deep;
The geese will be gabbling soon:
The whole of the land is asleep.

May I never leave this world
Until my ill-luck is gone;
Till I have cows and sheep
And the lad that I love for my own:
I would not think it long,
The night I would lie at his breast,
And the daughters of spite, after that,
Might say the thing they liked best.

Love takes the place of hate,
If a girl have beauty at all:
On a bed that was narrow and high,
A three-month I lay by the wall:
When I bethought on the lad
That I left on the brow of the hill,
I wept from dark until dark,
And my cheeks have the tear-tracks still.

And, O young lad that I love,
I am no mark for your scorn;
All you can say of me
Is undowered I was born:
And if I've no fortune in hand,
Nor cattle and sheep of my own,
This I can say, O lad,
I am fitted to lie my lone!
                    Version: Padraic Colum

THE YELLOW BITTERN
Cathal Buidhe MacGiolla Gunna (d. 1750)

The yellow bittern that never broke out
    In a drinking bout might as well have drunk;

His bones are thrown on a naked stone
   Where he lived alone like a hermit monk.
O yellow bittern! I pity your lot,
   Though they say that a sot like myself is curst—
I was sober a while, but I'll drink and be wise,
   For fear I should die in the end of thirst.

It's not for the common birds that I'd mourn,
   The blackbird, the corncake or the crane,
But for the bittern that's shy and apart
   And drinks in the marsh from the lone bog-drain.
Oh! if I had known you were near your death,
   While my breath held out I'd have run to you,
Till a splash from the Lake of the Son of the Bird
   Your soul would have stirred and waked anew.

My darling told me to drink no more
   Or my life would be o'er in a little short while;
But I told her 'tis drink gives me health and strength,
   And will lengthen my road by many a mile.
You see how the bird of the long smooth neck
   Could get his death from the thirst at last—
Come, son of my soul, and drink your cup,
   For you'll get no sup when your life is past. . . .

THE STARS STAND UP IN THE AIR

The stars stand up in the air
The sun and the moon are gone,
The strand of its waters is bare,
And her sway is swept from the swan.

The cuckoo was calling all day,
Hid in the branches above,
How my stórín is fled away,
'Tis my grief that I gave her my love!

Three things through love I see—
Sorrow and sin and death—
And my mind reminding me
That this doom I breathe with my breath.

But sweeter than violin or lute
Is my love—and she left me behind.
I wish that all music were mute,
And I to my beauty were blind.

She's more shapely than swan by the strand,
She's more radiant than grass after dew,
She's more fair than the stars where they stand—
'Tis my grief that her ever I knew!

Versions: Thomas MacDonagh

KILCASH

What shall we do for timber?
   The last of the woods is down.
Kilcash and the house of its glory
   And the bell of the house are gone,
The spot where that lady waited
   Who shamed all women for grace
When earls came sailing to greet her
   And Mass was said in the place.

My grief and my affliction
   Your gates are taken away,
Your avenue needs attention,
   Goats in the garden stray.
The courtyard's filled with water
   And the great earls where are they?
The earls, the lady, the people
   Beaten into the clay.

No sound of duck or geese there,
    Hawk's cry or eagle's call,
No humming of the bees there
    That brought honey and wax for all,
Nor even the song of the birds there
    When the song goes down in the west,
No cuckoo on top of the boughs there,
    Singing the world to rest.

There's mist there tumbling from branches,
    Unstirred by night and by day,
And darkness falling from heaven,
    For our fortune has ebbed away,
There's no holly nor hazel nor ash there,
    The pasture's rock and stone,
The crown of the forest has withered,
    And the last of its game is gone.

I beseech of Mary and Jesus
    That the great come home again
With long dances danced in the garden,
    Fiddle music and mirth among men,
That Kilcash the home of our fathers
    Be lifted on high again,
And from that to the deluge of waters
    In bounty and peace remain.

                    Version: Frank O'Connor

FAIR CASSIDY

I left my prayers and the kneeling pilgrims
And went wild running down the holy Reek
And all who saw me said: 'That is Cassidy
Who abandoned God for a girl's cheek.'

The first time I saw her I was a student
Reading my prayerbook, I raised my eyes

But they betrayed me, raced to embrace her,
And I had not slept at the next sunrise.

When I was at College they taught me English
And praised my accent, but with that first sight
The only language that I knew was love-talk
And all my thoughts were turned to birds in flight.

I have no land, no stock nor money
To win that girl to me, I cannot pray,
But I'd mount the Reek on my bleeding knees
If I could have her on my wedding-day.

She could cheat my heart to believe in marvels,
That no grass would grow, that no moon would shine,
That the stars are lightless, that she could love me;
And oh! Christ in Heaven that she were mine.

The sun will cool and the moon will darken
And fishes swim in an empty sea,
The floods will rise above the mountains
And Cassidy still be in slavery.

She passes by and I curse the mother
Who bore that daughter to torture me—
Ah sweet, if we could elope together
I'd risk my neck on the gallows tree.

There is no hill and there's no valley,
No road, no bog that she passes by
But is filled with music, heart-breaking music,
And may Christ have mercy on Cassidy.
                    Version: Donagh MacDonagh

CLONMEL JAIL

O a year from tomorrow I left my own people,
I went down to Ardpatrick, the ribbons in my hat.
Some Whiteboys were there then, they were fighting the English
And now I'm sad and lonely in the jail of Clonmel.

My bridle and saddle are gone from me this long time,
My hurley well hidden behind my own door,
My slither's being played with by the boys of the valley
The one I could hit a goal with as good as another.

O Kerrymen, please pray for me, soft and lovely were your voices,
Little I thought ever that I never would return to you
And to think our three heads will be spiked and on show here
In the snows of the winter's night and any other weather that comes
    to us.

To Iveragh if you ever go, take the news to my people
That I'm lost to this world now and will be dead beyond Friday.
Make sure there's a good wake for me, a good coffin to carry me in:
That's the end of O'Donnell and forever say a prayer for him.

Version: Valentin Iremonger

Thomas Moore

1779–1852

THE SONG OF FIONNUALA

Silent, O Moyle, be the roar of thy water,
    Break not, ye breezes, your chain of repose,
While, murmuring mournfully, Lir's lonely daughter
    Tells to the night-star her tale of woes.
When shall the swan, her death-note singing,
    Sleep, with wings in darkness furled?
When will heaven, its sweet bell ringing,
    Call my spirit from this stormy world?

Sadly, O Moyle, to thy winter-wave weeping,
    Fate bids me languish long ages away;
Yet still in her darkness doth Erin lie sleeping,
    Still doth the pure light its dawning delay.
When will that day-star, mildly springing,
    Warm our isle with peace and love?
When will heaven, its sweet bell ringing,
    Call my spirit to the fields above?

from LALLA ROOKH

Fly to the desert, fly with me,
Our Arab tents are rude for thee;
But, oh! the choice what heart can doubt,
Of tents with love, or thrones without?

Our rocks are rough, but smiling there
The acacia waves her yellow hair,
Lonely and sweet, nor loved the less
For flowering in a wilderness.

Our sands are bare, but down their slope
The silvery-footed antelope
As gracefully and gaily springs
As o'er the marble court of kings.

Then come—thy Arab maid will be
The loved and lone acacia tree,
The antelope, whose feet shall bless
With their light sound thy loneliness.

from THE FUDGE FAMILY IN PARIS

After dreaming some hours of the land of Cockaigne,
That Elysium of all that is *friand* and nice,
Where for hail they have *bon-bons* and claret for rain,
And the skaters in winter show off on cream-ice;
Where so ready all nature its cookery yields,
Macaroni au parmesan grows in the fields;
Little birds fly about with the true pheasant taint,
And the geese are all born with a liver complaint!
I rise—put on neck-cloth—stiff, tight as can be—
For a lad who goes into the world, Dick, like me,
Should have his neck tied up, you know—there's no doubt of it—
Almost as tight as some lads who go out of it.
With whiskers well oil'd, and with boots that 'hold up
The mirror to nature'— so bright you could sup
Off the leather like china; with coat, too, that draws
On the tailor, who suffers, a martyr's applause!
With head bridled up, like a four-in-hand leader,
And stays—devil's in them—too tight for a feeder,
I strut to the old Café Hardy which yet

Beats the field at *a déjeuner à la fourchette*.
There, Dick, what a breakfast! oh, not like your ghost
Of a breakfast in England, your curst tea and toast;
But a side-board, you dog, where one's eye roves about,
Like a Turk's in the Haram, and thence singles out
One pâte of larks, just to tune up the throat,
One's small limbs of chicken, done *en papillote,*
One's erudite cutlets, drest all ways but plain,
Or one's kidneys—imagine, Dick—done with champagne!
Then, some glasses of Beaune, to dilute, or, mayhap,
Chambertin, which you know's the pet tipple of Nap,
And which Dad, by the by, that legitimate stickler,
Much scruples to taste, but *I*'m not so particular.—
Your coffee comes next, by prescription: and then, Dick,'s
The coffee's ne'er-failing and glorious appendix . . .
A neat glass of *parfait-amour*, which one sips
Just as if bottled velvet tipp'd over one's lips.

A PASTORAL BALLAD by John Bull

*After the arrival of the packet bringing the account of the defeat of the
Catholic Question, in the House of Commons, orders were sent to the
Pigeon House to forward 5,000,000 rounds of musket-ball cartridge
to the different garrisons round the country.*
Freeman's Journal, Dublin, March 12, 1827

I have found out a gift for my Erin,
    A gift that will surely content her;—
Sweet pledge of a love so endearing!
    Five millions of bullet I've sent her.

She ask'd me for Freedom and Right,
    But ill she her wants understood;
Ball cartridges, morning and night,
    Is a dose that will do her more good.

There is hardly a day of our lives
  But we read, in some amiable trials,
How husbands make love to their wives
  Through the medium of hemp and of phials.

One thinks, with his mistress or mate
  A good halter is sure to agree—
That love-knot which, early and late,
  I have tried, my dear Erin, on thee.

While another, whom Hymen has bless'd
  With a wife that is not over placid,
Consigns the dear charmer to rest,
  With a dose of the best Prussic acid.

Thus, Erin! my love do I show—
  Thus quiet thee, mate of my bed!
And, as poison and hemp are too slow,
  Do thy business with bullets instead . . .

George Darley

1795–1846

from NEPENTHE

O blest unfabled Incense Tree
That burns in glorious Araby,
With red scent chalicing the air,
Till earth-life grow Elysian there!

Half buried to her flaming breast
In this bright tree, she makes her nest,
Hundred-sunned Phoenix! when she must
Crumble at length to hoary dust!

Her gorgeous death-bed! her rich pyre
Burnt up with aromatic fire!
Her urn, sight high from spoiler men!
Her birthplace when self-born again!

The mountainless green wilds among,
Here ends she her unechoing song!
With amber tears and odorous sighs
Mourned by the desert where she dies!

THE SEA-RITUAL

Prayer unsaid, and Mass unsung,
Deadman's dirge must still be rung:
   Dingle-dong, the dead-bells sound!
   Mermen chant his dirge around!

Wash him bloodless, smooth him fair,
Stretch his limbs, and sleek his hair:
   Dingle-dong, the dead-bells go!
   Mermen swing them to and fro!

In the wormless sand shall he
Feast for no foul glutton be:
    Dingle-dong, the dead-bells chime!
    Mermen keep the tone and time!

We must with a tombstone brave
Shut the shark out from his grave:
    Dingle-dong, the dead-bells toll!
    Merman dirgers ring his knoll!

Such a slab will we lay o'er him
All the dead shall rise before him!
    Dingle-dong, the dead-bells boom!
    Mermen lay him in his tomb!

SIREN CHORUS

Troop home to silent grots and caves,
    Troop home! and mimic as you go
The mournful winding of the waves
    Which to their dark abysses flow.

At this sweet hour all things beside
    In amorous pairs to covert creep,
The swans that brush the evening tide
    Homeward in snowy couples keep.

In his green den the murmuring seal
    Close by his sleek companion lies,
While singly we to bedward steal,
    And close in fruitless sleep our eyes.

In bowers of love men take their rest,
    In loveless bowers we sigh alone,
With bosom-friends are others blest,
    But we have none! but we have none!

James Clarence Mangan

1803–1849

AND THEN NO MORE

I saw her once, one little while, and then no more:
'Twas Eden's light on Earth a while, and then no more.
Amid the throng she passed along the meadow-floor:
Spring seemed to smile on Earth awhile, and then no more;
But whence she came, which way she went, what garb she wore
I noted not; I gazed a while, and then no more!

I saw her once, one little while, and then no more:
'Twas Paradise on Earth a while, and then no more.
Ah! what avail my virgils pale, my magic lore?
She shone before mine eyes awhile, and then no more.
The shallop of my peace is wrecked on Beauty's shore.
Near Hope's fair isle it rode awhile, and then no more!

I saw her once, one little while, and then no more:
Earth looked like Heaven a little while, and then no more.
Her presence thrilled and lighted to its inner core
My desert breast a little while, and then no more.
So may, perchance, a meteor glance at midnight o'er
Some ruined pile a little while, and then no more!

I saw her once, one little while, and then no more:
The earth was Peri-land awhile, and then no more.
Oh, might I see but once again, as once before,
Through chance or wile, that shape awhile, and then no more!
Death soon would heal my griefs! This heart, now sad and sore,
Would beat anew a little while, and then no more.

SIBERIA

In Siberia's wastes
   The Ice-wind's breath
Woundeth like the toothed steel;
Lost Siberia doth reveal
   Only blight and death.

Blight and death alone.
   No summer shines.
Night is interblent with Day
In Siberia's wastes alway
   The blood blackens, the heart pines.

In Siberia's wastes
   No tears are shed,
For they freeze within the brain
Nought is felt but dullest pain,
   Pain acute, yet dead;

Pain as in a dream,
   When years go by
Funeral-paced, yet fugitive,
When man lives, and doth not live,
   Doth not live—nor die.

In Siberia's wastes
   Are sands and rocks.
Nothing blooms of green or soft
But the snow-peaks rise aloft
   And the gaunt ice-blocks.

And the exile there
   Is one with those;
They are part, and he is part,
For the sands are in his heart,
   And the killing snows.

Therefore, in these wastes
  None curse the Czar.
Each man's tongue is cloven by
The North Blast, that heweth nigh
  With sharp scimitar.

And such doom each drees
  Till, hunger-gnawn,
And cold-slain, he at length sinks there,
Yet scarce more a corpse than ere
  His last breath was drawn.

THE NAMELESS ONE

Roll forth, my song, like the rushing river
  That sweeps along to the mighty sea;
God will inspire me while I deliver
        My soul of thee!

Tell thou the world, when my bones lie whitening
  Amid the lost homes of youth and eld,
That there was once one whose veins ran lightning
        No eye beheld.

Tell how his boyhood was one drear night-hour,
  How shone for him, through his griefs and gloom,
No star of all Heaven sends to light our
        Path to the tomb.

Roll on, my song, and to after ages
  Tell how, disdaining all earth can give,
He would have taught men, from Wisdom's pages,
        The way to live.

And tell how trampled, derided, hated,
  And worn by weakness, disease, and wrong,
He fled for shelter to God, who mated
        His soul with song—

With song which always, sublime or vapid,
   Flowed like a rill in the morning-beam,
Perchance not deep, but intense and rapid—
         A mountain stream.

Tell how this Nameless, condemned for years long
   To herd with demons from Hell beneath,
Saw things that made him, with groans and tears, long
         For even death.

Go on to tell how, with genius wasted,
   Betrayed in friendship, befooled in love,
With spirit shipwrecked, and young hopes blasted,
         He still, still strove.

Till, spent with toil, dreeing death for others,
   And some whose hands should have wrought for him;
(If children live not for sires and mothers),
         His mind grew dim.

And he fell far through that pit abysmal,
   The gulf and grave of Maginn and Burns,
And pawned his soul for the devil's dismal
         Stock of returns.

But yet redeemed it in days of darkness,
   And shapes and signs of the final wrath,
When death, in hideous and ghastly starkness,
         Stood on his path.

And tell how now, amid wreck and sorrow,
   And want, and sickness, and houseless nights,
He bides in calmness the silent morrow,
         That no ray lights.

And lives he still, then? Yes! Old and hoary
   At thirty-nine, from despair and woe,
He lives, enduring what future story
         Will never know.

Him grant a grave to, ye pitying noble,
  Deep in your bosoms! There let him dwell!
He, too, had tears for all souls in trouble,
          Here and in Hell.

REST ONLY IN THE GRAVE

I rode till I reached the House of Wealth—
'Twas filled with riot and blighted health.

I rode till I reached the House of Love—
'Twas vocal with sighs beneath and above!

I rode till I reached the House of Sin—
There were shrieks and curses without and within.

I rode till I reached the House of Toil—
Its inmates had nothing to bake or boil.

I rode in search of the House of Content
But never could reach it, far as I went!

The House of Quiet, for strong and weak
And poor and rich, I have still to seek—

That House is narrow, and dark, and small—
But the only Peaceful House of all.

John Swanick Drennan

1809–1893

ON THE TELESCOPIC MOON

A lifeless solitude—an angry waste,
Searing our alien eyes with horrors bare;
No fertilizing cloud—no genial air
To mitigate its savageness of breast;
The light itself all undiffusive there;
Motionless terror clinging to the crest
Of steepmost pinnacles; as by despair
Unfathomable caverns still possessed!
How shall we designate such world forlorn?
What nook of Heaven abhors this portent dark?
Lo! Where the *Moon* reveals her gentle ray,
Waking the nightingale's and poet's lay;
Speeding benign the voyager's return;
And lighting furtive kisses to their mark.

EPIGRAMS

I

L'AMITIÉ ET L'AMOUR

With nought to hide or to betray
    She eyed me frank and free.
But, oh, the girl that looked away
    Was dearer far to me!

II

A golden casket I designed
    To hold a braid of hair;

My Love was false, and now I find
A coil of serpents there.

III

Love signed the contract blithe and leal,
Time shook the sand, Death set the seal.

Samuel Ferguson

1810–1886

LAMENT FOR THE DEATH OF THOMAS DAVIS

I walked through Ballinderry in the spring-time,
    When the bud was on the tree,
And I said, in every fresh-ploughed field beholding
    The sowers striding free,
Scattering broadcast forth the corn in golden plenty
    On the quick, seed-clasping soil,
'Even such, this day, among the fresh-stirred hearts of Erin,
    Thomas Davis, is thy toil!'

I sat by Ballyshannon in the summer,
    And saw the salmon leap;
And I said, as I beheld the gallant creatures
    Spring glittering from the deep,
Thro' the spray, and thro' the prone heaps striving onward
    To the calm clear streams above,
'So seekest thou thy native founts of freedom, Thomas Davis,
    In thy brightness of strength and love!'

I stood in Derrybawn in the autumn,
    And I heard the eagle call,
With a clangorous cry of wrath and lamentation
    That filled the wide mountain hall,
O'er the bare deserted place of his plundered eyrie;
    And I said, as he screamed and soared,
'So callest thou, thou wrathful-soaring Thomas Davis,
    For a nation's rights restored.'

And, alas! to think but now, and thou art lying,
    Dear Davis, dead at thy mother's knee;
And I, no mother near, on my own sick-bed,
    That face on earth shall never see;

I may lie and try to feel that I am dreaming,
   I may lie and try to say, 'Thy will be done'—
But a hundred such as I will never comfort Erin
   For the loss of that noble son!

Young husbandman of Erin's fruitful seed-time,
   In the fresh track of danger's plough!
Who will walk the heavy, toilsome perilous furrow
   Girt with freedom's seed-sheets now?
Who will banish with the wholesome crop of knowledge
   The daunting weed and the bitter thorn,
Now that thou thyself art but a seed for hopeful planting
   Against the resurrection morn?

Young salmon of the flood-time of freedom
   That swells round Erin's shore,
Thou wilt leap against their loud, oppressive torrent
   Of bigotry and hate no more;
Drawn downward by their prone material instinct,
   Let them thunder on their rocks, and foam—
Thou hast leaped, aspiring soul, to founts beyond their raging,
   Where troubled waters never come.

But I grieve not, eagle of the empty eyrie,
   That thy wrathful cry is still;
And that the songs alone of peaceful mourners
   Are heard to-day on Erin's hill.
Better far, if brothers' wars are destined for us—
   (God avert that horrid day, I pray!)—
That ere our hands be stained with slaughter fratricidal,
   Thy warm heart should be cold in clay.

But my trust is strong in God, who made us brothers,
   That he will not suffer these right hands,
Which thou hast joined in holier rites than wedlock,
   To draw opposing brands.
O many a tuneful tongue that thou madest vocal,
   Would lie cold and silent then,

And songless long once more should often-widowed Erin
    Mourn the loss of her brave young men.

O brave young men, my love, my pride, my promise,
    'Tis on you my hopes are set,
In manliness, in kindliness, in justice,
    To make Erin a nation yet;
Self-respecting, self-relying, self-advancing,
    In union or in severance, free and strong—
And if God grant this, then, under God, to Thomas Davis
    Let the greater praise belong!

Aubrey De Vere

1814–1902

THE LITTLE BLACK ROSE

The Little Black Rose shall be red at last;
　What made it black but the March wind dry,
And the tear of the widow that fell on it fast?
　It shall redden the hills when June is nigh.

The Silk of the Kine shall rest at last;
　What drove her forth but the dragon-fly?
In the golden vale she shall feed full fast,
　With her mild gold horn and her slow, dark eye.

The wounded wood-dove lies dead at last!
　The pine long bleeding, it shall not die!
This song is secret. Mine ear it passed
　In a wind o'er the plains at Athenry.

IN RUIN RECONCILED

I heard a woman's voice that wailed
　Between the sandhills and the sea:
The famished sea-bird past me sailed
　Into the dim infinity.

I stood on boundless, rainy moors:
　Far off I saw a great Rock loom;
The grey dawn smote its iron doors;
　And then I knew it was a Tomb.

Two queenly shapes before the grate
　Watched, couchant on the barren ground;
Two regal shapes in ruined state,
　One Gael, one Norman; both discrowned.

Thomas Caulfield Irwin

1823–1892

from SWIFT

XI

It was a dim October day,
  When clouds hung low on roof and spire,
  He dashed his horse, to gallop pressed,
  Along the old road leading west,
Where Liffey's waters shimmering lay
  Beneath the noonlight's struggling fire.

XII

Aleft, the slopes of tillage spread;
  And further, higher to the south,
  The sloping slate-grey mountains rose,
  Sun-pencill'd in the noon's repose,
And by his path the river bed,
  Deep sanded with the summer drought.

XIII

The city sunk in smoke behind,
  Before, the air rose blue and lone.
  At times, from ivied hedge and wall,
  Faint shrilled the robin's crystal call;
And, from the west, the careless wind
  Was blowing in a monotone.

XVI

At length, beneath its woody gloom,
  Old Marley's cloister ends his way.

He lights—he knocks. The pigeon's plaint
   Swoons fitfully above and faint;
And glimmers through the garden's bloom
   The river's sheet of glassy grey.

XVII

Lo! from her memoried laurel bower,
   Where oft she sat alone, to hear
   His coming, she is hastening now,
   To meet him with a joyous brow,
Though saddened by th' impending hour,
   And shuddering with an unknown fear.

XVIII

She enters—springs to meet him. God!
   Can passion demonize a brow
   Of spirit-splendour! In a breath
   The letter's thrown; and he, like death,
Is gone, Hark! Ringing from the road
   His horse's trampling echoes now.

WITH THE DAWN

HUSBAND

Why have you risen, to stand with naked feet
And thin robe stirring in the airs of night,
Looking from the casement?

WIFE

          It is sweet
To view upon the broad sea, glimmering white,
Sails, in the low moonlight.

HUSBAND

I dream'd that you were lost to me afar,
And I had just recovered you once more.
Why linger you?—

WIFE

       To watch that large star
Sparkle our cradled child's calm slumber o'er.
Soft as the little wave that sweet and frore
Rises and sinks upon the sandy shore,—
  He breathes; and on his face there comes a smile,
  Just as the dawn's pale gold has touched, the while,
Yon faint cloud cradled on the distant deep.
  The calm sea-level turns from white to rose;
  And, as the space a richer glory grows,
The earliest bird sings faintly far away
  Upon the poplar by the ocean steep.

HUSBAND

Awake him not, oh, dear one, till 'tis day;
  To be alive, and suffer not, is sleep.

William Allingham

1824–1889

THE EVICTION

(*from* Laurence Bloomfield in Ireland)

In early morning twilight, raw and chill,
Damp vapours brooding on the barren hill,
Through miles of mire in steady grave array
Threescore well-arm'd police pursue their way;
Each tall and bearded man a rifle swings,
And under each greatcoat a bayonet clings;
The Sheriff on his sturdy cob astride
Talks with the chief, who marches by their side,
And, creeping on behind them, Paudeen Dhu
Pretends his needful duty much to rue.
Six big-boned labourers, clad in common frieze,
Walk in the midst, the Sheriff's staunch allies;
Six crowbar men, from distant county brought,—
Orange, and glorying in their work, 'tis thought,
But wrongly,—churls of Catholics are they,
And merely hired at half-a-crown a day.

The Hamlet clustering on its hill is seen,
A score of petty homesteads, dark and mean;
Poor always, not despairing until now;
Long used, as well as poverty knows how,
With life's oppressive trifles to contend.
This day will bring its history to an end.
Moveless and grim against the cottage walls
Lean a few silent men: but someone calls
Far off; and then a child 'without a stitch'
Runs out of doors, flies back with piercing screech,
And soon from house to house is heard the cry
Of female sorrow, swelling loud and high,

Which makes the men blaspheme between their teeth.
Meanwhile, o'er fence and watery field beneath,
The little army moves through drizzling rain;
A 'Crowbar' leads the Sheriff's nag; the lane
Is enter'd, and their plashing tramp draws near:
One instant, outcry holds its breath to hear;
'Halt!'—at the doors they form in double line,
And ranks of polish'd rifles wetly shine.

The Sheriff's painful duty must be done;
He begs for quiet—and the work's begun.
The strong stand ready; now appear the rest,
Girl, matron, grandsire, baby on the breast,
And Rosy's thin face on a pallet borne;
A motley concourse, feeble and forlorn.
One old man, tears upon his wrinkled cheek,
Stands trembling on a threshold, tries to speak,
But, in defect of any word for this,
Mutely upon the doorpost prints a kiss,
Then passes out for ever. Through the crowd
The children run bewilder'd, wailing loud;
Where needed most, the men combine their aid;
And, last of all, is Oona forth convey'd,
Reclined in her accustom'd strawen chair,
Her aged eyelids closed, her thick white hair
Escaping from her cap; she feels the chill,
Looks round and murmurs, then again is still.

Now bring the remnants of each household fire.
On the wet grounds the hissing coals expire;
And Paudeen Dhu, with meekly dismal face,
Receives the full possession of the place.

Whereon the Sheriff, 'We have legal hold.
Return to shelter with the sick and old.
Time shall be given; and there are carts below
If any to the workhouse choose to go.'

A young man makes him answer, grave and clear,
'We're thankful to you! but there's no one here
Goin' back into them houses: do your part.
Nor we won't trouble Pigot's horse and cart.'
At which name, rushing into th' open space,
A woman flings her hood from off her face,
Falls on her knees upon the miry ground,
Lifts hands and eyes, and voice of thrilling sound,—
'Vengeance of God Almighty fall on you,
James Pigot!—may the poor man's curse pursue,
The widow's and the orphan's curse, I pray,
Hang heavy round you at your dying day!'
Breathless and fix'd one moment stands the crowd
To hear this malediction fierce and loud.

But now (our neighbour Neal is busy there)
On steady poles he lifted Oona's chair,
Well-heap'd with borrow'd mantles; gently bear
The sick girl in her litter, bed and all;
Whilst others hug the children weak and small
In careful arms, or hoist them pick-a-back;
And, 'midst the unrelenting clink and thwack
Of iron bar on stone, let creep away
The sad procession from that hill-side grey,
Through the slow-falling rain. In three hours more
You find, where Ballytullagh stood before,
Mere shatter'd walls, and doors with useless latch,
And firesides buried under fallen thatch.

THE DREAM

I heard the dogs howl in the moonlight night;
I went to the window to see the sight;
All the Dead that ever I knew
Going one by one and two by two.

On they pass'd, and on they pass'd;
Townsfellows all, from first to last;
Born in the moonlight of the lane,
Quenched in the heavy shadow again.

Schoolmates, marching as when we play'd
At soldiers once—but now more staid;
Those were the strangest sight to me
Who were drown'd, I knew, in the awful sea.

Straight and handsome folk; bent and weak too;
Some that I loved, and gasp'd to speak to;
Some but a day in their churchyard bed;
Some that I had not known were dead . . .

On, on a moving bridge they made
Across the moon-stream, from shade to shade,
Young and old, women and men;
Many long forgot, but remember'd then.

And first there came a bitter laughter;
A sound of tears the moment after;
And then a music so lofty and gay,
That every morning, day by day,
I strive to recall it if I may.

William Larminie

1850–1899

THE NAMELESS DOON

Who were the builders? Question not the silence
That settles on the lake for evermore,
Save when the sea-bird screams and to the islands
The echo answers from the steep-cliffed shore.
O half-remaining ruin, in the lore
Of human life a gap shall all deplore
Beholding thee; since thou art like the dead
Found slain, no token to reveal the why,
The name, the story. Someone murdered
We know, we guess; and gazing upon thee,
And, filled by thy long silence of reply,
We guess some garnered sheaf of tragedy;—
Of tribe or nation slain so utterly
That even their ghosts are dead, and on their grave
Springeth no bloom of legend in its wildness;
And age by age weak washing round the islands
No faintest sigh of story lisps the wave.

Anglo-Irish Songs and Ballads

SONG

(*from* She Stoops to Conquer)

Let school-masters puzzle their brain
With grammar, and nonsense, and learning;
Good liquor, I stoutly maintain,
Gives *genus* a better discerning.
Let them brag of their Heathenish Gods,
Their Lethes, their Styxes, and Stygians;
Their Quis, and their Quaes, and their Quods,
They're all but a parcel of Pigeons.
                              Toroddle, toroddle, toroll.

When Methodist preachers come down,
A'preaching that drinking is sinful,
I'll wager the rascals a crown,
They always preach best with a skinful.
But when you come down with your pence,
For a slice of their scurvy religion,
I'll leave it to all men of sense,
But you my good friend are the pigeon.
                              Toroddle, toroddle, toroll.

Then come, put the jorum about,
And let us be merry and clever,
Our hearts and our liquors are stout,
Here's the Three Jolly Pigeons for ever.
Let some cry up woodcock or hare,
Your bustards, your ducks, and your widgeons;
But of all the birds in the air,
Here's a health to the Three Jolly Pigeons.
                              Toroddle, toroddle, toroll.

OLIVER GOLDSMITH

THE KILRUDDERY HUNT

In seventeen hundred and forty-four
The fifth of December, I think 'twas no more,
At five in the morning by most of the clocks,
We rode from Kilruddery in search of a fox.
The Loughlinstown landlord, the brave Owen Bray,
And Johnny Adair, too, were with us that day;
Joe Debil, Hal Preston, those huntsmen so stout—
Dick Holmes, some few others, and so we set out.

We cast off our hounds for an hour or more,
When Wanton set up a most tuneable roar;
'Hark, Wanton,' cried Joe, and the rest were not slack,
For Wanton's no trifler esteemed by the pack;
Old Bounty and Collier came readily in,
And every hound joined in the musical din;
Had Diana been there, she'd been pleased to the life,
And one of the lads got a goddess to wife.

Ten minutes past nine was the time of the day
When Reynard broke cover, and this was his way—
As strong from Killegar, as if he could fear none,
Away he brushed round by the house of Kilternan,
To Carrickmines thence, and to Cherrywood then,
Steep Shankhill he climbed, and to Ballyman glen,
Bray Common he crossed, leap'd Lord Anglesey's wall,
And seemed to say, 'Little I care for you all.'

He ran Bushes Grove up to Carbury Byrnes—
Joe Debil, Hal Preston, kept leading by turns;
The earth it was open, yet he was so stout,
Tho' he might have got in, still he chose to keep out;
To Malpas high hills was the way that he flew,
At Dalkey's stone common we had him in view;
He drove on to Bullock, he slunk Glenageary,
And so onto Monkstown, where Larry grew weary.

Thro' Rochestown wood like an arrow he passed,
And came to the steep hills of Dalkey at last;
There gallantly plunged himself into the sea,
And said in his heart, 'None can now follow me.'
But soon, to his cost, he perceived that no bounds
Could stop the pursuit of the staunch-mettled hounds;
His policy here did not serve him a rush,
Five couples of Tartars were hard at his brush.

To recover the shore then again was his drift;
But ere he could reach to the top of the clift,
He found both of speed and of daring a lack,
Being waylaid and killed by the rest of the pack.
At his death there were present the lads I have sung,
Save Larry, who, riding a garron, was flung.
Thus ended at length a most delicate chase,
That held us five hours and ten minutes' space.

THOMAS MOZEEN

THE GAY OLD HAG

Will you come a boating, my gay old hag,
Will you come a boating, my tight old hag,
Will you come a boating, down the Liffey floating?
I'll make a pair of oars of your two long shins.

Crush her in the corner the gay old hag,
Crush her in the corner the tight old hag,
Crush her in the corner and keep her snug and warm,
Put powder in her horn, she's a fine old hag.

Napoleon's on dry land, says the gay old hag,
Napoleon's on dry land, says the tight old hag,
Napoleon's on dry land, with a sword in his right hand,
He's a gallant Ribbon man, says the gay old hag.

My mother's getting young, says the gay old hag,
My mother's getting young, says the gay old hag,
My mother's getting young and she'll have another son
To make the orange run, says the gay old hag.

Remember '98, says the gay old hag,
When our Boys you did defeat, says the gay old hag,
Then our Boys you did defeat, but we'll beat you out compleat,
Now you're nearly out of date, says the fine old hag.

PHARAO'S DAUGHTER

In Agypt's land contaygious to the Nile,
Old Pharao's daughter went to bathe in style,
She tuk her dip and came unto the land,
And for to dry her royal pelt she ran along the strand:

A bull-rush tripped her, whereupon she saw
A smiling babby in a wad of straw,
She took it up and said in accents mild,
'Tare-an-ages, girls, which o'yees own the child?'

MICHAEL MORAN—'ZOZIMUS'

THE NIGHT BEFORE LARRY WAS STRETCHED

The night before Larry was stretched,
    The boys they all paid him a visit;
A bait in their sacks, too, they fetched;
    They sweated their duds till they riz it:
For Larry was ever the lad,
    When a boy was condemned to the squeezer,
Would fence all the duds that he had
    To help a poor friend to a sneezer,
    And warm his gob 'fore he died.

The boys they came crowding in fast,
    They drew all their stools round about him,
Six glims round his trap-case were placed,
    He couldn't be well waked without 'em.
When one of us asked could he die
    Without having duly repented,
Says Larry, 'That's all in my eye;
    And first by the clargy invented,
    To get a fat bit for themselves.'

'I'm sorry, dear Larry,' says I,
    'To see you in this situation;
And, blister my limbs if I lie,
    I'd as lieve it had been my own station.'
'Ochone! it's all over,' says he,
    'For the neckcloth I'll be forced to put on,
And by this time tomorrow you'll see
    Your poor Larry as dead as a mutton,
    Because, why, his courage was good.

'And I'll be cut up like a pie,
    And my nob from my body be parted.'
'You're in the wrong box, then', says I,
    'For blast me if they're so hard-hearted:
A chalk on the back of your neck
    Is all that Jack Ketch dares to give you;
Then mind not such trifles a feck,
    For why should the likes of them grieve you?
    And now, boys, come tip us the deck.'

The cards being called for, they played,
    Till Larry found one of them cheated;
A dart at his napper he made
    (The boy being easily heated):
'Oh, by the hokey, you thief,
    I'll scuttle your nob with my daddle!
You cheat me because I'm in grief,
    But soon I'll demolish your noddle,
    And leave you your claret to drink.'

Then the clergy came in with his book,
    He spoke him so smooth and so civil;
Larry tipped him a Kilmainham look,
    And pitched his big wig to the Devil;
Then sighing, he threw back his head
    To get a sweet drop of the bottle,
And pitiful sighing, he said:
        'Oh, the hemp will be soon round my throttle
        And choke my poor windpipe to death.

'Though sure it's the best way to die,
    Oh, the Devil a better a-livin'!
For, sure, when the gallows is high
    Your journey is shorter to Heaven:
But what harasses Larry the most,
    And makes his poor soul melancholy
Is to think of the time when his ghost
        Will come in a sheet to sweet Molly—
        Oh, sure it will kill her alive!'

So moving these last words he spoke,
    We all vented our tears in a shower;
For my part, I thought my heart broke,
    To see him cut down like a flower.
On his travels we watched him next day;
    Oh, the throttler! I thought I could kill him;
But Larry not one word did say,
        Nor changed till he come to 'King William'—
        Then, *musha!*, his colour grew white.

When he came to the nubbling chit,
    He was tucked up so neat and so pretty,
The rumbler jogged off from his feet,
    And he died with his face to the city;
He kicked, too,—but that was all pride,
    For soon you might see 'twas all over;
Soon after the noose was untied,
        And at darky we waked him in clover,
        And sent him to take a ground sweat.

THE BOYS OF MULLABAUN

On a Monday morning early as my wandering steps did lead me,
Down by a farmer's station through the meadows and green lawns,
I heard great lamentations, the small birds they were making,
Saying, 'We'll have no more engagements with the Boys of
    Mullabaun.'

Squire Jackson he is raging for honour and for fame,
He never turned traitor nor betrayed the rights of man,
But now we are in danger, for a vile deceiving stranger
Has ordered transportation for the Boys of Mullabaun.

I beg your pardon, ladies, I ask it as a favour,
I hope there is no treason in what I'm going to say,
I'm condoling late and early, my very heart is breaking
For a noble esquire's lady that lives near Mullabaun.

To end my lamentation I am in consternation;
No one can roam for recreation until the day do dawn;
Without a hesitation we're charged with combination
And sent for transportation with the Boys of Mullabaun.

'JOHNNY, I HARDLY KNEW YE!'

While going the road to sweet Athy,
    Hurroo! hurroo!
While going the road to sweet Athy,
    Hurroo! hurroo!
While going the road to sweet Athy,
A stick in my hand and a drop in my eye,
A doleful damsel I heard cry:
    'Och, Johnny, I hardly knew ye!
      With drums and guns, and guns and drums
        The enemy nearly slew ye;
      My darling dear, you look so queer,
        Och, Johnny, I hardly knew ye!

'Where are your eyes that looked so mild?
    Hurroo! hurroo!
Where are your eyes that looked so mild?
    Hurroo! hurroo!
Where are your eyes that looked so mild,
When my poor heart you first beguiled?
Why did you skedaddle from me and the child?
    Och, Johnny, I hardly knew ye!
                    With drums, etc.

'Where are the legs with which you run?
    Hurroo! hurroo!
Where are the legs with which you run?
    Hurroo! hurroo!
Where are the legs with which you run
When you went to shoulder a gun?
Indeed, your dancing days are done!
    Och, Johnny, I hardly knew ye!
                    With drums, etc.

'It grieved my heart to see you sail,
    Hurroo! hurroo!
It grieved my heart to see you sail,
    Hurroo! hurroo!
It grieved my heart to see you sail,
Though from my heart you took leg-bail;
Like a cod you're doubled up head and tail.
    Och Johnny, I hardly knew ye!
                    With drums, etc.

'You haven't an arm and you haven't a leg,
    Hurroo! hurroo!
You haven't an arm and you haven't a leg,
    Hurroo! hurroo!
You haven't an arm and you haven't a leg,
You're an eyeless, noseless, chickenless egg;
You'll have to be put wid a bowl to beg;
    Och, Johnny, I hardly knew ye!
                    With drums, etc.

'I'm happy for to see you home,
    Hurroo! hurroo!
I'm happy for to see you home,
    Hurroo! hurroo!
I'm happy for to see you home,
All from the island of Sulloon,[1]
So low in flesh, so high in bone;
    Och, Johnny, I hardly knew ye!
                With drums, etc.

'But sad as it is to see you so,
    Hurroo! hurroo!
But sad as it is to see you so,
    Hurroo! hurroo!
But sad as it is to see you so,
And to think of you now as an object of woe,
Your Peggy 'll still keep ye on as her beau;
    Och, Johnny, I hardly knew ye!
      With drums and guns, and guns and drums,
        The enemy nearly slew ye;
      My darling dear, you look so queer,
        Och, Johnny, I hardly knew ye!

[1] Ceylon

COLLEEN RUE

As I roved out one summer's morning, speculating most curiously,
To my surprise, I soon espied a charming fair one approaching me;
I stood awhile in deep meditation, contemplating what should I do,
But recruiting all my sensations, I thus accosted the Colleen Rue:

'Are you Aurora, or the beauteous Flora, Euterpasia, or Venus
    bright?
Or Helen fair, beyond compare, that Paris stole from her Grecian's
    sight?
Thou fairest creature, you have enslaved me, I am intoxicated by
    Cupid's clue,

Whose golden notes and infatuation deranged my ideas for you,
    Colleen Rue.'

'Kind sir, be easy, and do not tease me, with your false praise so
    jestingly,
Your dissimulations and invitations, your fantastic praises, seducing
    me.
I am not Aurora, or the beauteous Flora, but a rural maiden to all
    men's view,
That's here condoling my situation, and my appellation is the
    Colleen Rue.'

'Was I Hector, that noble victor, who died a victim of Grecian skill,
Or was I Paris, whose deeds were various, as an arbitrator on Ida's
    hill,
I would roam through Asia, likewise Arabia, through Pennsylvania,
    seeking you,
The burning regions, like famed Vesuvius, for one embrace of the
    Colleen Rue.'

'Sir, I am surprised and dissatisfied at your tantalizing insolence,
I am not so stupid, or enslaved by Cupid, as to be duped by your
    eloquence,
Therefore desist from your solicitations, I am engaged, I declare it's
    true,
To a lad I love beyond all earthly treasures, and he'll soon embrace
    his Colleen Rue.'

SKIN THE GOAT'S CURSE ON CAREY

Before I set sail, I will not fail
    To give that lad my blessing,
And if I had him here there's not much fear
    But he'd get a good top dressing;
By the hat on my head but he'd lie on his bed
    Till the end of next September,

I'd give him good cause to rub his jaws
    And Skin the Goat remember.

But as I won't get the chance to make Carey dance,
    I'll give him my benedictions,
So from my heart's core may he evermore
    Know nothing but afflictions,
May every buck flea from here to Bray
    Jump through the bed that he lies on,
And by some mistake may he shortly take
    A flowing pint of poison.

May his toes fill with corns like puckawn's horns
    Till he can neither wear slippers or shoes,
With a horrid toothache may he roar like a drake
    And jump like a mad kangaroo.
May a horrid big rat make a hole in his hat
    And chew all the hair off his head,
May the skin of a pig be made into a wig
    And stuck on him when he is dead . . .

May his wife be jealous and pitch up the bellows,
    And measure him over the head,
May he get the Devil's fright, that will turn him left and right,
    Every night till it knocks him stone dead,
May a horrid baboon jump out of the moon
    And tear his old carcase asunder,
And the day he'll sail, may snow and hail
    Accompany rain and thunder . . .

When the equator is crossed, may the rudder be lost,
    And his vessel be wafted ashore,
To some cannibal isle near the banks of the Nile,
    Where savages jump and roar;
With a big sharp knife may they take his life,
    While his vessel is still afloat,
And pick his bones as clean as stones,
    Is the prayer of poor Skin the Goat.

THE STREAMS OF BUNCLODY

Oh were I at the moss house, where the birds do increase,
At the foot of Mount Leinster or some silent place,
By the streams of Bunclody, where all pleasures do meet,
And all I would ask is one kiss from you, sweet.

If I was in Bunclody I would think myself at home,
'Tis there I would have a sweetheart, but here I have none,
Drinking strong liquor in the height of my cheer,
Here's a health to Bunclody and the lass I love dear.

The cuckoo is a pretty bird, it sings as it flies,
It brings us good tidings, and tells us no lies,
It sucks the young bird's eggs to make its voice clear,
And the more it cries cuckoo the summer draws near.

If I was a clerk and could write a good hand,
I would write to my true love that she might understand,
I am a young fellow that is wounded in love,
That lived by Bunclody, but now must remove.

If I was a lark and had wings I could fly
I would go to yon arbour where my love she does lie,
I'd proceed to yon arbour where my true love does lie,
And on her fond bosom contented I would die.

'Tis why my love slights me, as you may understand,
That she has a freehold, and I have no land,
She has great store of riches and a large sum of gold,
And everything fitting a house to uphold.

So adieu, my dear father, adieu, my dear mother,
Farewell to my sister, farewell to my brother;
I am bound for America, my fortune to try,
When I think on Bunclody, I'm ready to die.

SHE MOVED THROUGH THE FAIR

My young love said to me, 'My brothers won't mind,
And my parents won't slight you for your lack of kind.'
Then she stepped away from me, and this she did say,
'It will not be long, love, till our wedding day.'

She stepped away from me and she moved through the fair,
And fondly I watched her go here and go there,
Then she went her way homeward with one star awake,
As the swan in the evening moves over the lake.

The people were saying no two were e'er wed
But one had a sorrow that never was said,
And I smiled as she passed with her goods and her gear,
And that was the last that I saw of my dear.

I dreamt it last night that my young love came in,
So softly she entered, her feet made no din;
She came close beside me, and this she did say,
'It will not be long, love, till our wedding day.'

PADRAIC COLUM

THE HAY HOTEL

There is a window stuffed with hay
Like herbage in an oven cast;
And there we came at break of day
To soothe ourselves with light repast:
And men who worked before the mast
And drunken girls delectable:
A future symbol of our past
You'll, maybe, find the Hay Hotel.

Where are the great Kip Bullies gone,
The Bookies and outrageous Whores

Whom we so gaily rode upon
When youth was mine and youth was yours:
Tyrone Street of the crowded doors
And Faithful Place so infidel?
It matters little who explores
He'll only find the Hay Hotel.

Dick Lynam was a likely lad,
His back was straight; has he gone down?
And for a pal Jem Plant he had
Whose navel was like half a crown.
They were the talk of all Meck town;
And Norah Seymour loved them well;
Of all their haunts of lost renown
There's only left the Hay Hotel.

Fresh Nellie's gone and Mrs Mack,
May Oblong's gone and Number Five,
Where you could get so good a back
And drinks were so superlative;
Of all their nights, O Man Alive!
There is not left an oyster shell
Where greens are gone the greys will thrive;
There's only left the Hay Hotel.

There's nothing left but ruin now
Where once the crazy cabfuls roared;
Where new-come sailors turned the prow
And Love-logged cattle-dealers snored:
The room where old Luke Irwin whored,
The stairs on which John Elwood fell:
Some things are better unencored:
There's only left the Hay Hotel.

Where is Piano Mary, say,
Who dwelt where Hell's Gates leave the street,
And all the tunes she used to play
Along your spine beneath the sheet?

She was a morsel passing sweet
And warmer than the gates of hell.
Who tunes her now between the feet?
Go ask them at the Hay Hotel.

Nay; never ask this week, fair Lord,
If, where they are now, all goes well,
So much depends on bed and board
They give them in the Hay Hotel.

OLIVER ST. JOHN GOGARTY

THE ONDT AND THE GRACEHOPER

He larved ond he larved on he merd such a nauses
The Gracehoper feared he would mixplace his fauces.
I forgive you, grondt Ondt, said the Gracehoper, weeping,
For their sukes of the sakes you are safe in whose keeping.
Teach Floh and Luse polkas, show Bienie where's sweet
And be sure Vespatilla fines fat ones to heat.
As I once played the piper I must now pay the count
So saida to Moyhammlet and marhaba to your Mount!
Let who likes lump above so what flies be a full 'un;
I could not feel moregruggy if this was prompollen.
I pick up your reproof, the horsegift of a friend,
For the prize of your save is the price of my spend.
Can castwhores pulladeftkiss if oldpollocks forsake 'em
Or Culex feel etchy if Pulex don't wake him?
A locus to loue, a term it t'embarass,
These twain are the twins that tick *Homo Vulgaris*.
Has Aquileone nort winged to go syf
Since the Gwyfyn we were in his farrest drewbryf
And that Accident Man not beseeked where his story ends
Since longsephyring sighs sought heartseast for their orience?
We were Wastenot with Want, precondamned, two and true,

Till Nolans go volants and Bruneyes come blue.
Ere those gidflirts now gadding you quit your mocks for my gropes
An extense must impull, an elapse must elopes,
Of my tectucs takestock, tinktact, and ail's weal;
As I view by your farlook hale yourself to my heal.
Partiprise my thinwhins whiles my blink points unbroken on
Your whole's whercabroads with Tout's trightyright token on.
My in risible universe youdly haud find
Sulch oxtrabeeforeness meat soveal behind.
Your feats end enormous, your volumes immense,
(May the Graces I hoped for sing your Ondtship song sense!),
Your genus its worldwide, your spacest sublime!
But, Holy Saltmartin, why can't you beat time?

JAMES JOYCE

GOING TO MASS LAST SUNDAY

Going to Mass last Sunday my true love passed me by,
I knew her mind was altered by the rolling of her eye;
And when I stood in God's dark light my tongue could word no
    prayer
Knowing my saint had fled and left her reliquary bare.

Sweet faces smiled from holy glass, demure in saintly love,
Sweet voices ripe with Latin grace rolled from the choir above;
But brown eyes under Sunday wear were all my liturgy;
But how can she hope for heaven who has so deluded me?

When daffodils were altar gold her lips were light on mine
And when the hawthorn was bright we drank the year's new wine;
The nights seemed stained-glass windows lit with love that paled the
    sky,
But love's last ember perishes in the winter of her eye.

Drape every downcast day now in purple cloth of Lent,
Smudge every forehead now with ash, that she may yet repent,

Who going to Mass last Sunday could pass so proudly by
And show her mind was altered by the rolling of an eye.

BALLAD TO A TRADITIONAL REFRAIN

Red brick in the suburbs, white horse on the wall,
Eyetalian marbles in the City Hall:
O stranger from England, why stand so aghast?
May the Lord in His mercy be kind to Belfast.

This jewel that houses our hopes and our fears
Was knocked up from the swamp in the last hundred years;
But the last shall be first and the first shall be last:
May the Lord in His mercy be kind to Belfast.

We swore by King William there'd never be seen
An All-Irish Parliament at College Green,
So at Stormont we're nailing the flag to the mast:
May the Lord in His mercy be kind to Belfast.

O the bricks they will bleed and the rain it will weep,
And the damp Lagan fog lull the city to sleep;
It's to hell with the future and live on the past:
May the Lord in His mercy be kind to Belfast.

MAURICE JAMES CRAIG

W. B. Yeats

1865–1939

ADAM'S CURSE

We sat together at one summer's end,
That beautiful mild woman, your close friend,
And you and I, and talked of poetry.
I said, 'A line will take us hours maybe;
Yet if it does not seem a moment's thought,
Our stitching and unstitching has been naught.
Better go down upon your marrow-bones
And scrub a kitchen pavement, or break stones
Like an old pauper, in all kind of weather;
For to articulate sweet sounds together
Is to work harder than all these, and yet
Be thought an idler by the noisy set
Of bankers, schoolmasters, and clergymen
The martyrs call the world.'
      And thereupon
That beautiful mild woman for whose sake
There's many a one shall find out all heartache
On finding that her voice is sweet and low
Replied, 'To be born woman is to know—
Although they do not talk of it at school—
That we must labour to be beautiful.'

I said, 'It's certain there is no fine thing
Since Adam's fall but needs much labouring.
There have been lovers who thought love should be
So much compounded of high courtesy
That they would sigh and quote with learned looks
Precedents out of beautiful old books;
Yet now it seems an idle trade enough.'

We sat grown quiet at the name of love;
We saw the last embers of daylight die,
And in the trembling blue-green of the sky
A moon, worn as if it had been a shell
Washed by time's waters as they rose and fell
About the stars and broke in days and years.

I had a thought for no one's but your ears:
That you were beautiful, and that I strove
To love you in the old high way of love;
That it had all seemed happy, and yet we'd grown
As weary-hearted as that hollow moon.

THE FASCINATION OF WHAT'S DIFFICULT

The fascination of what's difficult
Has dried the sap out of my veins, and rent
Spontaneous joy and natural content
Out of my heart. There's something ails our colt
That must, as if it had not holy blood
Nor on Olympus leaped from cloud to cloud,
Shiver under the lash, strain, sweat and jolt
As though it dragged road-metal. My curse on plays
That have to be set up in fifty ways,
On the day's war with every knave and dolt,
Theatre business, management of men.
I swear before the dawn come round again
I'll find the stable and pull out the bolt.

MEMORY

One had a lovely face,
And two or three had charm,
But charm and face were in vain
Because the mountain grass
Cannot but keep the form
Where the mountain hare has lain.

THE ROAD AT MY DOOR

An affable Irregular,
A heavily-built Falstaffian man,
Comes cracking jokes of civil war
As though to die by gunshot were
The finest play under the sun.

A brown Lieutenant and his men,
Half dressed in national uniform,
Stand at my door, and I complain
Of the foul weather, hail and rain,
A pear-tree broken by the storm.

I count those feathered balls of soot
The moor-hen guides upon the stream,
To silence the envy in my thought;
And turn towards my chamber, caught
In the cold snows of a dream.

THE STARE'S NEST BY MY WINDOW

The bees build in the crevices
Of loosening masonry, and there
The mother birds bring grubs and flies.
My wall is loosening; honey-bees,
Come build in the empty house of the stare.

We are closed in, and the key is turned
On our uncertainty; somewhere
A man is killed, or a house burned,
Yet no clear fact to be discerned:
Come build in the empty house of the stare.

A barricade of stone or of wood;
Some fourteen days of civil war;

Last night they trundled down the road
That dead young soldier in his blood:
Come build in the empty house of the stare.

We had fed the heart on fantasies,
The heart's grown brutal from the fare;
More substance in our enemities
Than in our love; O honey-bees,
Come build in the empty house of the stare.

NINETEEN HUNDRED AND NINETEEN

(1)

Many ingenious lovely things are gone
That seemed sheer miracle to the multitude,
Protected from the circle of the moon
That pitches common things about. There stood
Amid the ornamental bronze and stone
An ancient image made of olive wood—
And gone are Phidias' famous ivories
And all the golden grasshoppers and bees.

We too had many pretty toys when young:
A law indifferent to blame or praise,
To bribe or threat; habits that made old wrong
Melt down, as it were wax in the sun's rays;
Public opinion ripening for so long
We thought it would outlive all future days.
O what fine thought we had because we thought
That the worst rogues and rascals had died out.

All teeth were drawn, all ancient tricks unlearned,
And a great army but a showy thing;
What matter that no cannon has been turned
Into a ploughshare? Parliament and king

Thought that unless a little powder burned
The trumpeters might burst with trumpeting
And yet it lack all glory; and perchance
The guardsmen's drowsy chargers would not prance.

Now days are dragon-ridden, the nightmare
Rides upon sleep: a drunken soldiery
Can leave the mother, murdered at her door,
To crawl in her own blood, and go scot-free;
The night can sweat with terror as before
We pierced our thoughts into philosophy,
And planned to bring the world under a rule,
Who are but weasels fighting in a hole.

He who can read the signs nor sink unmanned
Into the half-deceit of some intoxicant
From shallow wits; who knows no work can stand,
Whether health, wealth or peace of mind were spent
On master-work of intellect or hand,
No honour leave its mighty monument,
Has but one comfort left: all triumph would
But break upon his ghostly solitude.

But is there any comfort to be found?
Man is in love and loves what vanishes,
What more is there to say? That country round
None dared admit, if such a thought were his,
Incendiary or bigot could be found
To burn that stump on the Acropolis,
Or break in bits the famous ivories
Or traffic in the grasshoppers or bees.

(II)

When Loie Fuller's Chinese dancers enwound
A shining web, a floating ribbon of cloth,
It seemed that a dragon of air
Had fallen among dancers, had whirled them round

Or hurried them off on its own furious path;
So the Platonic Year
Whirls out new right and wrong,
Whirls in the old instead;
All men are dancers and their tread
Goes to the barbarous clangour of a gong.

(III)

Some moralist or mythological poet
Compares the solitary soul to a swan;
I am satisfied with that,
Satisfied if a troubled mirror show it,
Before that brief gleam of its life be gone,
An image of its state;
The wings half spread for flight,
The breast thrust out in pride
Whether to play, or to ride
Those winds that clamour of approaching night.

A man in his own secret meditation
Is lost amid the labyrinth that he has made
In art or politics;
Some Platonist affirms that in the station
Where we should cast off body and trade
The ancient habit sticks,
And that if our works could
But vanish with our breath
That were a lucky death,
For triumph can but mar our solitude.

The swan has leaped into the desolate heaven:
That image can bring wildness, bring a rage
To end all things, to end
What my laborious life imagined, even
The half-imagined, the half-written page;
O but we dreamed to mend
Whatever mischief seemed

To afflict mankind, but now
That winds of winter blow
Learn that we were crack-pated when we dreamed.

(IV)

We, who seven years ago
Talked of honour and of truth,
Shriek with pleasure if we show
The weasel's twist, the weasel's tooth.

(V)

Come let us mock at the great
That had such burdens on the mind
And toiled so hard and late
To leave some monument behind,
Nor thought of the levelling wind.

Come let us mock at the wise;
With all those calendars whereon
They fixed old aching eyes,
They never saw how seasons run,
And now but gape at the sun.

Come let us mock at the good
That fancied goodness might be gay,
And sick of solitude
Might proclaim a holiday:
Wind shrieked—and where are they?

Mock mockers after that
That would not lift a hand maybe
To help good, wise or great
To bar that foul storm out, for we
Traffic in mockery.

Violence upon the road: violence of horses;
Some few have handsome riders, are garlanded
On delicate sensitive ear or tossing mane,
But wearied running round and round in their courses
All break and vanish, and evil gathers head:
Herodias' daughters have returned again,
A sudden blast of dusty wind and after
Thunder of feet, tumult of images,
Their purpose in the labyrinth of the wind;
And should some crazy hand dare touch a daughter
All turn with amorous cries, or angry cries,
According to the wind, for all are blind.
But now wind drops, dust settles; thereupon
There lurches past, his great eyes without thought
Under the shadow of stupid straw-pale locks,
That insolent fiend Robert Artisson
To whom the love-lorn Lady Kyteler brought
Bronzed peacock feathers, red combs of her cocks.

THE SECOND COMING

Turning and turning in the widening gyre
The falcon cannot hear the falconer;
Things fall apart; the centre cannot hold;
Mere anarchy is loosed upon the world,
The blood-dimmed tide is loosed, and everywhere
The ceremony of innocence is drowned;
The best lack all conviction, while the worst
Are full of passionate intensity.

Surely some revelation is at hand;
Surely the Second Coming is at hand.
The Second Coming! Hardly are these words out
When a vast image out of *Spiritus Mundi*

Troubles my sight: somewhere in sands of the desert
A shape with lion body and the head of a man,
A gaze blank and pitiless as the sun,
Is moving its slow thighs, while all about it
Reel shadows of the indignant desert birds.
The darkness drops again; but now I know
That twenty centuries of stony sleep
Were vexed to nightmare by a rocking cradle,
And what rought beast, its hour come round at last,
Slouches towards Bethlehem to be born?

THE GREAT DAY

Hurrah for revolution and more cannon-shot!
A beggar upon horseback lashes a beggar on foot.
Hurrah for revolution and cannon come again!
The beggars have changed places, but the lash goes on.

THE CURSE OF CROMWELL

You ask what I have found, and far and wide I go:
Nothing but Cromwell's house, and Cromwell's murderous crew,
The lovers and the dancers are beaten into the clay,
And the tall men and the swordsmen and the horsemen, where are
    they?
And there is an old beggar wandering in his pride—
His fathers served their fathers before Christ was crucified.
            O what of that, O what of that,
            What is there left to say?

All neighbourly content and easy talk are gone,
But there's no good complaining, for money's rant is on,
He that's mounting up must on his neighbour mount,
And we and all the Muses are things of no account.

They have schooling of their own, but I pass their schooling by,
What can they know that we know that know the time to die?
>   *O what of that, O what of that,*
>   *What is there left to say?*

But there's another knowledge that my heart destroys,
As the fox in the old fable destroyed the Spartan boy's,
Because it proves that things both can and cannot be;
That the swordsmen and the ladies can still keep company,
Can pay the poet for a verse and hear the fiddle sound,
That I am still their servant though all are underground.
>   *O what of that, O what of that,*
>   *What is there left to say?*

I came on a great house in the middle of the night,
Its open lighted doorway and its windows all alight,
And all my friends were there and made me welcome too;
But I woke in an old ruin that the winds howled through;
And when I pay attention I must out and walk
Among the dogs and horses that understand my talk.
>   *O what of that, O what of that,*
>   *What is there left to say?*

A. E. (George Russell)

1867–1935

GERMINAL

Call not thy wanderer home as yet
  Though it be late.
Now is his first assailing of
  The invisible gate.
Be still through that light knocking. The hour
  Is thronged with fate.

To that first tapping at the invisible door
  Fate answereth.
What shining image or voice, what sigh
  Or honied breath,
Comes forth, shall be the master of life
  Even to death.

Satyrs may follow after. Seraphs
  On crystal wing
May blaze. But the delicate first-comer
  It shall be King.
They shall obey, even the mightiest,
  That gentle thing.

All the strong powers of Dante were bowed
  To a child's mild eyes,
That wrought within him that travail
  From depths up to skies,
Inferno, Purgatorio
  And Paradise.

Amid the soul's grave councillors
  A petulant boy
Laughs under the laurels and purples, the elf
  Who snatched at his joy,

Ordering Caesar's legions to bring him
   The world for his toy.

In ancient shadows and twilights
   Where childhood had strayed,
The world's great sorrows were born
   And its heroes were made.
In the lost boyhood of Judas
   Christ was betrayed.

Let thy young wanderer dream on:
   Call him not home.
A door opens, a breath, a voice
   From the ancient room,
Speaks to him now. Be it dark or bright
   He is knit with his doom.

EXILES

The gods have taken alien shapes upon them
Wild peasants driving swine
In a strange country. Through the swarthy faces
The starry faces shine.

Under grey tattered skies they strain and reel there:
Yet cannot all disguise
The majesty of fallen gods, the beauty,
The fire beneath their eyes.

They huddle at night within low clay-built cabins;
And, to themselves unknown,
They carry with them diadem and sceptre
And move from throne to throne.

J. M. Synge

1871–1909

THE PASSING OF THE SHEE
After looking at one of A. E.'s pictures

Adieu, sweet Angus, Maeve and Fand,
Ye plumed yet skinny Shee,
That poets played with hand in hand
To learn their ecstasy.

We'll search in Red Dan Sally's ditch,
And drink in Tubber fair,
Or poach with Red Dan Philly's bitch
The badger and the hare.

ON AN ISLAND

You've plucked a curlew, drawn a hen,
Washed the shirts of seven men,
You've stuffed my pillow, stretched the sheet,
And filled the pan to wash your feet,
You've cooped the pullets, wound the clock,
And rinsed the young men's drinking crock;
And now we'll dance to jigs and reels,
Nailed boots chasing girls' naked heels,
Until your father'll start to snore,
And Jude, now you're married, will stretch on the floor.

IS IT A MONTH

Is it a month since I and you
In the starlight of Glen Dubh
Stretched beneath a hazel bough
Kissed from ear and throat to brow,

Since your fingers, neck, and chin
Made the bars that fenced me in,
Till Paradise seemed but a wreck
Near your bosom, brow, and neck
And stars grew wilder, growing wise,
In the splendour of your eyes!
Since the weasel wandered near
Whilst we kissed from ear to ear
And the wet and withered leaves
Blew about your cap and sleeves,
Till the moon sank tired through the ledge
Of the wet and windy hedge?
And we took the starry lane
Back to Dublin town again.

HE UNDERSTANDS THE GREAT CRUELTY
OF DEATH

My flowery and green age was passing away, and I feeling a chill in
the fires had been wasting my heart, for I was drawing near the
hillside above the grave.

Then my sweet enemy was making a start, little by little, to give
over her great wariness, the way she was wringing a sweet thing
out of my sharp sorrow. The time was coming when Love and
Decency can keep company, and Lovers may sit together and say
out all things are in their hearts. But Death had his grudge against
me, and he got up in the way, like an armed robber, with a pike in
his hand.

(after Petrarch)

RENDEZ-VOUS MANQUÉ DANS LA RUE RACINE

When your hour was rung at last
I stood as in terror to watch the turn,
And met two creaking coffins that passed.
Lord God, I am slow to learn!

Thomas MacDonagh

1878–1916

THE MAN UPRIGHT

I once spent an evening in a village
Where the people are all taken up with tillage,
Or do some business in a small way
Among themselves, and all the day
Go crooked, doubled to half their size,
Both working and loafing, with their eyes
Stuck in the ground or in a board,—
For some of them tailor, and some of them hoard
Pence in a till in their little shops,
And some of them shoe-soles—they get the tops
Ready-made from England, and they die cobblers—
All bent up double, a village of hobblers
And slouchers and squatters, whether they straggle
Up and down, or bend to haggle
Over a counter, or bend at a plough,
Or to dig with a spade, or to milk a cow,
Or to shove the goose-iron stiffly along
The stuff on the sleeve-board, or lace the fong
In the boot on the last, or to draw the wax-end
Tight cross-ways—and so to make or to mend
What will soon be worn out by the crooked people.
The only thing straight in the place was the steeple,
I thought at first. I was wrong in that;
For there past the window at which I sat
Watching the crooked little men
Go slouching, and with the gait of a hen
An odd little woman go pattering past,
And the cobbler crouching over his last
In his window opposite, and next door
The tailor squatting inside on the floor—
While I watched them, as I have said before,

And thought that only the steeple was straight,
There came a man of a different gait—
A man who neither slouched nor pattered,
But planted his steps as if each step mattered;
Yet walked down the middle of the street
Not like a policeman on his beat,
But like a man with nothing to do
Except walk straight upright like me and you.

Seamus O'Sullivan

1879–1958

THE LAMPLIGHTER

Here to the leisured side of life,
Remote from traffic, free from strife,
A cul-de-sac, a sanctuary
Where old quaint customs creep to die
And only ancient memories stir,
At evening comes the lamplighter;
With measured steps, without a sound,
He treads the unalterable round,
Soundlessly touching one by one
The waiting posts that stand to take
The faint blue bubbles in his wake;
And when the night begins to wane
He comes to take them back again,
Before the chilly dawn can blight
The delicate frail buds of light.

IN NORTH GREAT GEORGE'S STREET
(*A Thought from Moschus*)

Ah me, the aspidistra grows dusty behind the window pane,
And the delicate tracery of the fan-light is obscured from light;
Yet these shall, perchance be dusted, and shine brightly again;
But they, the gallant, the witty and the brave,
Whaley and Egan, and all who fought the oncoming of death and
    night,
These death has taken. They lie forever, each in a forgotten grave.

Joseph Campbell

1879–1944

DARKNESS

Darkness.
I stop to watch a star shine in the boghole—
A star no longer, but a silver ribbon of light.
I look at it, and pass on.

THE GOMBEEN

Behind a web of bottles, bales,
Tobacco, sugar, coffin nails
The gombeen like a spider sits,
Surfeited; and, for all his wits,
As meagre as the tally-board
On which his usuries are scored.

The mountain people come and go
For wool to weave or seed to sow,
White flour to bake a wedding cake,
Red spirits for a stranger's wake.
No man can call his soul his own
Who has the Devil's spoon on loan.

And so behind his web of bales,
Horse halters, barrels, pucaun sails
The gombeen like a spider sits,
Surfeited; and, for all his wits,
As poor as one who never knew
The treasure of the early dew.

IDEAL AND REALITY

I thirst for violins, as drunkards thirst
For wine; I hunger for great verse, plain-served
In ordinaries where poor bards foregather.
Or dished on plates of gold in theatres.
I'd give these living eyes to see the Sphinx,
The sun-bleached columns of the Parthenon,
The doves about the Lion of San Mark,
Angelo's frescoes, Goya's canvases.
And here am I, mured in a prison cell;
No picture seen, save what obscenities
Old lags have drawn with dirt on white-washed bricks
To satisfy desire, or hieroglyphs
Of some field-bred, jail-sick Republican
Telling his tale of days for a bomb thrown;
No clustered shaft, no pointed arch, no dome
Dim with Byzantine colour, no Greek frieze.
Great in its unashamed simplicity—
Only the meanness of four narrow walls
And dirty window. Prophet-like, I walk
The oaken floor, a desert of dry sand,
Searching for amber honeycombs of verse,
For crystal-wells of muted violins,
And find no treasure. What thing comes to me
But harsh discordance? On the basement crane
The steel chain rasps; a porridge tray is slammed;
The landing sentry clicks his rifle bolt
To keep his wits awake; nail-booted feet
Batter a Munster hornpipe overhead;
A toilet flushed; someone, endlessly,
Shouts in a snuffling, strident, Meath Street voice
For Johnny Pigeon, till the tyrannized ear
Rebels, and curses Johnny Pigeon's name;
The sweepers sweep the compound; buckets clink;
A new mouthorgan plays an ancient waltz;
And, master of a school of minor notes,
The tap-tap of a ringmaker is heard,
Beating his penny in a distant wing.

AD LIMINA

The ewes and lambs, loving the far hillplaces,
Cropping by choice the succulent tops of heather,
Drinking the pure water of cloudborn lochlands,
Resting under erratics fostered with Abel—
Come to my haggard gate, my very doorstep.

The birds of freest will and strongest wingbeat,
Sad curlew, garrulous stonechat, hawk and coaltit,
Haunting lone bog or scalp or broken ruin,
Poising the rough thrust of air's excesses—
Come to my haggard gate, my very doorstep.

The trout in the river, below the hanging marllot,
Swift, with ancestral fear of hook and shadow,
The elvers of cold drain and slough, remembering
The warm tangles of Caribbee and Sargasso—
Come to my haggard gate, my very doorstep.

Even the stoats and rats, who know a possessor
Of the rare sixth sense, the bardic insight,
Match, and more, for their devilish perversions,
And the deer, shyest of shy at autumn rutting—
Come to my haggard gate, my very doorstep.

Am I not a lucky man, trusted, Franciscan,
That these spacious things gentle or hostile,
Following God's urge, denying their nature,
Harbingers of high thoughts and fathers of poems—
Come to my haggard gate, my very doorstep.

Padraic Colum

1881–1972

THE BOOK OF KELLS

First, make a letter like a monument—
An upright like the fast-held hewn stone
Immovable, and half-rimming it
The strength of Behemoth his neck-bone,
And underneath that yoke, a staff, a rood
Of no less hardness than the cedar wood.

Then, on a page made golden as the crown
Of sainted man, a scripture you enscroll
Blackly, firmly, with the quickened skill
Lessoned by famous masters in our school,
And with an ink whose lustre will keep fresh
For fifty generations of our flesh.

And limn below it the Evangelist
In raddled coat, on bench abidingly,
Simple and bland: Matthew his name or Mark,
Or Luke or John; the book is by his knee,
And thereby its similitudes: Lion,
Or Calf, or Eagle, or Exalted Man.

The winds that blow around the world—the four
Winds in their colours on your pages join—
The Northern Wind—its blackness interpose;
The Southern Wind—its blueness gather in;
In redness and in greenness manifest
The splendours of the Winds of East and West.

And with these colours on a ground of gold
Compose a circuit will be seen by men
As endless patience, but is nether web

Of endless effort— a strict pattern:
Illumination lighting interlace
Of cirque and scroll, of panel and lattice.

A single line describes them and enfolds,
One line, one course where term there is none,
Which in its termlessness is envoying
The going forth and the return one.
With man and beast and bird and fish therein
Transformed to species that have never been.

With mouth a-gape or beak a-gape each stands
Initial to a verse of miracle,
Of mystery and of marvel (Depth of God!)
That Alpha or Omega may not spell,
Then finished with these wonders and these signs,
Turn to the figures of your first outlines.

Axal, our angel, has sustained you so
In hand, in brain; now to him seal that thing
With figures many as the days of man,
And colours, like the fire's enamelling—
That baulk, that letter you have greatly reared
To stay the violence of the entering Word!

James Joyce

1882–1941

ECCE PUER

Of the dark past
A child is born
With joy and grief
My heart is torn.

Calm in his cradle
The living lies.
May love and mercy
Unclose his eyes!

Young life is breathed
On the glass;
The world that was not
Comes to pass.

A child is sleeping:
An old man gone.
O, father forsaken,
Forgive your son!

James Stephens

1882–1950

TO THE FOUR COURTS, PLEASE

The driver rubbed at his nettly chin
With a huge loose forefinger, crooked and black;
And his wobbly violet lips sucked in,
And puffed out again and hung down slack:
A black fang shone through his lop-sided smile,
In his little pouched eye flickered years of guile.

And the horse, poor beast! It was ribbed and forked;
And its ears hung down, and its eyes were old;
And its knees were knuckly; and, as we talked,
It swung the stiff neck that could scarcely hold
Its big skinny head up—then I stepped in,
And the driver climbed to his seat with a grin.

God help the horse, and the driver too!
And the people and beasts who have never a friend!
For the driver easily might have been you,
And the horse be me by a different end!
And nobody knows how their days will cease!
And the poor, when they're old, have little of peace!

Robinson Jeffers

1887–1962

ANTRIM

No spot of earth where men have so fiercely for ages of time
Fought and survived and cancelled each other,
Pict and Gael and Dane, McQuillan, Clandonnel, O'Neill,
Savages, the Scot, the Norman, the English,
Here in the narrow passage and the pitiless north, perpetual
Betrayals, relentless resultless fighting.
A random fury of dirks in the dark: a struggle for survival
Of hungry blind cells of life in the womb.
But now the womb has grown old, her strength has gone forth;
    a few red carts in a fog creak flax to the dubs,
And sheep in the high heather cry hungrily that life is hard;
    a plaintive peace; shepherds and peasants.

We have felt the blades meet in the flesh in a hundred ambushes
And the groaning blood bubble in the throat;
In a hundred battles the heavy axes bite the deep bone,
The mountain suddenly stagger and be darkened.
Generation on generation we have seen the blood of boys
And heard the moaning of women massacred,
The passionate flesh and nerves have flamed like pitchpine and fallen
And lain in the earth softly dissolving.
I have lain and been humbled in all these graves, and mixed new flesh
    with the old and filled the hollow of my mouth
With maggots and rotten dust and ages of repose, I lie here and plot
    the agony of resurrection.

Francis Ledwidge

1891–1917

A TWILIGHT IN MIDDLE MARCH

Within the oak a throb of pigeon wings
Fell silent, and grey twilight hushed the fold,
And spiders' hammocks swung on half-oped things
That shook like foreigners upon our cold.
A gipsy lit a fire and made a sound
Of moving tins, and from an oblong moon
The river seemed to gush across the ground
To the cracked metre of a marching tune.

And then three syllables of melody
Dropped from a blackbird's flute, and died apart
Far in the dewy dark. No more but three,
Yet sweeter music never touched a heart
Neath the blue domes of London. Flute and reed
Suggesting feelings of the solitude
When will was all the Delphi I would heed,
Lost like a wind within a summer wood
From little knowledge where great sorrows brood.

JUNE

Broom out the floor now, lay the fender by,
And plant this bee-sucked bough of woodbine there,
And let the window down. The butterfly
Floats in upon the sunbeam, and the fair
Tanned face of June, the nomad gipsy, laughs
Above her widespread wares, the while she tells
The farmers' fortunes in the fields, and quaffs
The water from the spider-peopled wells.

The hedges are all drowned in green grass seas,
And bobbing poppies flare like Elmo's light,
While siren-like the pollen-stained bees
Drone in the clover depths. And up the height
The cuckoo's voice is hoarse and broke with joy.
And on the lowland crops the crows make raid,
Nor fear the clappers of the farmer's boy,
Who sleeps, like drunken Noah, in the shade.

And loop this red rose in that hazel ring
That snares your little ear, for June is short
And we must joy in it and dance and sing.
And from her bounty draw her rosy worth.
Ay! soon the swallows will be flying south,
The wind wheel north to gather in the snow,
Even the roses split on youth's red mouth
Will soon blow down the road all roses go.

LAMENT FOR THOMAS MACDONAGH

He shall not hear the bittern cry
In the wild sky, where he is lain,
Nor voices of the sweeter birds
Above the wailing of the rain.

Nor shall he know when loud March blows
Thro' slanting snows her fanfare shrill,
Blowing to flame the golden cup
Of many an upset daffodil.

But when the Dark Cow leaves the moor,
And pastures poor with greedy weeds,
Perhaps he'll hear her low at morn
Lifting her horn in pleasant meads.

Thomas MacGreevy

1894–1967

NOCTURNE OF THE SELF-EVIDENT PRESENCE

Fortunate,
Being articulate,
The alps
Rise
In ice
To heights
Of large stars
And little;
To courts
Beneath other courts
With walls of white starlight.
They have stars for pavements,
The valley is an area,
And I a servant,
A servant of servants,
Of metaphysical bereavements,
Staring up
Out of the gloom.

I see no immaculate feet on those pavements,
No winged forms,
Foreshortened,
As by Reubens or Domenichino,
Plashing the silvery air,
Hear no cars,

Elijah's or Apollo's
Dashing about
Up there.
I see alps, ice, stars and white starlight
In a dry, high silence.

HOMAGE TO HIERONYMUS BOSCH

A woman with no face walked into the light;
A boy, in a brown-tree norfolk suit
Holding on
Without hands
To her seeming skirt.

She stopped,
And he stopped,
And I, in terror, stopped, staring.

Then I saw a group of shadowy figures behind her.
It was a wild wet morning
But the little world was spinning on.
Liplessly, somehow, she addressed it:
The book must be opened
And the park too.

I might have tittered
But my teeth chattered
And I saw that the words, as they fell,
Lay, wriggling, on the ground.

There was a stir of wet wind
And the shadowy figures began to stir
When one I had thought dead
Filmed slowly out of his great dignity on a tomb near by
And they all shuddered
He bent as if to speak to the woman
But the nursery governor flew up out of the well of Saint Patrick,
Confiscated by his mistress,
And, his head bent,
Staring out over his spectacles,
And scratching the gravel furiously,
Hissed—

      The words went *pingg*! like bullets,
      Upwards, past his spectacles—

Say nothing, I say, say nothing, say nothing!
And he who had seemed to be coming to life
Gasped,
Began hysterically, to laugh and cry,
And, with a gesture of impotent and half-petulant despair,
Filmed back into his effigy again.

High above the Bank of Ireland
Unearthly music sounded,
Passing westwards.

Then, from the drains,
Small sewage rats slid out.
They numbered hundreds of thousands, tens, thousands.
Each bowed obsequiously to the shadowy figures
Then turned and joined in a stomach dance with his sisters and
    brothers.
Being a multitude they danced irregularly.
There was rat laughter,
Deeper here and there,
And occasionally she-rats grew hysterical.
The shadowy figures looked on, agonized.
The woman with no face gave a cry and collapsed.
The rats danced on her
And on the wriggling words
Smirking.
The nursery governer flew back into the well
With the little figure without hands in the brown-tree clothes.

Robert Graves

b. 1895

THE LAUREATE

Like a lizard in the sun, though not scuttling
When men approach, this wretch, this thing of rage,
Scowls and sits rhyming in his horny age.

His time and truth he has not bridged to ours,
But shrivelled by long heliotropic idling
He croaks at us his out-of-date humours.

Once long ago here was a poet; who died.
See how remorse twitching his mouth proclaims
It was no natural death, but suicide.

Arrogant, lean, unvenerable, he
Still turns for comfort to the western flames
That glitter a cold span above the sea.

IN HER PRAISE

This they know well: the Goddess yet abides.
Though each new lovely woman whom she rides,
Straddling her neck a year or two or three,
Should sink beneath such weight of majesty
And, groping back to mankind, betray
The headlong power that whitened all her way
With a broad track of trefoil—leaving you
Her chosen lover, ever again thrust through
With daggers, your purse rifled, your rings gone;
Nevertheless they call you to live on
To parley with the pure, oracular dead,

To hear the wild pack whimpering overhead,
To watch the moon tugging at her cold tides.
Woman is mortal woman. She abides.

POINT OF NO RETURN

When the alcoholic passed the crucial point
Of no return, he sold his soul to priests
Who, mercifully, would not deny him drink
But remitted a thousand years of purgatory
On this condition: that he must now engage
A woman's pity, beseeching her to cure him,
Wearing her down with betterment and relapse,
Till he has won a second soul for glory,
At the point of no return.

THE BROKEN GIRTH

Bravely from Fairyland he rode, on furlough,
Astride a tall bay given him by the Queen
From whose couch he had leaped not a half-hour since,
Whose lilies-of-the-valley shone from his helm.

But alas, as he paused to assist five Ulstermen
Sweating to raise a recumbent Ogham pillar,
Breach of a saddle-girth tumbled Oisín
To common Irish earth. And at once, it is said,
Old age came on him with grief and frailty.

St. Patrick asked: would he not confess the Christ?—
Which for that Lady's sake he loathed to do,
But northward loyally turned his eyes in death.
It was Fenians bore the unshriven corpse away

For burial, keening.
                    Curse me all squint-eyed monks
Who misconstrue the passing of Finn's son:
Old age, not Fairyland, was his delusion.

HAG-RIDDEN

I awoke in profuse sweat, arms aching,
Knees bruised and soles cut to the raw—
Preserved no memory of that night
But whipcracks and my own voice screaming.
Through what wild, flinty wastes of fury,
Hag of the Mill,
Did you ride your madman?

F. R. Higgins

1896–1941

CHINESE WINTER

From these bare trees
The sticks of last year's nests
Print sad characters against the moon;
While wind-blown moonlight,
Stripping fields to silver,
Scrawls December on each frozen pool.

Light washed on every tree
Roots it in black shadow,
As last year's love now roots me in black night;
And where love danced
Footprints of fiery moments
Flash out memorials in silent ice.

FATHER AND SON

Only last week, walking the hushed fields
Of our most lovely Meath, now thinned by November,
I came to where the road from Laracor leads
To the Boyne river—that seemed more lake than river,
Stretched in uneasy light and stript of reeds.

And walking longside an old weir
Of my people's, where nothing stirs—only the shadowed
Leaden flight of a heron up the lean air—
I went unmanly with grief, knowing how my father,
Happy though captive in years, walked last with me there.

Yes, happy in Meath with me for a day
He walked, taking stock of herds hid in their own breathing;

And naming colts, gusty as wind, once steered by his hand,
Lightnings winked in the eyes that were half shy in greeting
Old friends—the wild blades, when he gallivanted the land.

For that proud, wayward man now my heart breaks—
Breaks for that man whose mind was a secret eyrie,
Whose kind hand was sole signet of his race,
Who curbed me, scorned my green ways, yet increasingly loved me
Till Death drew its grey blind down his face.

And yet I am pleased that even my reckless ways
Are living shades of his rich calms and passions—
Witnesses for him and for those faint namesakes
With whom now he is one, under yew branches,
Yes, one in a graven silence no bird breaks.

O YOU AMONG WOMEN

When pails empty the last brightness
Of the well, at twilight-time,
And you are there among women—
O mouth of silence,
Will you come with me, when I sign,
To the far green wood, that fences
A lake inlaid with light?

To be there, O, lost in each other,
While day melts in airy water,
And the drake-headed pike—a shade
In the waves' pale stir!
For love is there, under the breath,
As a coy star is there in the quiet
Of the wood's blue eye.

Austin Clarke

b. 1896

THE STRAYING STUDENT

On a holy day when sails were blowing southward,
A bishop sang the Mass at Inishmore,
Men took one side, their wives were on the other
But I heard the woman coming from the shore:
And wild in despair my parents cried aloud
For they saw the vision draw me to the doorway.

Long had she lived in Rome when Popes were bad,
The wealth of every age she makes her own,
Yet smiled on me in eager admiration,
And for a summer taught me all I know,
Banishing shame with her great laugh that rang
As if a pillar caught it back alone.

I learned the prouder counsel of her throat,
My mind was growing bold as light in Greece;
And when in sleep her stirring limbs were shown,
I blessed the noonday rock that knew no tree:
And for an hour the mountain was her throne,
Although her eyes were bright with mockery.

They say I was sent back from Salamanca
And failed in logic, but I wrote her praise
Nine times upon a college wall in France.
She laid her hand at darkfall on my page
That I might read the heavens in a glance
And I knew every star the Moors had named.

Awake or in my sleep, I have no peace now,
Before the ball is struck, my breath has gone,
And yet I tremble lest she may deceive me

And leave me in this land, where every woman's son
Must carry his own coffin and believe,
In dread, all that the clergy teach the young.

TENEBRAE

This is the hour that we must mourn
With tallows on the black triangle,
Night has a napkin deep in fold
To keep the cup; yet who dare pray
If all in reason should be lost,
The agony of man betrayed
At every station of the cross?

O when the forehead is too young,
Those centuries of mortal anguish,
Dabbed by a consecrated thumb
That crumbles into dust, will bring
Despair with all that we can know;
And there is nothing left to sing,
Remembering our innocence.

I hammer on that common door,
Too frantic in my superstition,
Transfix with nails that I have broken,
The angry notice of the mind.
Close as the thought that suffers him,
The habit every man in time
Must wear beneath his ironed shirt.

An open mind disturbs the soul,
And in disdain I turn my back
Upon the sun that makes a show
Of half the world, yet still deny
The pain that lives within the past,
The flame sinking upon the spike,
Darkness that man must dread at last.

MARRIAGE

Parents are sinful now, for they must whisper
Too much in the dark. Aye, there's the rub! What grace
Can snatch the small hours from that costly kiss?
Those who slip off the ring, try to be chaste
And when they cannot help it, steal the crumbs
From their own wedding breakfast, spare expense
And keep in warmth the children they have nourished.
But shall the sweet promise of the sacrament
Gladden the heart, if mortals calculate
Their pleasures by the calendar? Night-school
Of love where all, who learn to cheat, grow pale
With guilty hope at every change of moon!

IRISH-AMERICAN DIGNITARY

Glanced down at Shannon from the sky-way
With his attendant clergy, stayed night
In Dublin, but whole day with us
To find his father's cot, now dust
And rubble, bless new church, school buildings
At Glantworth, drive to Spangle Hill
And cut first sod, hear, answer, fine speeches,
Accept a learned gown, freedom
Of ancient city, so many kissing
His ring—God love him!—almost missed
The waiting liner: that day in Cork
Had scarcely time for knife and fork.

THE JEST

Half spirit, the older
I am, the bolder,

Yet add for a jest
That you may think
Not beat your breast,
Invisible ink.

ANCIENT LIGHTS

When all of us wore smaller shoes
And knew the next world better than
The knots we broke, I used to hurry
On missions of my own by Capel
Street, Bolton Street and Granby Row
To see what man has made. But darkness
Was roomed with fears. Sleep, stripped by woes
I had been taught, beat door, leaped landing,
Lied down the bannisters of naught.

Being sent to penance, come Saturday,
I shuffled slower than my sins should.
My fears were candle-spiked at side-shrines,
Rays lengthened them in stained-glass. Confided
To night again, my grief bowed down,
Heard hand on shutter-knob. Did I
Take pleasure, when alone—how much—
In a bad thought, immodest look
Or worse, unnecessary touch?

Closeted in the confessional,
I put on flesh, so many years
Were added to my own, attempted
In vain to keep Dominican
As much i' the dark as I was, mixing
Whispered replies with his low words;
Then shuddered past the crucifix,
The feet so hammered, daubed-on blood-drip,
Black with lip-scrimmage of the damned.

Once as I crept from the church-steps,
Beside myself, the air opened
On purpose. Nature read in a flutter
An evening lesson above my head.
Atwirl beyond the leadings, corbels,
A cage-bird came among sparrows
(The moral inescapable)
Plucked, roof-mired, all in mad bits. O
The pizzicato of its wires!

Goodness of air can be proverbial:
That day, by the kerb at Rutland Square,
A bronze bird fabled out of trees,
Mailing the spearheads of the railings,
Sparrow at nails I hailed the skies
To save the tiny dropper, found
Appetite gone. A child of clay
Had blustered it away. Pity
Could raise some littleness from dust.

What Sunday clothes can change us now
Or humble orders in black and white?
Stinking with centuries the act
Of thought. So think, man, as Augustine
Did, dread the ink-bespattered ex-monk,
And keep your name. No, let me abandon
Night's jakes. Self-persecuted of late
Among the hatreds of rent Europe,
Poetry burns at a different stake.

Still, still I remember aweful downpour
Cabbing Mountjoy Street, spun loneliness
Veiling almost the Protestant Church,
Two backyards from my very home.
I dared to shelter at locked door.
There, walled by heresy, my fears
Were solved. I had absolved myself;
Feast-day effulgence, as though I gained
For life a plenary indulgence.

The sun came out, new smoke flew up,
The gutters of the Black Church rang
With services. Waste water mocked
The ballcocks: down-pipes sparrowing,
And all around the spires of Dublin
Such swallowing in the air, such cowling
To keep high offices pure: I heard
From shore to shore, the iron gratings
Take half our heavens with a roar.

THE LOST HEIFER

When the black herds of the rain were grazing
In the gap of the pure cold wind
And the watery haze of the hazel
Brought her into my mind,
I thought of the last honey by the water
That no hive can find.

Brightness was drenching through the branches
When she wandered again,
Turning the silver out of dark grasses
Where the skylark had lain,
And her voice coming softly over the meadow
Was the mist becoming rain.

INSCRIPTION FOR A HEADSTONE

What Larkin bawled to hungry crowds
Is murmured now in dining-hall
And study. Faith bestirs itself
Lest infidels in their impatience
Leave it behind. Who could have guessed
Batons were blessings in disguise,

When every ambulance was filled
With half-killed men and Sunday trampled
Upon unrest? Such fear can harden
Or soften heart, knowing too clearly
His name endures on our holiest page,
Scrawled in a rage by Dublin's poor.

BURIAL OF AN IRISH PRESIDENT
(*Dr. Douglas Hyde*)

The tolling from St. Patrick's
Cathedral was brangled, repeating
Itself in top-back room
And alley of the Coombe,
Crowding the dirty streets,
Upbraiding all our pat tricks
Tricoloured and beflowered,
Coffin of our President,
Where fifty mourners bowed,
Was trestled in the gloom
Of arch and monument,
Beyond the desperate tomb
Of Swift. Imperial flags,
Corunna, Quatre Bras,
Inkermann, Pretoria,
Their pride turning to rags,
Drooped, smoke-thin as the booming
Of cannon. The simple word
From heaven was vaulted, stirred
By candles. At the last bench
Two Catholics, the French
Ambassador and I, knelt down.
The vergers waited. Outside.
The hush of Dublin town,
Professors of cap and gown,
Costello, his Cabinet,

In Government cars, hiding
Around the corner, ready
Tall hat in hand, dreading
Our Father in English. Better
Not hear that 'which' for 'who'
And risk eternal doom.

A SERMON ON SWIFT
Friday, 11.30 a.m. April 28th, 1967

Gentle of hand, the Dean of St. Patrick's guided
My silence up the steps of the pulpit, put around
My neck the lesser microphone.
                            'I feel
That you are blessing me, Mr. Dean.'
                                    Murmur
Was smile.
            In this first lay sermon, must I
Not speak the truth? Known scholars, specialists,
From far and near, were celebrating the third
Centenary of our great satirist.
They spoke of the churchman who kept his solemn gown,
Full-bottom, for Sunday and the Evening Lesson,
But hid from lectern the chuckling rhymster who went,
Bald-headed, into the night when modesty
Wantoned with beau and belle, his pen in hand.
Dull morning clapped his oldest wig on. He looked from
The Deanery window, spied the washerwomen
Bundling along, the hay carts swaying from
The Coombe, dropping their country smells, the hackney—
Clatter on cobbles—ready to share a quip
Or rebus with Sheridan and Tom Delaney,
Read an unfinished chapter to Vanessa
Or Stella, then rid his mind of plaguey curling—
Tongs, farthingales and fal-de-lals. A pox on
Night-hours when wainscot, walls, were dizziness,

Tympana, maddened by inner terror, celled
A man who did not know himself from Cain.
A Tale of a Tub, Gulliver's Travels, fables
And scatological poems, I pennied them on
The Quays, in second-hand book-stalls, when I was young,
Soon learned that humour, unlike the wit o' the Coffee
House, the Club, lengthens the features, smile hid by
A frown.
   Scarce had I uttered the words,
          'Dear Friends,'
Dear Swiftians'—
     when from the eastern window
The pure clear ray, that Swift had known, entered the
Shady church and touched my brow. So blessed
Again, I gathered 'em up, four-letter words,
Street-cries, from the Liberties.
        Ascend,
Our Lady of Filth, Cloacina, soiled goddess
Of paven sewers. Let Roman fountains, a-spray
With themselves, scatter again the imperious gift
Of self-in-sight.
     Celia on a close-stool
Stirs, ready to relace her ribs. Corinna,
Taking herself to pieces at midnight, slips from
The bed at noon, putting together soilures
And soft sores. Strephon half rouses from a dream
Of the flooding Tiber on his marriage-night,
When Chloe stoops out unable to contain her
Twelve cups of tea. Women are unsweet at times,
No doubt, yet how can willynilly resist
The pleasures of defaulting flesh?
       My Sermon
Waits in the plethora of Rabelais, since
March veered with the rusty vane of Faith. I had reached
The house of Aries. Soon in the pure ray,
I am aware of my ancestor, Archbishop
Browne, hastily come from Christ Church, to dispel
Error and Popish superstition. He supped

Last night with Bishop Bale of Ossory,
Robustious as his plays, and, over the talk
And malmsey, forgot the confiscated wealth
Of abbeys.

          In prose, plain as pike, pillory,
In octosyllabic verse turning the two-way
Corner of rhyme, Swift wrote of privy matters
That have to be my text. The Lilliputian
March-by of the crack regiments saluting
On high the double pendulosity
Of Gulliver, glimpsed through a rent in his breeches;
The city square in admiration below. But who
Could blame the Queen when that almighty
Man hosed the private apartments of her palace,
Hissed down the flames of carelessness, leaving
The royal stables unfit for Houyngnms, or tell (in
A coarse aside) what the gigantic maidens
Of Brobdignab did in their playfulness with
The tiny Lemuel when they put him astride
A pap, broader than the mizzen mast of his
Wrecked ship, or hid him in the tangle below?

Reasonable century of Bolingbroke,
Hume, hundred-quilled Voltaire. Satyr and nymph
Disported in the bosk, prim avenues
Let in the classical sky. The ancient temples
Had been restored. Sculptures replaced the painted
Images of the saints. Altars were fuming,
And every capital was amaranthed.
Abstraction ruled the decumana of verse,
Careful caesura kept the middle silence
No syllable dared to cross.

               Swift gave his savings
To mumbling hand, to tatters. Bare kibes ran after
Hoof as he rode beside the Liffey to sup
At Celbridge, brood with Vanessa in a star-bloomed
Bower on Tory politics, forget
Queen Anne, stride from a coffee-house in Whitehall

And with his pamphlets furrow the battle-fields
Of Europe once more, tear up the blood-signed contracts
Of Marlborough, Victualler of Victories;
While in St. Patrick's Cathedral the candling clerk
Shifted the shadows from pillar to pillar, shuffling
His years along the aisles with iron key.
Last gift of an unwilling patriot, Swift willed
To us a mansion of forgetfulness. I lodged
There for a year until Erata led me
Beyond the high-walled garden of Memory,
The Fountain of Hope, to the rewarding Gate,
Reviled but no longer defiled by harpies. And there
In Thomas Street, night to the busy stalls,
Divine Abstraction smiled.

                     My hour, above
Myself, draws to an end. Satiric rhymes
Are safe in the Deanery. So I must find
A moral, search among my wits.

                             I have

It.

   In his sudden poem *The Day of Judgement*
Swift borrowed the allegoric bolt of Jove,
Damned and forgave the human race, dismissed
The jest of life. Here is his secret belief
For sure: the doctrine of Erigena,
Scribing his way from West to East, from bang
Of monastery door, click o' the latch,
His sandals worn out, unsoled, a voice proclaiming
The World's mad business—Eternal Absolution.

R. N. D. Wilson

1899–1953

ELEGY IN A PRESBYTERIAN BURYING-GROUND

In Memoriam: J. L. D.

(I)

The meeting-house is not what it used to be
Since the new church was built,
But the white-washed walls still make a pleasant setting
For the ash-trees at the gate,
And the round windows—though the red panes are gone—
Have dignity upon the simple wall,
And the door, level to the grass, without steps or porchway
Might open yet to all.

(II)

The white pavilions of gateposts, stained with damp
And with rusty iron (where the gate had hung)
Still point the way to the stable, where horse and pony could
    nuzzle,
Till the second sermon was done,
And the elders came out, to draw the shafts of the traps up,
And load their wives and children into the well
With their bibles and their black dresses and farmyard faces.
Farewell, farewell!

(III)

I could have buried a poet here under these hedges
And left him happy. Son of the manse he was,
And drew his integrity from these white-walled precincts,
His rhetoric from his father's pulpit phrase.

Though he himself had made his Covenant elsewhere,
An older, darker and more troubled one,
With the certainty of a leaf, of a stone, of a dewdrop,
He knew his Election.

(IV)

He would remember the nooks where the first primroses
Christened the moss, and the freckled thrush would come
Mating its melody with his own grave elegiacs
To turn a Scottish psalm.
And whenever the men stood up, with their backs to the pulpit,
Hiding their faces from Jehovah's glare,
He would be with them, though he prayed another
And more contentious prayer.

(V)

There are some townlands more in league with heather
And the dark mountain, than with fields where men
Have sowed and planted; and his rebel spirit
Still sought the farthest glen,
Whose Sabbath was a solitude, whose gossip
Was the wind's whisper. There he broke the bread
Of meaning, in a silence, that his verses
So well interpreted.

(VI)

Yet he would grieve with me for the dereliction
That has overtaken this place,
For he cared for it. And the burying-ground beside it
Held many of his race.
He would not be surprised to find it sadly neglected,
Who was himself so negligent of fame.
And I?
—I would be proud to be the stoneyard mason
Who had incised his name.

John Lyle Donaghy

1902–1946

WINTER

The feathery forests are blown back, frost rends
   The mountain-spar and moulds
The thrift leaf where the lean wild cat descends
   Out of his Grampian holds;
The wild white goat forsakes the clamorous height,
   In the half dawn comes down
And rears his horns against the lily light
   And bleats out through the town;
The redwing leaves the Scandinavian skies
   And snowflowers fallen by night
Through his black cover-twigs and cross-sea hies
   With long untwittering flight;
The last mute martin from the roof-tiles slips
   Upon his southward way,
And now my spirit, unbodied, seeks your lips,
   Breathed outward silently—
   How shall my feet then stay?

PORTRAIT

Nor yet do I, your knowing lover,
Know why your eyes appear to me
Like sea-grey basalt in a sea
Full-flooded, and no more can tell
Why in the scarcely visible
Lines that are beneath your eyes
I should conceive a small town lies
With wooden tower and narrow way
Shielded there from more decay.

As little all may I discover
What's the flax-node of your chin,
Why at the place your breasts begin
I should at sudden moments see
Two boughs of a young hazel tree
That start together and apace
Grow like white clouds in fresh-sunned space,
Least, how, when you will move about,
I see the head well-waves break out.

DUCK

Two wild duck of the upland spaces:
This morning, when the mists had lifted
Half above the bell-noised stream,
They rose in laboured circles, climbing
High into the light, wings plying
Stiffly through the vaporous air;
Till when the victor sun had mounted,
They dropped back into rushy cover.

Noon again, they flew, loud-winged,
This time along a heather byway,
That cuts up to the shallow reaches,
Where they met the secret harm,
Whirled suddenly and fell together,
Fell both beside one clump of rushes,
Dying at the mossy root,
Before the nosing dog had found them.

*

A brace of wild duck deftly fettered
The hot hail has done its worst
With sinewy neck, and glossy feathers:
One lies with neck outstretched, eyes staring,
One with head laid under breast,
Both quiet on the old brown dresser.

DEATHWARD

Winter fells—
mizzen-shroud of the larch
black-frost pinnacles of fir—

wreck in the surge—

I shape my mouth with a snow-fang
turned to the cold foam,
dying into death—
                    March, 1939.

Patrick MacDonogh

1902–1961

NOW THE HOLY LAMP OF LOVE

Now the holy lamp of love
Or unholy if they will,
Lifts her amber light above
Cornamona's hill.
Children playing round about
Decent doors at edge of dark
Long ago have ceased to shout.
Now the fox begins to bark.

Cradling hands are all too small
And your hair is drenched with dew;
Love though strong can build no wall
From the hungry fox for you.
Holy men have said their say
And those holy men are right,
God's own fox will have his way
This night or some other night.

NO MEAN CITY

Though naughty flesh will multiply
Our chief delight is in division;
Whatever of Divinity
We are all Doctors of Derison.
Content to risk a far salvation
For the quick coinage of a laugh
We cut, to make wit's reputation,
Our total of two friends by half.

from ESCAPE TO LOVE

VI

Alone and Godless, stopped by the sudden edge
Of the great quarry slicing the limestone height,
He sees, as from his own life's ultimate ledge,
Symbols of fear and love where slow black families
Creep home from church, home from huge mysteries,
From terrible love home to love's kitchen cares.
New sense of isolation, unawares,
Half-open doors to dim divinities,
To his unwelcome godhead thrust out of sight
By a long indolent act of sacrilege.
He, the unsatisfied, hating the arid light,
Uncharmed, that lit the scrubbed boards of one creed,
Refusing the encumbered heritage, loaded with doubt,
Half-envying, half-despising these poor heirs
Enriched by faith. Political orphan, too,
Fouled by his forbears' history he knew
Himself the enemy of that narrow breed,
But no friend to the breed that threw them out.

VII

Below in the sun-dazed field there's something stirs,—
Two God-fed Christians, freed for sweet Sunday sport,
Each with his murderous hound. Deep in the bursting furze
The dogs are suddenly slipped,—Oh, but the start is short!
Apex of all earth's inescapable woes
The ousted hare streaks for the corner hedge
And death's sharp angle narrows to its close.
High on a lost world's last and perilous edge
Blind sympathy of flesh shared the expected hell
Of that warm palpitant body torn apart;
Blind instinct to save ran into empty air
Two hundred feet of it, and as he fell,
(Who knows the ingredients of a miracle?)
Wire in the gapped hedge saved the uncaptured hare . . .

Ewart Milne

b. 1903

VANESSA VANESSA

Three roads were shadowy and the sky over.
One road was mine with many people marching far.
One road so solitary it seemed untrodden, a road alone.

The third was rutted, old with Time and tracks, the parent road.
And at the fork of the roads Two stood: one waiting,
The other looking and wondering, anxious how she might choose.

But the waiting one, this was I, knew
There was no choice to make, or if there were
It was already too late, for her mould was setting.
And it was in that shadowy land as if my hands reached out
Not once but twice, pleadingly: once with, ah, such desire
To bring her along my road: once with sterner zeal
To set her on that lone, that solitary second path.

Twice: but each time my hands went through and fell
As if through greylit nothing: where her breasts were, arms were,
All was as shadows, though from the waist down something shrank
    in fear.
And slowly along the third, the parent road she went,
Shade fading within the shadows, lost to me, to herself,
To the world: lost and looking back.

THE MARTYRED EARTH

Thistledown blows over the poisoned fields,
The corn grows but the harvests are stunted,
The land, the land is tired,

A thin honey melts for all the fanning of the bees,
And the islands are finished.

Rivers empty chemical wastes into the seas,
On their ocean feeding grounds the fish cannot feed,
The herrings die and the herring fleet is disbanded,
There is no shiphaven under the eroded hill,
No hiding place from angry cloud or headland hungry gulls

And over Africa men wake from sleep to death.
The Zambesi roars and the locust and tse-tse rule,
Fever mist rises on the Mountains of the Moon,
The white mosquito fills his bank with black blood,
And a continent wails, without rest, without end.

Without rest, without end the desert enroaches,
Mother earth speaks with no uncertain voice;
And if, here and there, the creeping sands are driven back
In a painful restoration slow as the growth of young firs,
Elsewhere man's savage exploitation continues.

But flesh shall rust in the red clay,
And not an imprint remain of great glories built
Out of the earth's rape, and the entombing her black flowers;
As of cities and civilizations greater than Rome than Egypt
Nothing unburied remains. The dust is moving fast.

Patrick Kavanagh

1904–1967

EPIC

I have lived in important places, times
When great events were decided, who owned
That half a rood of rock, a no-man's land
Surrounded by our pitchfork-armed claims.
I heard the Duffys shouting 'Damn your soul'
And old McCabe stripped to the waist, seen
Step the plot defying blue cast-steel—
'Here is the march along these iron stones'
That was the year of the Munich bother. Which
Was more important? I inclined
To lose my faith in Ballyrush and Gortin
Till Homer's ghost came whispering to my mind
He said: I made the Iliad from such
A local row. Gods make their own importance.

SHANCODUFF

My black hills have never seen the sun rising,
Eternally they look north towards Armagh.
Lot's wife would not be salt if she had been
Incurious as my black hills that are happy
When dawn whitens Glassdrummond chapel.

My hills hoard the bright shillings of March
While the sun searches in every pocket.
They are my Alps and I have climbed the Matterhorn
With a sheaf of hay for three perishing calves
In the field under the Big Forth of Rocksavage.

The sleety winds fondle the rushy beards of Shancoduff
While the cattle-drovers sheltering in the Featherna Bush
Look up and say: 'Who owns them hungry hills
That the water-hen and snipe must have forsaken?
A poet? Then by heavens he must be poor.'
I hear and is my heart not badly shaken?

SPRAYING THE POTATOES

The barrels of blue potato-spray
Stood on a headland of July
Beside an orchard wall where roses
Were young girls hanging from the sky.

The flocks of green potato-stalks
Were blossoms spread for sudden flight,
The Kerr's Pinks in a frivelled blue,
The Arran Banners wearing white.

And over that potato field
A hazy veil of woven sun.
Dandelions growing on headlands, showing
Their unloved hearts to everyone.

And I was there with the knapsack sprayer
On the barrel's edge poised. A wasp was floating
Dead on a sunken briar leaf
Over a copper-poisoned ocean.

The axle-roll of a rut-locked cart
Broke the burnt stick of noon in two.
An old man came through a cornfield
Remembering his youth and some Ruth he knew.

He turned my way. 'God further the work.'
He echoed an ancient farming prayer.
I thanked him. He eyed the potato drills.
He said: 'You are bound to have good ones there.'

We talked and our talk was a theme of kings,
A theme for strings. He hunkered down
In the shade of the orchard wall. O roses
The old man dies in the young girl's frown.

And poet lost to potato-fields,
Remembering the lime and copper smell
Of the spraying barrels he is not lost
Or till blossomed stalks cannot weave a spell.

from THE GREAT HUNGER

(IX)

He gave himself another year,
Something was bound to happen before then—
The circle would break down
And he would curve the new one to his own will.
A new rhythm is a new life
And in it marriage is hung and money.
He would be a new man walking through unbroken meadows
Of dawn in the year of One.

The poor peasant talking to himself in a stable door—
An ignorant peasant deep in dung.
What can the passers-by think otherwise?
Where is his silver bowl of knowledge hung?
Why should men be asked to believe in a soul
That is only the mark of a hoof in guttery gaps?
A man is what is written on the label.
And the passing world stares but no one stops
To look closer. So back to the growing crops
And the ridges he never loved.
Nobody will ever know how much tortured poetry the pulled weeds
    on the ridge wrote
Before they withered in the July sun,

Nobody will ever read the wild, sprawling, scrawling mad woman's
    signature,
The hysteria and the boredom of the enclosed nun of his thought.
Like the afterbirth of a cow stretched on a branch in the wind
Life dried in the veins of these women and men:
The grey and grief and unlove,
The bones in the backs of their hands,
And the chapel pressing its low ceiling over them.

Sometimes they did laugh and see the sunlight,
A narrow slice of divine instruction.
Going along the river at the bend of Sunday
The trout played in the pools encouragement
To jump in love though death bait the hook.
And there would be girls sitting on the grass banks of lanes.
Stretch-legged, and lingering staring—
A man might take one of them if he had the courage.
But 'No' was in every sentence of their story
Except when the public-house came in and shouted its piece.

The yellow buttercups and the bluebells among the whin bushes
On rocks in the middle of ploughing
Was a bright spoke in the wheel
Of the peasant's mill.
The goldfinches on the railway paling were worth looking at—
A man might imagine then
Himself in Brazil and these birds the birds of paradise
And the Amazon and the romance traced on the school map lived
    again.

Talk in evening corners and under trees
Was like an old book found in a king's tomb.
The children gathered round like students and listened
And some of the saga defied the draught in the open tomb
And was not blown.

SANCTITY

To be a poet and not know the trade,
To be a lover and repel all women;
Twin ironies by which great saints are made,
The agonizing pincer-jaws of Heaven.

IN MEMORY OF MY MOTHER

You will have the road gate open, the front door ajar
The kettle boiling and a table set
By the window looking out at the sycamores—
And your loving heart lying in wait

For me coming up among the poplar trees.
You'll know my breathing and my walk
And it will be a summer evening on those roads
Lonely with leaves of thought.

We will be choked with the grief of things growing,
The silence of dark-green air
Life too rich—the nettles, docks and thistles
All answering the prodigal's prayer.

You will know I am coming though I send no word
For you were lover who could tell
A man's thoughts—my thoughts—though I hid them—
Through you I knew Woman and did not fear her spell.

I HAD A FUTURE

O I had a future
A future.

Gods of the imagination bring back to life
The personality of those streets,
Not any streets
But the streets of nineteen-forty.

Give the quarter-seeing eyes I looked out of
The animal-remembering mind
The fog through which I walked towards
    The mirage
That was my future.

The women I was to meet
They were nowhere within sight.

And then the pathos of the blind soul,
How without knowing stands in its own
    kingdom.
Bring me a small detail
How I felt about money,
Not frantic as later,
There was the future.

Show me the stretcher-bed I slept on
In a room in Drumcondra Road,
Let John Betjeman call for me in a car.

It is summer and the eerie beat
Of madness in Europe trembles the
Wings of the butterflies along the canal.

O I had a future.

THE HOSPITAL

A year ago I fell in love with the functional ward
Of a chest hospital: square cubicles in a row

Plain concrete, wash basins—an art lover's woe,
Not counting how the fellow in the next bed snored.
But nothing whatever is by love debarred,
The common and banal her heat can know.
The corridor led to a stairway and below
Was the inexhaustible adventure of a gravelled yard.

This is what love does to things: the Rialto Bridge,
The main gate that was bent by a heavy lorry,
The seat at the back of a shed that was a suntrap.
Naming these things is the love-act and its pledge;
For we must record love's mystery without claptrap,
Snatch out of time the passionate transitory.

LINES WRITTEN ON A SEAT ON
THE GRAND CANAL

O commemorate me where there is water,
Canal water preferably, so stilly
Greeny at the heart of summer. Brother
Commemorate me thus beautifully,
Where by a lock Niagarously roars
The falls for those who sit in the tremendous silence
Of mid-July. No one will speak in prose
Who finds his way to these Parnassian islands.
A swan goes by head low with many apologies,
Fantastic light looks through the eyes of bridges—
And look! a barge comes bringing from Athy
And other far-flung towns mythologies.
O commemorate me with no hero-courageous
Tomb—just a canal-bank seat for the passer-by.

Brian Coffey

b. 1905

from MUSE, JUNE, RELATED
To the memory of Denis Devlin

Blooms such as wither at finger-touch
hid her
while the hawk, blue shark,
prowled the corn.

The cedars had trapped the sun
when he turned
scythe to field
where she bent her head.

Her palms warm strands
for questing ants,
her limbs the forest mounds,
his the silence,
a spring sighed in its depths.

When sun went out
she had been touched
so she lay quiet eyes
whose liner
slips through harbour arms.

If he turned his head
in his course,
he saw her through branches
a slip of light
until the leaves took her.

He went imagining
her tears at morning

spent on the green.
In song he poised her,
lauded victory
over his muse.

What he fancied ended
she smiled as begun,
knowing him no freeman,
him reginal
astray from the perfect scene.

Samuel Beckett

b. 1906

GNOME

Spend the years of learning squandering
Courage for the years of wandering
Through the world politely turning
From the loutishness of learning

ALBA

before morning you shall be here
and Dante and the Logos and all strata and mysteries
and the branded moon
beyond the white plane of music
that you shall establish before morning
       grave suave singing silk
       stoop to the black firmament of areca
       rain on the bamboos flower of smoke alley of willows
who though you stoop with fingers of compassion
to endorse the dust
shall not add to your bounty
whose beauty shall be a sheet before me
a statement of itself drawn across the tempest of emblems
so that there is no sun and no unveiling
and no host
only I and then the sheet
and bulk dead

'I WOULD LIKE MY LOVE TO DIE'

I would like my love to die
and the rain to be falling on the graveyard

295

and on me walking the streets
mourning she who sought to love me.
from the French (1948)

from WATT

The crocuses and the larch turning green every year a week before
the others and the pastures red with uneaten sheep's placentas and
the long summer days and the newmown hay and the woodpigeon
in the morning and the cuckoo in the afternoon and the corncake
in the evening and the wasps in the jam and the smell of the gorse
and the look of the gorse and the apples falling and the children
walking in the dead leaves and the larch turning brown a week
before the others and the chestnuts falling and the howling winds
and the sea breaking over the pier and the first fires and the hooves
on the road and the consumptive postman whistling *The Roses Are
Blooming in Picardy* and the standard oillamp and of course the
snow and to be sure the sleet and bless your heart the slush and every
fourth year the February débâcle and the endless April showers and
the crocuses and then the whole bloody business starting all over
again.

from WORDS AND MUSIC

Age is when to a man
Huddled o'er the ingle
Shivering for the hag
To put the pan in the bed
And bring the toddy
She comes in the ashes
Who loved could not be won
Or won not loved
Or some other trouble
Comes in the ashes
Like in that old light
The face in the ashes
That old starlight
On the earth again.

Padraic Fallon

b. 1906

ASSUMPTION

Some Syrian rainmaker
Invoking a minor image of power found her
Intrude, O enormous magic, and his hands
Dissolve in showers over many lands;
Earth turned woman, or woman into earth, he
Left this wild image to Syrian sorcery.
But O how they tamed her, the Greeks, the civilizing
Mythologizing Alexandrian schoolmen
And the soft Italians with the Christian eyes
Who ferried her over the tideless Mediterranean;
The muted breasts, the quiet, and on the top
A face bright as a waterdrop.

Assumed into heaven, she,
A statue among statuary,
Consumes in her single fire the line
Of barbarous virgins who dwelt between
Trinities in their season.
Heaven and earth are in division;
The gross fertilities, the ram, the bull,
Left out-of-doors while in her shuttered parlour
When she bares the nipple
No rye rises, no wheaten flower;
Only her dreams stir
The peacock presences of air.

This mild lady
Calms the gross ambitions with a steady
Country look. No drums, no dances,
No midnight fires, no sacrifice of princes;
She takes her pail among the cows
And bolts her fowl in the fowl house;

Evoe, if the sun-headed god is gone, there's still
The house to be done, white linen hung
Upon the hedge. The serene axle
Goes round and round in a crucifixion,
But earth is a pot of flowers. Foreign tongues
Commune above her in a drift of wings.

THE YOUNG FENIANS

They looked so good;
They were the coloured lithographs
Of Murat, Bernadotte and Ney
And the little Corsican.
Mars had made them from our dead
And given to each his martial head.

The cavalry and plumes would come,
No doubt about it;
Every half-acre man with a sword,
The boy with a drum;
And down the Alps of every local hill
The bannered horses ride to kill.

O'Connell helpless in the house;
The old gazeboes at their talk,
All to no purpose;
Tone must rise and Emmet walk,
Edward troop out of Kildare;
The time had come; the day was fair.

Flags flew from our every word;
The new names sang from litanies,
Saviours each one;
They were the eagles in the morning sun;
A country rising from its knees
To upset all the histories.

George Reavey

b. 1907

NEVER

When the bones walk out of me
Down the hill and the flesh falls limp
And lies all still as the wind blows back
And ever until . . .

Never, I'll say, by the stoneless wall;
By the touchless tree, never, I'll say;
Never, by the lightless eye in the vast blind hall,
By the tasteless dew
                 and earth's huge black ball;
Never, never, I'll say, shall I ever be
Without sleep at my side
                 on this slope of all.

THE BRIDGE OF HERACLITUS
(To René Magritte)

There was a bridge that Rozinante would not cross,
Though Don Quixote spurred him to the task;
The tempting plains did not avail,
Nor the promised sky's perennial invitation;
In the limpid waters seeming slow and calm
Real eddies surged, decades', days' increasing flow;
And Don Quixote urging Rozinante to excel,
Was in the waters' mirror washed another man,
His goal half-won, but Dulcinea still his talisman.

John Hewitt

b. 1907

THE RAM'S HORN

I have turned to the landscape because men disappoint me:
the trunk of a tree is proud; when the woodmen fell it,
it still has a contained Ionic solemnity:
it is a rounded event without the need to tell it.

I have never been compelled to turn away from the dawn
because it carries treason behind its wakened face:
even the horned ram, glowering over the bog-hole,
though symbol of evil, will step through the blown grass with grace.

Animal, plant, or insect, stone or water,
are, every minute, themselves; they behave by law.
I am not required to discover motives for them,
or strip my heart to forgive the rat in the straw.

I live my best in the landscape, being at ease there;
the only trouble I find I have brought in my hand.
See, I let it fall with a rustle of stems in the nettles,
and never for a moment suppose that they understand.

THE FRONTIER

At the frontier the long train slows to a stop:
small men in uniform drift down the corridor,
thumb passports, or withdraw for consultation;
the customs officers chalk the bags and leave us to shut them.

We pass here into another allegiance,
expect new postage stamps, new prices, manifestoes,
and brace ourselves for the change. But the landscape does not alter;
we had already entered these mountains an hour ago.

AN IRISHMAN IN COVENTRY

A full year since, I took this eager city,
the tolerance that laced its blatant roar,
its famous steeples and its web of girders,
as image of the state hope argued for,
and scarcely flung a bitter thought behind me
on all that flaws the glory and the grace
which ribbons through the sick, guilt-clotted legend
of my creed-haunted, Godforsaken race.
My rhetoric swung round from steel's high promise
to the precision of the well-gauged tool,
tracing the logic in the vast glass headlands,
the clockwork horse, the comprehensive school.

Then, sudden, by occasion's chance concerted,
in enclave of my nation, but apart,
the jigging dances and the lilting fiddle
stirred the old rage and pity in my heart.
The faces and the voices blurring round me,
the strong hands long familiar with the spade,
the whiskey-tinctured breath, the pious buttons,
called up a people endlessly betrayed
by our own weakness, by the wrongs we suffered
in that long twilight over bog and glen,
by force, by famine and by glittering fables
which gave us martyrs when we needed men,
by faith which had no charity to offer,
by poisoned memory, and by ready wit,
with poverty corroded into malice,
to hit and run and howl when it is hit.

This is our fate: eight hundred years' disaster,
crazily tangled as the Book of Kells;
the dream's distortion and the land's division,
the midnight raiders and the prison cells.
Yet like Lir's children banished to the waters
our hearts still listen for the landward bells.

Louis MacNeice

1907–1963

from AUTUMN JOURNAL

(XVI)

Nightmare leaves fatigue:
    We envy men of action
Who sleep and wake, murder and intrigue
    Without being doubtful, without being haunted.
And I envy the intransigence of my own
    Countrymen who shoot to kill and never
See the victim's face become their own
    Or find his motive sabotage their motives.
So reading the memoirs of Maud Gonne,
    Daughter of an English mother and a soldier father,
I note how a single purpose can be founded on
    A jumble of opposites:
Dublin Castle, the vice-regal ball,
    The embassies of Europe,
Hatred scribbled on a wall,
    Gaols and revolvers.
And I remember, when I was little, the fear
    Bandied among the servants
That Casement would land at the pier
    With a sword and a horde of rebels;
And how we used to expect, at a later date,
    When the wind blew from the west, the noise of shooting
Starting in the evening at eight
    In Belfast in the York Street district;
And the voodoo of the Orange bands
    Drawing an iron net through darkest Ulster,
Flailing the limbo lands—
    The linen mills, the long wet grass, the ragged hawthorn.
And one read black where the other read white, his hope
    The other man's damnation:

Up the Rebels, To Hell with the Pope,
    And God Save—as you prefer—the King or Ireland.
The land of scholars and saints:
    Scholars and saints my eye, the land of ambush,
Purblind manifestoes, never-ending complaints,
    The born martyr and the gallant ninny;
The grocer drunk with the drum,
    The land-owner shot in his bed, the angry voices
Piercing the broken fanlight in the slum,
    The shawled woman weeping at the garish altar.
Kathaleen ni Houlihan! Why
    Must a country, like a ship or a car, be always female,
Mother or sweetheart? A woman passing by,
    We did but see her passing.
Passing like a patch of sun on the rainy hill
    And yet we love her for ever and hate our neighbour
And each one in his will
    Binds his heirs to continuance of hatred.
Drums on the haycock, drums on the harvest, black
    Drums in the night shaking the windows:
King William is riding his white horse back
    To the Boyne on a banner.
Thousands of banners, thousands of white
    Horses, thousands of Williams
Waving thousands of swords and ready to fight
    Till the blue sea turns to orange.
Such was my country and I thought I was well
    Out of it, educated and domiciled in England,
Though yet her name keeps ringing like a bell
    In an under-water belfry.
Why do we like being Irish? Partly because
    It gives us a hold on the sentimental English
As members of a world that never was,
    Baptised with fairy water;
And partly because Ireland is small enough
    To be still thought of with a family feeling,
And because the waves are rough
    That split her from a more commercial culture;

And because one feels that here at least one can
    Do local work which is not at the world's mercy
And that on this tiny stage with luck a man
    Might see the end of one particular action.
It is self-deception of course;
    There is no immunity in this island either;
A cart that is drawn by somebody else's horse
    And carrying goods to somebody else's market.
The bombs in the turnip sack, the sniper from the roof,
    Griffith, Connolly, Collins, where have they brought us?
Ourselves alone! Let the round tower stand aloof
    In a world of bursting mortar!
Let the school-children fumble their sums
    In a half-dead language;
Let the censor be busy on the books; pull down the Georgian slums;
    Let the games be played in Gaelic.
Let them grow beet-sugar; let them build
    A factory in every hamlet;
Let them pigeon-hole the souls of the killed
    Into sheep and goats, patriots and traitors.
And the North, where I was a boy,
    Is still the North, veneered with the grime of Glasgow,
Thousands of men whom nobody will employ
    Standing at the corners, coughing.
And the street-children play on the wet
    Pavement—hopscotch or marbles;
And each rich family boasts a sagging tennis-net
    On a spongy lawn beside a dripping shrubbery.
The smoking chimneys hint
    At prosperity round the corner
But they make their Ulster linen from foreign lint
    And the money that comes in goes out to make more money.
A city built upon mud;
    A culture built upon profit;
Free speech nipped in the bud,
    The minority always guilty.
Why should I want to go back
    To you, Ireland, my Ireland?

The blots on the page are so black
    That they cannot be covered with shamrock.
I hate your grandiose airs,
    Your sob-stuff, your laugh and your swagger,
Your assumption that everyone cares
    Who is the king of your castle.
Castles are out of date,
    The tide flows round the children's sandy fancy;
Put up what flag you like, it is too late
    To save your soul with bunting.
Odi atque amo:
    Shall we cut this name on trees with a rusty dagger?
Her mountains are still blue, her rivers flow
    Bubbling over the boulders.
She is both a bore and a bitch;
    Better close the horizon,
Send her no more fantasy, no more longings which
    Are under a fatal tariff.
For common sense is the vogue
    And she gives her children neither sense nor money
Who slouch around the world with a gesture and a brogue
    And a faggot of useless memories.

THALASSA

Run out the boat, my broken comrades;
Let the old seaweed crack, the surge
Burgeon oblivious of the last
Embarkation of feckless men,
Let every adverse force converge—
Here we must needs embark again.

Run up the sail, my hearsick comrades;
Let each horizon tilt and lurch—
You know the worst: your wills are fickle,
Your values blurred, your hearts impure

And your past life a ruined church—
But let your poison be your cure.

Put out to sea, ignoble comrades,
Whose record shall be noble yet;
Butting through scarps of moving marble
The narwhal dares us to be free;
By a high star our course is set,
Our end is Life. Put out to sea.

?1963

Denis Devlin

1908–1959

ENCOUNTER

'Our saints are poets, Milton and Blake,
Who would rib men with pride against the spite
Of God,' the Englishman said, and in the silence
Hatred sparkled along our bones. He said:
'Celt, your saints adorn the poor with roses
And praise God for standing still.'

Between the two of us, François from Touraine,
Where women and the wheat ripen and fall due
Suavely at evening, smiled, teasing the breadcrumbs.
He whispered: 'Patience; listen to the world's
Growth, rustling in fire and childlike water!'

And I: 'Milton and Marvell, like the toady, Horace,
Praised the men of power for the good
They happened on, with bible and sword; the wretched
Hold out their begging-bowls at the wooden gates,
Too poor to weep, too poor to weep with tears.'

Boxflower scent. Fumes of burgundy.
Nagging children at the tables
A dream's remove from their fathers smoking
Along the boulevard laid with yellow evening.

LOUGH DERG

The poor in spirit on their rosary rounds,
The jobbers with their whiskey-angered eyes,
The pink bank clerks, the tip-hat papal counts,

And drab, kind women their tonsured mockery tries,
Glad invalids on penitential feet
Walk the Lord's majesty like their village street.

With mullioned Europe shattered, this Northwest,
Rude-sainted isle would pray it whole again:
(Peasant Apollo! Troy is worn to rest.)
Europe that humanized the sacred bane
Of God's chance who yet laughed in his mind
And balanced thief and saint: were they this kind?

Low rocks, a few weasels, lake
Like a field of burnt gorse; the rooks caw;
Ours, passive, for man's gradual wisdom take
Firefly instinct dreamed out into law;
The prophets' jeweled kingdom down at heel
Fires no Augustine here. Inert, they kneel;

All is simple and symbol in their world,
The incomprehended rendered fabulous.
Sin teases life whose natural fruits withheld
Sour the deprived nor bloom for timely loss:
Clan Jansen! less what magnanimity leavens
Man's wept-out, fitful, magniloquent heavens

Where prayer was praise, O Lord! the Temple trumpets
Cascaded down Thy sunny pavilions of air,
The scroll-tongued priests, the galvanic strumpets,
All clash and stridency gloomed upon Thy stair;
The pharisees, the exalted boy their power
Sensually psalmed in Thee, their coming hour!

And to the sun, earth turned her flower of sex,
Acanthus in the architects' limpid angles;
Close priests allegorized the Orphic egg's
Brood, and from the Academy, tolerant wranglers
Could hear the contemplatives of the Tragic Choir
Drain off man's sanguine, pastoral death-desire.

It was said stone dreams and animal sleeps and man
Is awake; but sleep with its drama on us bred
Animal articulate, only somnambulist can
Conscience like Cawdor give the blood its head
For the dim moors to reign through druids again.
O first geometer! tangent-feelered brain

Clearing by inches the encircled eyes,
Bolder than the peasant tiger whose autumn beauty
Sags in the expletive kill, or the sacrifice
Of dearth puffed positive in the stance of duty
With which these pilgrims would propitiate
Their fears; no leafy, medieval state

Of paschal cathedrals backed on earthy hooves
Against the craftsmen's primary-coloured skies
Whose gold was Gabriel on the patient roofs,
The parabled windows taught the dead to rise,
And Christ the Centaur in two natures whole,
With fable and proverb joinered body and soul.

Water withers from the oars. The pilgrims blacken
Out of the boats to masticate their sin
Where Dante smelled among the stones and bracken
The door to Hell (O harder Hell where pain
Is earthed, a casuist sanctuary of guilt!).
Spirit bureaucracy on a bet built

Part by this race when monks in convents of coracles
For the Merovingian centuries left their land,
Belled, fragrant; and honest in their oracles
Bespoke the grace to give without demand,
Martyrs Heaven winged nor tempted with reward.
And not ours, doughed in dogma, who never have dared

Will with surrogate palm distribute hope:
No better nor worse than I who, in my books,
Have angered at the stake with Bruno and, by the rope

Watt Tyler swung from, leagued with shifty looks
To fuse the next rebellion with the desperate
Serfs in the same need to eat and get;

Have praised, on its thunderous canvas, the Florentine smile
As man took to wearing his death, his own
Sapped crisis through cathedral branches (while
Flesh groped loud round dissenting skeleton)
In soul, reborn as body's appetite:
Now languisht back in body's amber light,

Now is consumed. O earthly paradise!
Hell is to know our natural empire used
Wrong, by mind's moulting, brute divinities.
The vanishing tiger's saved, his blood transfused.
Kent is for Jutes again and Glasgow town
Burns high enough to screen the stars and moon.

Well may they cry who have been robbed, their wasting
Shares in justice legally lowered until
Man his own actor, matrix, mould and casting,
Or man, God's image, sees, his idol spill.
Say it was pride that did it, or virtue's brief:
To them that suffer it is no relief.

All indiscriminate, man, stone, animal
Are woken up in nightmare. What John the Blind
From Patmos saw works and we speak it. Not all
The men of God nor the priests of mankind
Can mend or explain the good and broke, not one
Generous with love prove communion.

Behind the eyes the winged ascension flags,
For want of spirit by the market blurbed,
And if hands touch, such fraternity sags
Frightened this side the dikes of death disturbed
Like Aran Islands' bibulous, unclean seas:
Pieta: but the limbs ache; it is not peace.

Then to see less, look little, let hearts' hunger
Feed on water and berries. The pilgrims sing:
Life will fare well from elder to younger,
Though courage fail in a world-end, rosary ring.
Courage kills its practioners and we live,
Nothing forgotten, nothing to forgive.

We pray to ourself. The metal moon, unspent
Virgin eternity sleeping in the mind,
Excites the form of prayer without content;
Whitehorn lightens, delicate and blind,
The negro mountain, and so, knelt on her sod,
This woman beside me murmuring *My God! My God!*

ASCENSION

It happens through the blond window, the trees
With diverse leaves divide the light, light birds;
Aengus, the god of Love, my shoulders brushed
With birds, you could say lark or thrush or thieves

And not be right yet—or ever right—
For it was God's Son foreign to our moor:
When I looked out the window, all was white,
And what's beloved in the heart was sure,

With such a certainty ascended He,
The Son of Man who deigned Himself to be:
That when we lifted out of sleep, there was
Life with its dark, and love above the laws.

ANK'HOR VAT

The antlered forests
Move down to the sea.
Here the dung-filled jungle pauses

Buddha has covered the walls of the great temple
With the vegetative speed of his imagery

Let us wait, hand in hand

No Western god or saint
Ever smiled with the lissom fury of this god
Who holds in doubt
The wooden stare of Apollo
Our Christian crown of thorns:

There is no mystery in the luminous lines
Of that high, animal face
The smile, sad, humouring and equal
Blesses without obliging
Loves without condescension;
The god, clear as spring-water
Sees through everything, while everything
Flows through him

A fling of flowers here
Whose names I do not know
Downy, scarlet gullets
Green legs yielding and closing

While, at my mental distance from passion,
The prolific divinity of the temple
Is a quiet lettering on vellum.

Let us lie down before him
His look will flow like oil over us.

VENUS OF THE SALTY SHELL

Round a cleft in the cliffs to come upon
The Athenians standing with their friendly gods
Serious on the shore.

The fresh violet of the Middle Sea
Blooms and is gone; and there
The tremble of a difference from the foam
Foam forms a shell which bears
The smiling idol of Love
Brightness shadowy through brightness.

The space of a moment love lightens the body
Only when love comes free as air
Like the goddess on the dove-drawn shell
Riding upon the speckled hawthorn waves
Into the rocky ways of the sea-republic.
Look at that hand gently to the breast!
She smiles as if turning all the orchards of summer
Into one brittle petal to touch.

The old men do not remember
The women of their youth,
The young men bend at point like setters.
There is need; she, the desired-with-cries,
Fanned by the ivory air, on the ache of birth
Advances as though her nakedness
Were the first glad woman's for these men

And nearer and the cries of the men
Stop, they are struck still.
The doves, the hawthorn merge in the wrack and foam.

W. R. Rodgers

1909–1969

THE LOVERS

After the tiff there was stiff silence, till
One word, flung in centre like single stone,
Starred and cracked the ice of her resentment
To its edge. From that stung core opened and
Poured up one outward and widening wave
Of eager and extravagant anger.

AN IRISH LAKE

There in the hard light
Dark birds, pink-footed, dab and pick
Among the addery roots and marrowy stones,
And the blown waves blink and hiccup at the lake's
Lip. A late bee blares and drones on inland
Into a cone-point of silence, and I
Lying at the rhododendron's foot
Look through five finger's grille at the lake
Shaking, at the bare and backward plain, and
The running and bending hills that carry
Like a conveyer belt the bright snail-line
Of clouds along the sky all day unendingly.

There, far from the slack noose of rumour
That tightens into choking fact, I relax,
And sounds and sights and scents sail slowly by.
But suddenly, like delicate and tilted italics,
The up-standing birds stretch urgently away
Into the sky as suddenly grown grey.
Night rounds on Europe now. And I must go.
Before its hostile faces peer and pour

Over the mind's rim enveloping me,
And my so-frightened thoughts dart here and there
Like trout among their grim stony gazes.

THE PARTY

So they went, leaving a picnic-litter of talk
And broken glitter of jokes, the burst bags of spite:
In comes Contempt, the caretaker, eye on ceiling,
Broom in armpit, and with one wide careless cast
Sweeps the stuttering rubbish out of memory,
Opens the shutters, puts out the intimate lamp,
And, a moment, gazes on the mute enormities
Of distant dawn. And far doors bang in mind, idly.

FIELD DAY

The old farmer, nearing death, asked
To be carried outside and set down
Where he could see a certain field
'And then I will cry my heart out,' he said.

It troubles me, thinking about that man;
What shape was the field of his crying
In Donegal?

I remember a small field in Down, a field
Within fields, shaped like a triangle.
I could have stood there and looked at it
All day long.

And I remember crossing the frontier between
France and Spain at a forbidden point, and seeing
A small triangular field in Spain,
And stopping

Or walking in Ireland down any rutted by-road
To where it hit the highway, there was always
At this turning-point and abuttment
A still centre, a V-shape of grass
Untouched by cornering traffic,
Where country lads larked at night.

I think I know what the shape of the field was
That made the old man weep.

Donagh MacDonagh

1912–1968

HUNGRY GRASS

Crossing the shallow holdings high above sea
Where few birds nest, the luckless foot may pass
From the bright safety of experience
Into the terror of the hungry grass.

Here in a year when poison from the air
First withered in despair the growth of spring
Some skull-faced wretch whom nettle could not save
Crept on four bones to his last scattering;

Crept, and the shrivelled heart which drove his thought
Towards platters brought in hospitality
Burst as the wizened eyes measured the miles
Like dizzy walls forbidding him the city.

Little the earth reclaimed from that poor body;
But yet, remembering him, the place has grown
Bewitched, and the thin grass he nourishes
Racks with his famine, sucks marrow from the bone.

PROTHALAMIUM

And so much I lose her whose mind
Fitted so sweetly and securely into mine
That words seeded and blossomed in an instant,
Whose body was one of my fine
Morning visions come alive and perfect?
Must she slip out of my arms so
And I never revel again in the twilight of her hair

Or see the world grow
Marvellous within her eye. My hands
Are empty; and suddenly I think
That on some night like this, when rain is soft
And moths flutter at the window, seeking a chink,
I'll lose her utterly, a bedded bride
Gold ring and contract bound,
The night filled with terrifying music
And she not hearing a sound.

Charles Donnelly

1914-1937

LAST POEM

Between rebellion as a private study and the public
Defiance, is simple action only which will flicker
Catlike, for spring. Whether at nerve-roots is secret
Iron, there's no diviner can tell, only the moment can show.
Simple and unclear moment, on a morning utterly different
And under circumstances different from what you'd expected.

Your flag is public over granite. Gulls fly above it.
Whatever the issue of the battle is, your memory
Is public, for them to pull awry with crooked hands,
Moist eyes. And villages' reputations will be built on
Inaccurate accounts of your campaign. You're name for orators,
Figure stone-struck beneath damp Dublin sky.

In a delaying action, perhaps, on hillside in remote parish,
Outposts correctly placed, retreat secured to wood, bridge mined
Against pursuit, sniper may sight you carelessly contoured.
Or death may follow years in strait confinement, where diet
Is uniform as ceremony, lacking only fruit
Or on the barracks square before the sun casts shadow.

Name, subject of all considered words, praise and blame
Irrelevant, the public talk which sounds the same on hollow
Tongue as true, you'll be with Parnell and with Pearse.
Name alderman will raise a cheer with, teacher make reference
Oblique in class, and boys and women spin gum of sentiment
On qualities attributed in error.

Man, dweller in mountain huts, possessor of coloured mice,
Skilful in minor manual turns, patron of obscure subjects, of
Gaelic swordsmanship and medieval armoury.
The technique of the public man, the masked servilities are
Not for you. Master of military trade, you give
Like Raleigh, Lawrence, Childers, your services but not yourself.

Valentin Iremonger

b. 1918

THE DOG

All day the unnatural barking of dogs
Sounded in my ears. In O'Connell Street, among the crowd,
A dog barked at my heels but, when I looked, was gone.
Sitting at my window, later, at nearly three o'clock,
Glad for the quiet harmony of the afternoon,
A voice reached up like a long arm out of the street
To rap on the shutters of my ears but when I looked
The street's chaste line was unbroken, its perspective unstained.

Now, lying awake in bed, smoking,
Looking out the window, I can see him,
Lean-faced and shaggy, as the moonlight falls
Sideways into my room as into a chapel,
Where he squats on the lawn, tilting his lonely snout,
Raising his lost unnatural cry.

God send his master is not dead or none he loves
Being out of countenance has sent him for succour
And that I don't understand his plaintiveness:
But yet, God help me, I fear this unnatural barking
Has something to do with me and not with strangers
As quietly I lie, hearing the hours tick by
And the unsatisfied dog howling upon the lawn,
Breaking the night's maidenhead.

ICARUS

As, even today, the airman, feeling the plane sweat
Suddenly, seeing the horizon tilt up gravely, the wings shiver,

Knows that, for once, Daedalus has slipped up badly,
Drunk on the job, perhaps, more likely dreaming, high-flier Icarus,
Head butting down, skidding along the light-shafts
Back, over the tones of the sea-waves and the slipstream, heard
The gravel-voiced, stuttering trumpets of his heart.

Sennet among the crumbling court-yards of his brain the mistake
Of trusting somebody else on an important affair like this;
And, while the flat sea, approaching, buckled into oh! avenues
Of acclamation, he saw the wrong story fan out into history,
Truth, undefined, lost in his own neglect. On the hills,
The summer-shackled hills, the sun spanged all day;
Love and the world were young and there was no ending:

But star-chaser, big-time-going, chancer Icarus
Like a dog on the sea lay and the girls forgot him
And Daedalus, too busy hammering another job,
Remembered him only in pubs. No bugler at all
Sobbed taps for the young fool then, reported missing,
Presumed drowned, wing-bones and feathers on the tide
Drifting in casually, one by one.

INVOCATION

Ten bloody years with this quill lying
Almost idle on my table, I have sourly watched

The narrow summers go, the winters ride over,
Awaiting always, seized in a cold silence,

The genetic word, the arrogant vaticinal line.
And each spring, unmoving by an open window,

The room ringing with emptiness like an unswung bell,
My notebook, open, filled with abstract questions,

The bare trees outside expectant, I saw the crocus tell
The indolent fall of the autumn leaves, another year's

Bitter burning and the ice again forming.

Lie with me now, therefore, these wording days,
The ever-questing tragic-gesturing mind this spring exulting,

Lady I have icily waited for, whom I have known
By these aboding mountains, this lovely glen.

Anthony Cronin

b. 1925

from R.M.S. *TITANIC*

2

On the bog road the blackthorn flowers, the turf-stacks,
Chocolate brown, are built like bricks but softer,
And softer too the west of Ireland sky.
Turf smoke is chalked upon the darker blue
And leaves a sweet, rich poor man's smell in cloth.
Great ragged rhododendrons sprawl through gaps

And pink and white the chestnut blossom tops
The tumbled granite wall round the demesne.
The high-brass-bound De Dion coughing past,
O'Connor Don and the solicitor,
Disturbs the dust but not the sleeping dogs.

Disturbs the memories in an old man's head.
We only live one life, with one beginning.
The coming degradations of the heart
We who wake with all our landfalls staring
Back at us in the dawn, must hold our breaths for.
The west is not awake to where Titanic
Smokes in the morning, huge against the stars.

BAUDELAIRE IN BRUSSELS

Gas-lamps abandoned by the night burn on
Grotesquely as the daylight stirs the street,
And pain as bright as dawn behind the eyes
Is pulsing as the wings of madness beat.
The archetype prays to Poe to pray to God

For time to pay his debts and die of peace:
No mind can hold too many truths at once.
All contradictions cry out for release.
All contradictions: nothing equals pride
Except our hatred for ourselves: too late
God punishes in the person of his mother
One who endured before he chose his fate.

Pearse Hutchinson

b. 1927

MALAGA
(for Sammy Sheridan)

The scent of unseen jasmine on the warm night beach.

The tram along the sea-road all the way from town
through its wide open sides drank unseen jasmine down.
Living was nothing all those nights but that strong flower,
whose hidden voice on darkness grew to such mad power
I could have sworn for once I travelled through full peace
and even love at last had perfect calm release
only by breathing in the unseen jasmine scent,
that ruled us and the summer every hour we went.

The tranquil unrushed wine drunk on the daytime beach.
Or from an open room all that our sight could reach
was heat, sea, light, unending images of peace;
and then at last the night brought jasmine's great release—
not images but calm uncovetous content,
the wide-eyed heart alert at rest in June's own scent.

In daytime's humdrum town from small child after child
we bought cluster on cluster of the star flower's wild
white widowed heads, re-wired on strong weed stalks they'd
   trimmed
to long green elegance; but still the whole month brimmed
at night along the beach with a strong voice like peace;
and each morning the mind stayed crisp in such release.

Some hint of certainty, still worth longing I could teach,
lies lost in a strength of jasmine down a summer beach.

GAELTACHT

Bartley Costello, eighty years old,
sat in his silver-grey tweeds on a kitchen chair,
at his door in Carraroe, the sea only yards away,
smoking a pipe, with a pint of porter beside his boot:
'For the past twenty years I've eaten nothing only
periwinkles, my own hands got them off those rocks.
You're a quarter my age, if you'd stick to winkles
you'd live as long as me, and keep as spry.'

In the Liverpool Bar, at the North Wall,
on his way to join his children over there,
an old man looked at me, then down at his pint
of rich Dublin stout. He pointed at the black glass:
'Is lú í an Ghaeilge ná an t-uisce sa ngloine sin.'[1]

Beartla Confhaola, prime of his manhood,
driving between the redweed and the rock-fields,
driving through the sunny treeless quartz glory of Carna,
answered the foreigners' glib pity, pointing at the
small black cows: 'You won't get finer anywhere
than those black porry cattle.' In a pub near there,
one of the locals finally spoke to the townie:
'Labhraim le stráinséirí. Creidim gur chóir bheith
ag labhairt le stráinséirí.'[2] Proud as a man who'd claim:
'I made an orchard of a rock-field,
bougainvillea clamber my turf-ricks.'

A Dublin tourist on a red-quarter strand
hunting firewood found the ruins of a boat,
started breaking the struts out—an old man came,
he shook his head, and said:
'Aa, a mhac: ná bí ag briseadh báid.'[3]

[1] 'The Gaelic is less than the water in the glass.'
[2] 'I speak with strangers. I believe it's right to be speaking with strangers.'
[3] 'Ah, son: don't be breaking boats.'

The low walls of rock-fields in the west
are a beautiful clean white. There are chinks between
the neat white stones to let the wind through safe,
you can see the blue sun through them.
But coming eastward in the same county,
the walls grow higher, get grey:
an ugly grey. And the chinks disappear:
through those walls you can see nothing.

Then at last you come to the city,
beautiful with salmon basking becalmed black below
a bridge over the pale-green Corrib; and ugly
with many shopkeepers looking down on men like
Bartley Costello and Beartla Confhaola because they
speak in Irish, eat periwinkles, keep
small black porry cattle, and on us
because we are strangers.

Richard Murphy

b. 1927

GIRL AT THE SEASIDE

I lean on a lighthouse rock
Where the seagowns flow,
A trawler slips from the dock
Sailing years ago.

Wine, tobacco and seamen
Cloud the green air;
A head of snakes in the rain
Talks away desire.

A sailor kisses me
Tasting of mackerel;
I analyse misery
Till mass bells peal.

I wait for clogs on the cobbles,
Dead feet at night;
Only a tempest blows
Darkness on sealight.

I've argued myself here
To the blue cliff-tops:
I'll drop through the sea-air
Till everything stops.

from THE BATTLE OF AUGHRIM

PLANTER

Seven candles in silver sticks,
Water on an oval table,

The painted warts of Cromwell
Framed in a sullen gold.
There was ice on the axe
When it hacked the king's head.
Moths drown in the dripping wax.

Slow sigh of the garden yews
Forty years planted.
May the God of battle
Give us this day our land
And the papists be trampled.
Softly my daughter plays
Sefauchi's Farewell.

Dark night with no moon to guard
Roads from the rapparees,
Food at a famine price,
Cattle raided, corn trod,
And the servants against us
With our own guns and swords.
Stress a hymn to peace.

Quiet music and claret cups,
Forty acres of green crops
Keep far from battle
My guest, with a thousand troops
Following his clan-call,
Red-mouthed O'Donnell.
I bought him: the traitor sleeps.

To whom will the land belong
This time tomorrow night?
I am loyal to fields I have sown
And the king reason elected:
Not to a wine-blotted birth-mark
Of prophecy, but hard work
Deepening the soil for seed.

Out of the earth, out of the air, out of the water
And slinking nearer the fire, in groups they gather:
Once he looked like a bird, but now a beggar.

This fish rainbows out of a pool: 'Give me bread!'
He fins along the lake-shore with the starved.
Green eyes glow in the night from clumps of weed.

The water is still. A rock, or the nose of an otter
Jars the surface. Whistle of rushes or bird?
It steers to the bank, it lands as a pikeman armed.

With flint and bundles of straw a limestone hall
Is gutted, a noble family charred in its sleep,
And they gloat by moonlight on a mound of rubble.

The highway trees are gibbets where seventeen rot
Who were caught last week in a cattle-raid.
The beasts are lowing. 'Listen!' 'Stifle the guard!'

In a pinewood thickness an earthed-over charcoal fire
Forges them guns. They melt lead stripped from a steeple
For ball. At the whirr of a snipe each can disappear

Terrified as a bird in a gorse-bush fire,
To delve like a mole, or mingle like a nightjar,
Into the earth, into the air, into the water.

LITTLE HUNGER

I drove to Little Hunger promontory
    looking for pink stone
in roofless houses huddled by the sea
    to buy to build my own.

Hovels to live in, ruins to admire
    from a car cruising by,
the weathered face caught in a sunset fire,
    hollowed with exility;

whose gradual fall my purchase would complete,
    clearing them off the land,
the seven cabins needed to create
    the granite house I planned.

Once mine, I'd work on their dismemberment,
    threshold, lintel, wall;
and pick a hearthstone from a rubble fragment
    to make it integral.

Thomas Kinsella

b. 1928

CHRYSALIDES

Our last free summer we mooned about at odd hours
Pedalling slowly through country towns, stopping to eat
Chocolate and fruit, tracing our vagaries on the map.

At night we watched in the barn, to the lurch of melodeon music,
The crunching boots of countrymen—huge and weightless
As their shadows—twirling and leaping over the yellow concrete.

Sleeping too little or too much, we awoke at noon
And were received with womanly mockery into the kitchen,
Like calves poking our faces in with enormous hunger.

Daily we strapped our saddlebags and went to experience
A tolerance we shall never know again, confusing
For the last time, for example, the licit and the familiar.

Our instincts blurred with change; a strange wakefulness
Sapped our energies and dulled our slow-beating hearts
To the extremes of feeling—insensitive alike

To the unique succession of our youthful midnights,
When by a window ablaze softly with the virgin moon
Dry scones and jugs of milk awaited us in the dark,

Or to lasting horror: a wedding flight of ants
Spawning to its death, a mute perspiration
Glistening like drops of copper in our path.

ANOTHER SEPTEMBER

Dreams fled away, this country bedroom, raw
With the touch of the dawn, wrapped in a minor peace,
Hears through an open window the garden draw
Long pitch black breaths, lay bare its apple trees,
Ripe pear trees, brambles, windfall-sweetened soil,
Exhale rough sweetness against the starry slates.
Nearer the river sleeps St. John's, all toil
Locked fast inside a dream with iron gates.

Domestic autumn, like an animal
Long used to handling by those countrymen,
Rubs her kind hide against the bedroom wall
Sensing a fragrant child come back again
—Not this half-tolerated consciousness,
Its own cold season never done,
But that unspeaking daughter, growing less
Familiar where we fell asleep as one.

Wakeful moth-wings blunder near a chair,
Toss their light shell at the glass, and go
To inhabit the living starlight. Stranded hair
Stirs on the still linen. It is as though
The black breathing that billows her sleep, her name,
Drugged under judgement, waned and—bearing daggers
And balances—down the lampless darkness they came,
Moving like women: Justice, Truth, such figures.

from NIGHTWALKER

I must lie down with them all soon and sleep,
And rise with them again when the new dawn
Has touched our pillows and our wet pallor
And roused us. We'll come scratching in our waistcoats
Down to the kitchen for a cup of tea;

Then with our briefcases, through wind or rain,
Past our neighbours' gardens—Melrose, Bloomfield—
To wait at the station, fluttering our papers,
Palping the cool wind, discussing and murmuring.
                              Is it not right to serve
Our banks and businesses and governments
As together we develop our community
On clear principles, with no fixed ideas?
And (twitching our thin umbrellas) acceptable
That during a transitional period
Development should express itself in forms
Without principle, based on fixed ideas . . .
                              Robed in spattered iron
At the harbour mouth she stands, Productive Investment,
And beckons the nations through our gold half-door:
Lend me your wealth, your cunning and your drive,
Your arrogant refuse;
                              let my people serve them
Bottled fury in our new hotels,
While native businessmen and managers
Drift with them, chatting, over to the window
To show them our growing city, give them a feeling
Of what is possible; our labour pool,
The tax concessions to foreign capital,
How to get a nice estate though German,
Even collect some of our better young artists.
                              Morose condemnation . . .
It is a weakness, and turns on itself.
                              Clean bricks
Are made of mud; we need them for our tower.

                              *

Spirit-skeletons are straggling into view
From the day's depths. You can pick them out
In the night sky, with a little patience:
                              Pale influences . . .
The wakeful Twins,
                              Bruder und Schwester

—Two young Germans I had in this morning
Wanting to transfer investment income;
The sister a business figurehead, her brother
Otterfaced, with exasperated smiles
Assuming—pressing until he achieved—response.
Handclasp; I do not exist; I cannot take
My eyes from their pallor. A red glare
Plays on their faces, livid with little splashes
Of blazing fat. The oven door closes.
                                        All about and above me
The officials on the corridors or in their rooms
Work, or overwork, with mixed motives
Or none. We dwell together in urgency;
Dominate, entering middle age; subserve,
Aborting vague tendencies with buttery smiles.
Among us, behind locked doors, the ministers
Are working, with a sureness of touch found early,
In the nation's birth—the blood of enemies
And brothers dried on their hide long ago.
Dragon old men, upright and stately and blind,
Or shuffling in the corridor finding a key,
Their youth cannot die in them; it will be found
Beating with violence when their bodies rot.
                                        What occupies them
As they sit in their rooms? What they already are?
Shadow-flesh . . . claimed by pattern still living,
Linked into constellations with their dead . . .
                                        Look! The Wedding Group:
The Groom, the Best Man, the Fox, and their three ladies
—A tragic tale: soon, the story tells,
Enmity sprang up between them, and the Fox
Took to the wilds. Then, to the Groom's sorrow,
His dear friend left him also, vowing hatred.
So they began destroying the Groom's substance
And he sent out to hunt the Fox, but trapped
His friend instead; mourning, he slaughtered him.
Shortly, in his turn, the Groom was savaged
On a Sunday morning, no one knows by whom

(Though it's known the Fox is a friend of Death and rues Nothing).
                              Over here, in the same quarter,
The Two Executioners—Groom and Weasel—
'77' burning into each brow;
And look, the vivid Weasel there again,
Dancing crookbacked under the Player King
—A tragicomical tale:
                    how the Fox, long after,
Found a golden instrument one day,
A great complex gold horn, left at his door;
He examined it with little curiosity,
Wanting no gold or music; observed the mouthpiece,
Impossible to play with fox's lips,
And gave it with dull humour to his old enemy
The Weasel—who recognized the horn
Of the Player King, and bared his needle teeth.
He took it, hammered on it with a stick
And pranced about in blithe pantomime,
His head cocked to enjoy the golden clouts,
While the Fox from time to time nodded his mask.

BALLYDAVID PIER

Noon. The luminous tide
Climbs through the heat, covering
Grey shingle. A film of scum
Searches first among litter,
Cloudy with (I remember)
Life; then crystal-clear shallows
Cool on the stones, silent
With shells and claws, white fish bones;
Farther out a bag of flesh,
Foetus of goat or sheep,
Wavers below the surface.

Allegory forms of itself:
The line of life creeps upward

Replacing one world with another,
The welter of its advance
Sinks down into clarity,
Slowly the more foul
Monsters of loss digest . . .

Small monster of true flesh
Brought forth somewhere
In bloody confusion and error
And flung into bitterness,
Blood washed white:
Does that structure satisfy?

The ghost tissue hangs unresisting
In allegorical waters,
Lost in self-search
—A swollen blind brow
Humbly crumpled over
Budding limbs, unshaken
By the spasms of birth or death.

The Angelus. Faint bell-notes
From some church in the distance
It is nothing. The vacant harbour
Is filling; it will empty.
The misbirth touches the surface
And glistens like quicksilver.

FIRST LIGHT

A prone couple still sleeps.
Light ascends like a pale gas
Out of the sea : dawn-
Light, reaching across the hill
To the dark garden. The grass
Emerges, soaking with grey dew.

Inside, in silence, an empty
Kitchen takes form, tidied and swept,
Blank with marriage—where shrill
Lover and beloved have kept
Another vigil far
Into the night, and raved and wept.

Upstairs a whimper or sigh
Comes from an open bedroom door
And lengthens to an ugly wail
—A child enduring a dream
That grows, at the first touch of day,
Unendurable.

ANCESTOR

I was going up to say something,
and stopped. Her profile against the curtains
was old, and dark like a hunting bird's.

It was the way she perched on the high stool,
staring into herself, with one fist
gripping the side of the barrier around her desk
—or her head held by something, from inside.
And not caring for anything around her
or anyone there by the shelves.
I caught a faint smell, musky and queer.

I may have made some sound—she stopped rocking
and pressed her fist in her lap; then she stood up
and shut down the lid of the desk, and turned the key.

She shoved a small bottle under her aprons
and came toward me, darkening the passageway.

Ancestor . . . among sweet- and fruit-boxes.
Her black heart . . .
                    Was that a sigh?
—brushing by me in the shadows,
with her heaped aprons, through the red hangings
to the scullery, and down to the back room.

John Montague

b. 1929

ALL LEGENDARY OBSTACLES

All legendary obstacles lay between
Us, the long imaginary plain,
The monstrous ruck of mountains
And, swinging across the night,
Flooding the Sacramento, San Joaquin,
The hissing drift of winter rain.

All day I waited, shifting
Nervously from station to bar
As I saw another train sail
By, the San Francisco Chief or
Golden Gate, water dripping
From great flanged wheels.

At midnight you came, pale
Above the negro porter's lamp.
I was too blind with rain
And doubt to speak, but
Reached from the platform
Until our chilled hands met.

You had been travelling for days
With an old lady, who marked
A neat circle on the glass
With her glove, to watch us
Move into the wet darkness
Kissing, still unable to speak.

THE WILD DOG ROSE

(1)

I go to say goodbye to the *Cailleach*[1]
that terrible figure who haunted my childhood
but no longer harsh, a human being
merely, hurt by event.
           The cottage,
circled by trees, weathered to admonitory
shapes of desolation by the mountain winds,
straggles into view. The rank thistles
and leathery bracken of untilled fields
stretch behind with—a final outcrop—
the hooped figure by the roadside,
its retinue of dogs
                which give tongue
as I approach, with savage, whinging cries
so that she slowly turns, a moving nest
of shawls and rags, to view, to stare
the stranger down.
             And I feel again
that ancient awe, the terror of a child
before the great hooked nose, the cheeks
dewlapped with dirt, the staring blue
of the sunken eyes, the mottled claws
clutching a stick
             but now hold
and return her gaze, to greet her,
as she greets me, in friendliness.
Memories have wrought reconciliation
between us, we talk in ease at last,
like old friends, lovers almost,
sharing secrets.
           Of neighbours
she quarreled with, who now lie

---

[1] *Cailleach*: Irish (and Scots Gaelic) for an old woman, a hag.

in Garvaghey graveyard, beyond all hatred;
of my family and hers, how she never married,
though a man came asking in her youth.
'You would be loath to leave your own'
she sighs, 'and go among strangers'—
his parish ten miles off.

                      For sixty years
since she has lived alone, in one place.
Obscurely honoured by such confidences,
I idle by the summer roadside, listening,
while the monologue falters, continues,
rehearsing the small events of her life.
The only true madness is loneliness,
the monotonous voice in the skull
that never stops
                  because never heard.

(II)

And there
where the dog rose shines in the hedge
she tells me a story so terrible
that I try to push it away,
my bones melting.
                  Late at night
a drunk came, beating at her door
to break it in, the bolt snapping
from the soft wood, the thin mongrels
rushing to cut, but yelping as
he whirls with his farm boots
to crush their skulls.
                  In the darkness
they wrestle, two creatures crazed
with loneliness, the smell of the
decaying cottage in his nostrils
like a drug, his body heavy on hers,
the tasteless trunk of a seventy year

old virgin, which he rummages while
she battles for life
                         bony fingers
reaching desperately to push
against his bull neck. 'I prayed
to the Blessed Virgin herself
for help and after a time
I broke his grip.'
                  He rolls
to the floor, snores asleep,
while she cowers until dawn
and the dogs' whimpering starts
him awake, to lurch back across
the wet bog.

(III)

                  And still
the dog rose shines in the hedge.
Petals beaten wide by rain, it
sways slightly, at the tip of a
slender, tangled, arching branch
which, with her stick, she gathers
into us.
         'The wild rose
is the only rose without thorns',
she says, holding a wet blossom
for a second, in a hand knotted
as the knob of her stick.
'Whenever I see it, I remember
the Holy Mother of God and
all she suffered.'
                  Briefly
the air is strong with the smell
of that weak flower, offering
its crumbling yellow cup
and pale bleeding lips

fading to white
                at the rim
of each bruised and heart-
shaped petal.

A GRAFTED TONGUE

(Dumb,
Bloodied, the severed
head now chokes to
speak another tongue:—

As in
a long suppressed dream,
some stuttering, garb—
led ordeal of my own)

An Irish
child weeps at school
repeating its English.
After each mistake

The master
gouges another mark
on the tally stick
hung about its neck

Like a bell
on a cow, a hobble
on a straying goat.
To slur and stumble

In shame
the altered syllables
of your own name;
to stray sadly home

344

And find
the turf cured width
of your parent's hearth
growing alien:

In cabin
and field, they still
speak the old tongue.
You may greet no one.

To grow
a second tongue, as
harsh a humiliation
as twice to be born.

Decades later,
that child's grandchild's
speech stumbles over lost
syllables of an old order.

THE SAME GESTURE

There is a secret room
of golden light where
everything—love, violence,
hatred is possible;
and, again love.

Such intimacy of hand
and mind is achieved
under its healing light
that the shifting of
hands is a rite

like court music.
We barely know our
selves there though

it is what we always were
—most nakedly are—

and must remember
when we leave, re-
suming our habits
with our clothes:
work, 'phone, drive

through late traffic
changing gears with
the same gesture as
eased your snowbound
heart and flesh.

Richard Weber

b. 1932

A VISIT TO BRIDGE HOUSE
(*for Austin Clarke*)

An old house with trees and twisting river.
From here you watch Ireland grow older
And calmly note down each change and failure.
The poor, the church, the newly rich,
The subterfuges of the state, desecration
Of the beautiful, both made and nature's:
Who would have thought the Muse could carry
Such burdens and retain her youthful beauty?

April, and the sky broods, awaiting rain.
Beyond the bridge, your light invites me
To a book-walled room and talk of greater days.
Your gentle voice escorts me in with questions.
Happily you recall the past with humorous talk
Of Yeats, Russell, Moore and others gone away,
All imaged in poses, phrases that slide
One into another till past and present are one.

Over tea the room recedes to taller talk
Of what someone said then—or when?—you turn
And ask your wife, who tells you definitely, gently.
'Well, anyway, he said to me . . .' you begin again.
I think of how your talk and writing differ,
The one so soft, dissolving scene into scene;
The other clear, concise, alive with light
Of Ireland on her most vagrant summer days.

I think of your art of giving life to language:
From graft with older wood a strong new tree.
A gift like your kingfisher, 'seldom seen',

Its bright blur arrowing from present to future.
Reminded of time, I rise to leave: you stop
Reluctantly, though such talk must tire.
You come to the door, invite me again, wave
And return to living these your youngest years.

James Simmons

b. 1933

EXPERIENCE

'I want to fight you,' he said in a Belfast accent.
Amazed and scared, with hurried words I resisted.
'Fighting solves nothing. Tell me how I've annoyed you,'
I said. But more insulted the man persisted.

In the lavatory he squared his fists and approached me:
'Now you can talk.' I backed over cold stone in
A room that contained us and joined us. 'It's all so silly,'
I pleaded, searching for spaces to be alone in.

I shrank from his strangeness, not only afraid.
But at last of course I suffered what could not be delayed,
The innocuous struggle, the fighting words, 'bastard' and 'fuck',
A torn shirt and my lip numb and bloody,
My anger and—strange—the feel of my own body
New to me, as I struck, as he struck.

A REFORMER TO HIS FATHER

We shared not one idea in thirty years
Of occasional bicker and chat. One night of loud
Useless argument, unique and useless tears
Of mine surprised us. We paused, astute and proud,
Unreconciled. I think I had stopped hearing
Your words, and heard around me the rest,
Unknown, remote and thought I was comparing
The sound of your worst with their best.
Subservient to love I bent my head

Stiffly. You laughed, nervous, elated, and laid
Nicotined fingers lightly on and said
Nothing. Never again, and now you are dead:
And still I labour to build a country fit
For heroes, knowing you'd want no part of it.

GOODBYE, SALLY

Shaken already, I know
I'll wake at night after you go
watching the soft shine of your skin,
feeling your little buttocks, oh my grief,
like two duck eggs in a handkerchief,
barely a woman but taking me all in.

I think our love won't die—
but there I go trying to justify!
What odds that we'll never meet again
and probably other girls will never
bring half your agony of pleasure?
Fidelity is a dumb pain.

God, but I'm lucky too,
the way I've muddled through
to ecstasy so often despite
exhaustion, drunkenness and pride.
How come that you were satisfied
and so was I that night?

It's true for drinker and lover,
the best stuff has no hangover.
You're right to spit on argument,
girl. Your dumbness on a walk
was better than my clown's talk.
You showed me what you meant.

Good mornings from every night
with you, thirsty and sore with appetite.
You never let me act my age.
Goodbye to all analysis and cause-
grubbing. The singer wants applause
not criticism as he leaves the stage.

Desmond O'Grady

b. 1935

THE DYING GAUL

The hour at last come round
   the stroke that scores the kill
taken, there follows a painless,
   partly nostalgic withdrawal—
a drag to the sideline—to a clean piece
   of this world's dying ground.

Lean legs nerve like an athlete's.
   Raised kneecaps gleam altar marble.
Thigh shanks knot. The curled
   weighty balls bag low and the gentle
penis limps childless. Tousled,
   his head's like a young brown bull's.

Reclining, at repose upon
   one unwound nude haunch,
pelvis and dragged-out legs
   draining, his belly's bunch
about the navel wrinkles.
   Life strains on his taut right arm.

The blood clots, the nerve
   sings and all his joints
jamb stuck. His grounded gaze,
   like the madman's private smile, confronts
the process' revelation—the ways
   death consummates, like love.

Brendan Kennelly

b. 1936

MY DARK FATHERS

My dark fathers lived the intolerable day
Committed always to the night of wrong,
Stiffened at the hearthstone, the woman lay,
Perished feet nailed to her man's breastbone.
Grim houses beckoned in the swelling gloom
Of Munster fields where the Atlantic night
Fettered the child within the pit of doom,
And everywhere a going down of light.

And yet upon the sandy Kerry shore
The woman once had danced at ebbing tide
Because she loved flute music—and still more
Because a lady wondered at the pride
Of one so humble. That was long before
The green plant withered by an evil chance;
When winds of hunger howled at every door
She heard the music dwindle and forgot the dance.

Such mercy as the wolf receives was hers
Whose dance became a rhythm in a grave,
Achieved beneath the thorny savage furze
That yellowed fiercely in a mountain cave.
Immune to pity, she, whose crime was love,
Crouched, shivered, searched the threatening sky,
Discovered ready signs, compelled to move
Her to her innocent appalling cry.

Skeletoned in darkness, my dark fathers lay
Unknown, and could not understand
The giant grief that trampled night and day,
The awful absence moping through the land.

Upon the headland, the encroaching sea
Left sand that hardened after tides of Spring,
No dancing feet disturbed its symmetry
And those who loved good music ceased to sing.

Since every moment of the clock
Accumulates to form a final name,
Since I am come of Kerry clay and rock,
I celebrate the darkness and the shame
That could compel a man to turn his face
Against the wall, withdrawn from light so strong
And undeceiving, spancelled in a place
Of unapplauding hands and broken song.

Michael Longley

b. 1939

A LETTER TO THREE IRISH POETS

returning over the nightmare ground
we found the place again ...

—KEITH DOUGLAS

(I)

This, the twentieth day of March
In the first year of my middle age,
Sees me the father of a son:
Now let him in your minds sleep on
Lopsided, underprivileged
And, out of his tight burrow edged,

Your godchild while you think of him
Or, if you can't accept the term,
Don't count the damage but instead
Wet, on me, the baby's head:
About his ears our province reels
Pulsating like his fontanel,

And I, with you, when I baptize
Must calculate, must improvise
The holy water and the font,
Anything else that he may want,
And, 'priest of the muses,' mock the
Malevolent *deus loci.*

(II)

Now that the distant islands rise
Out of the corners of my eyes
And the imagination fills

355

Bog-meadow and surrounding hills,
I find myself addressing you
As though I'd always wanted to:

In order to take you all in
I've had to get beneath your skin,
To colonize you like a land,
To study each distinctive hand
And, by squatter's rights, inhabit
The letters of its alphabet,

Although when I call him Daniel
(Mother and baby doing well),
Lost relations take their places,
Namesakes and receding faces:
Late travellers on the Underground
People my head like a ghost town.

(III)

Over the cobbles I recall
Cattle clattering to the North Wall
Till morning and the morning's rain
Rinsed out the zig-zags of the brain,
Conducting excrement and fear
Along that lethal thoroughfare:

Now every lost bedraggled field
Like a mythopoeic bog unfolds
Its gelignite and dumdums:
And should the whole idea become
A vegetable run to seed in
Even our suburban garden,

We understudy for the hare's
Disappearance around corners,
The approximate untold barks
Of the otters we call water-dogs—

356

A dim reflection of ourselves,
A muddy forepaw that dissolves.

(IV)

Blood on the kerbstones, and my mind
Dividing like a pavement,
Cracked by the weeds, by the green grass
That covers our necropolis,
The pity, terror. . . . What comes next
Is a lacuna in the text,

Only blots of ink conceding
Death or blackout as a reading:
For this, his birthday, must confound
Baedekers of the nightmare ground—
And room for him beneath the hedge
With succour, school and heritage

Is made tonight when I append
Each of your names and name a friend:
For yours, then, and the child's sake
I who have heard the waters break
Claim this my country, though today
Timor mortis conturbat me.

Seamus Heaney

b. 1939

DIGGING

Between my finger and my thumb
The squat pen rests; snug as a gun.

Under my window, a clean rasping sound
When the spade sinks into gravelly ground:
My father, digging. I look down

Till his straining rump among the flowerbeds
Bends low, comes up twenty years away
Stooping in rhythm through potato drills
Where he was digging.

The coarse boot nestled on the lug, the shaft
Against the inside knee was levered firmly.
He rooted out tall tops, buried the bright edge deep
To scatter new potatoes that we picked
Loving their cool hardness in our hands.

By God, the old man could handle a spade.
Just like his old man.

My grandfather cut more turf in a day
Than any other man on Toner's bog.
Once I carried him milk in a bottle
Corked sloppily with paper. He straightened up
To drink it, then fell to right away
Nicking and slicing neatly, heaving sods
Over his shoulder, going down and down
For the good turf. Digging.

The cold smell of potato mould, the squelch and slap
Of soggy peat, the curt cuts of an edge

Through living roots awaken in my head.
But I've no spade to follow men like them.

Between my finger and my thumb
The squat pen rests.
I'll dig with it.

REQUIEM FOR THE CROPPIES

The pockets of our greatcoats full of barley—
No kitchens on the run, no striking camp—
We moved quick and sudden in our own country.
The priest lay behind ditches with the tramp.
A people, hardly marching—on the hike—
We found new tactics happening each day:
We'd cut through reins and rider with the pike
And stampede cattle into infantry,
Then retreat through hedges where cavalry must be thrown.
Until, on Vinegar Hill, the fatal conclave.
Terraced thousands died, shaking scythes at cannon.
The hillside blushed, soaked in our broken wave.
They buried us without shroud or coffin
And in August the barley grew up out of the grave.

THE TOLLUND MAN

(i)

Some day I will go to Aarhus
To see his peat-brown head,
The mild pods of his eye-lids,
His pointed skin cap.

In the flat country nearby
Where they dug him out,
His last gruel of winter seeds
Caked in his stomach,

Naked except for
The cap, noose and girdle,
I will stand a long time.
Bridegroom to the goddess,

She tightened her torc on him
And opened her fen,
Those dark juices working
Him to a saint's kept body,

Trove of the turf-cutters'
Honeycombed workings.
Now his stained face
Reposes at Aarhus.

(II)

I could risk blasphemy,
Consecrate the cauldron bog
Our holy ground and pray
Him to make germinate

The scattered, ambushed
Flesh of labourers,
Stockinged corpses
Laid out in the farmyards,

Tell-tale skin and teeth
Flecking the sleepers
Of four young brothers, trailed
For miles along the lines.

Something of his sad freedom
As he rode the tumbril
Should come to me, driving,
Saying the names

Tollund, Grabaulle, Nebelgard,
Watching the pointing hands
Of country people,
Not knowing their tongue.

Out there in Jutland
In the old man-killing parishes
I will feel lost,
Unhappy and at home.

MOSSBAWN SUNLIGHT
for Mary Heaney

There was a sunlit absence.
The helmeted pump in the yard
heated its iron,
water honeyed

in the slung bucket
and the sun stood
like a griddle cooling
against the wall

of each long afternoon.
So, her hands scuffled
over the bakeboard,
the reddening stove

sent its plaque of heat
against her where she stood

in a floury apron
by the window.

Now she dusts the board
with a goose's wing,
now sits, broad-lapped,
with whitened nails

and measling shins:
here is a space
again, the scone rising
to the tick of two clocks.

And here is love
like a tinsmith's scoop
sunk past its gleam
in the meal-bin.

Seamus Deane

b. 1940

RETURN

The train shot through the dark.
Hedges leapt across the window-pane.
Trees belled in foliage were stranded,
Inarticulate with rain.
A blur of lighted farm implied
The evacuated countryside.

I am appalled by its emptiness.
Every valley glows with pain
As we run like a current through;
Then the memories darken again.
In this Irish past I dwell
Like sound implicit in a bell.

The train curves round a river,
And how tenderly its gouts of steam
Contemplate the nodding moon
The waters from the clouds redeem.
Two hours from Belfast
I am snared in my past.

Crusts of light lie pulsing
Diamanté with the rain
At the track's end. Amazing!
I am in Derry once again.
Once more I turn to greet
Ground that flees from my feet.

Derek Mahon

b. 1941

ECCLESIASTES

God, you could grow to love it, God-fearing, God-
    chosen purist little puritan that,
for all your wiles and smiles, you are (the
    dank churches, the empty streets,
the shipyard silence, the tied-up swings) and
    shelter your cold heart from the heat
of the world, from woman-inquisition, from the
    bright eyes of children. Yes, you could
wear black, drink water, nourish a fierce zeal
    with locusts and wild honey, and not
feel called upon to understand and forgive
    but only to speak with a bleak
afflatus, and love the January rains when they
    darken the dark doors and sink hard
into the Antrim hills, the bog meadows, the heaped
    graves of your fathers. Bury that red
bandana and stick, that banjo. This is your
    country, close one eye and be king.
Your people await you, their heavy washing
    flaps for you in the housing estates—
a credulous people. God, you could do it, God
    help you, stand on a corner stiff
with rhetoric, promising nothing under the sun.

CONSOLATIONS OF PHILOSOPHY
(*For Eugene Lambe*)

When we start breaking up in the wet darkness
And the rotten boards fall from us, and the ribs

Crack under the constriction of tree-roots
And the seasons slip from the fields unknown to us

Oh, then there will be the querulous complaining
From citizens who had never dreamed of this—
Who, shaken to the bone in their stout boxes
By the latest bright cars, will not inspect them

And, kept awake by the tremors of new building,
Will not be there to comment. When the broken
Wreath bowls are speckled with rain water
And the grass grows wild for want of a caretaker

Oh, then a few will remember with affection
Dry bread, mousetrap cheese and the satisfaction
Of picking long butts from a wet gutter
Like daisies from a clover field in summer.

A DARK COUNTRY

Starting again
After a long patience,
A long absence, is a slow
Riding of undertow,
A ship turning among buoys in dawn rain
To slide into a dockyard fluorescence;

Is a coming
Into a dark country
Beyond appraisal or report
The shape of the human heart.
You will go as you came, a twist of spring
Water through ferns, as febrile and as wintry;

But now move—
Circumspectly at first

But with a growing sense
Of the significance,
Crippling and ordering, of what you love,
Its unique power to create and assuage thirst—

Among these
Signs, these wild declivities
That have in the past
Betrayed you to a waste
Of rage, self-pity bordering on self-hate,
A blind man without comfort at the gate;

Recognizing,
As in a sunken city
Sea-changed at last, the surfaces
Of once familiar places.
With practice you might decipher the whole thing
Or enough to suffer the relief and the pity.

Michael Hartnett

b. 1941

DOMESTIC SCENE

Her iron beats
the smell of bread
from damp linen:
silver, crystal
and warm things.
Whatever bird
I used to be,
hawk or lapwing,
tern, or something
wild, fierce or shy—
these birds are dead.
And I come here
on tiring wings.
Odours of bread. . . .

FOR MY GRANDMOTHER, BRIDGID HALPIN

maybe morning lightens over
the coldest time in all the day,
but not for you: a bird's hover,
seabird, blackbird, or bird of prey,
was rain, or death, or lost cattle:
the day's warning, like red plovers
so etched and small the clouded sky.
was book to you, and true bible.
you died in utter loneliness,
your acres left to the childless.
You never saw the animals
of God, and the flower under

your feet: and the trees change a leaf:
and the red fur of a fox on
a quiet evening: and the long
birches falling down the hillside.

SONNET

I saw magic on a green country road—
That old woman, a bag of sticks her load,

Blackly down to her thin feet a fringed shawl,
A rosary of bone on her horned hand,
A flight of curlews scribing by her head,
And ash trees combing with their frills her hair.

Her eyes, wet sunken holes pierced by an awl,
Must have deciphered her adoring land:
And curlews, no longer lean birds, instead
Become ten scarlet comets in the air.

Some incantation from her canyoned mouth,
Irish, English, blew frost along the ground,
And even though the wind was from the South
The ashleaves froze without an ashleaf sound.

ENAMOURED OF THE MINISCULE

Enamoured of the miniscule
of the careful and compact
I fail to introduce the fact
of current misery into
the line: and careful of the rule
therefore cannot ask my proper dues,
become, not a poet of the heart,
but a leipreachan at his last,
making unwearable golden shoes.

Eiléan Ni Chuilleanáin

b. 1942

SWINEHERD

'When all this is over,' said the swineherd,
'I mean to retire, where
Nobody will have heard about my special skills
And conversation is mainly about the weather.

I intend to learn how to make coffee, at least as well
As the Portuguese lay-sister in the kitchen
And polish the brass fenders every day.
I want to lie awake at night
Listening to cream crawling to the top of the jug
And the water lying soft in the cistern.

I want to see an orchard where the trees grow in straight lines
And the yellow fox finds shelter between the navy-blue trunks,
Where it gets dark early in summer
And the apple-blossom is allowed to wither on the bough.'

WASH

Wash man out of the earth, shear off
The human shell.
Twenty feet down there's close cold earth
So clean.

Wash the man out of the woman:
The strange sweat from her skin, the ashes from her hair.
Stretch her to dry under the sun
The blue marks on her breast will fade.

Woman and world not yet
Clean as the cat
Leaping to the windowsill with a fish in her teeth;
Her flat curious eyes reflect the squalid room,
She begins to wash the water from the fish.

Augustus Young

b. 1943

THE LAST REFUGE

We brushed our hair back and our
Sideburns down, drainpipes
tight as the gripe, tongues too tough
for words longer than four letters. Flicknifes
and bicycles we had and mothers
pleading at the Juveniles; trouble because
we slashed the back seats in the gods.

Our hands ringed like prize cocks
trembled when caught by the sleeve.
We said: have you a fag? and Leave
us alone. Chained to our slogans we scratched
blackheads like pilgrims out of Bunyan.

When Elvis went soft, we gave away to women.
Joined up overseas. Wars and discharge won,
Registered love. This is our dominion—
slippers and hatchet before the television.

AFTER FIVE YEARS

Pulling up in my car, I went into the cottage,
wearing a tie. They didn't recognise me until I
took off my sportscoat. Well I knew the walls
and what they contained. I could account for the crack
in the cup I drank from. I could hear their voice
from a distance, knowing its nearness; hardly a word
new, hardly a smile that wasn't a clue
to another. And when they handed me the fiddle,

I played the tune they taught me, although the time
was off; the three brothers from the hill came in
to make me more at home. The strange cat
on the range was the only sign that I had been
away. He was offspring of the generation in between.

ELEGY FOR A SCHOOL-FRIEND

Swam too far out: the swell took him.
Whitehorses carried off the waves
into cave echoes. The tide fell:
a rock broke the sea.

On the headstone the legend is
NÍ BÁS ACHT Á FÁS, not dead but
growing. We tend the grave and care-
fully thin the weeds.

Rain erodes the rock. At nightfall,
white as mushroom to my torch, she
in most mourning, his bas-relief
name chisels to dust.

Eavan Boland

b. 1945

THE WAR HORSE

This dry night nothing unusual
About the clip, clop casual

Iron of his shoes as he stamps death
Like a mint on the innocent coinage of earth.

I lift the window, watch the ambling feather
Of hoof and fetlock, loosed from its daily tether

In the tinker camp on the Enniskerry Road
Pass, his breath hissing, his snuffling head

Down. He is gone; no great harm is done,
Only a leaf of our laurel hedge is torn,

Of distant interest like a bombed limb,
Only a rose which now will never climb

The stone of our house, expendable, a mere
Line of defence against him, a volunteer

You might say, only a crocus, its bulbous head
Blown from growth, one of the screamless dead.

But we, we are safe, our unformed fear
Of fierce commitment gone; why should we care

If a rose, a hedge, a crocus are uprooted
Like corpses, remote, crushed, mutilated?

He stumbles on like a rumour of war, huge,
Threatening, while neighbours use the subterfuge

Of curtains, he stumbles down our street
Thankfully passing us. I pause, wait

Then to breathe relief, lean on the sill
And for a second only my blood is still

With atavism. That rose he trampled stays
Ribboned across our hedge, recalling days

Of burned countryside, illicit braid—
A cause ruined before, a world betrayed.

Richard Ryan

b. 1946

EL DORADO

Under a swaying
crucifix cursing,
bitten by flies,

an army is slicing
its way through
flowers as the

hummingbird darts
away and the snake
melts back into

its hot pools.
Far above, on
the cool roof

of the world,
the temples glitter
through cloud and

tall priests chant
urgently under their
great god of gold.

But their prayers
are unheard as, gold
gleaming in their

fevered eyes, the
white strangers begin
to close in, and

briefly their tall
cross catches the
last of the light—

twin gods conversing—
before yet another
world sinks, dying

under that iron cross.
Soldiers of Christ
they ransack the

buildings for women
and gold, but above
them the white condor

lifts, its great wings
stained with the blood
of the dying sun, to

drift slowly away.

DEAFNESS
(for my sister)

It is when I hear Mozart,
some birds, the scraping
of wind through pine and
she is there; sounds crowd
round her silence like clay.

It is then I hear the note—
an inkling of the sound
of death: not the mere being
without, but the not knowing,
at all . . .

Hugh Maxton

b. 1947

WAKING

(in memory of my father, died November 1960)

Someone is breathing in the room
apart from me. It is my father;
I recognise the hiss of his nostrils
closing, closing. . . . It is late;
he is doing Milltown work,
we can use the extra money.
That stub in his hand is a rent book
high as a bible, thin as his widow.
Below that, in the shadow, I imagine
the soft metal of his heart
(a gold cog, slipping) finally burred,
refusing to bite. The angle
of his nose, the slight furrow
of moustache escape me. All I have
is that sound fathered in darkness
carrying a reek of tobacco-y linen,
the taste of his lip.
                He rustles
like a curtain. Outside it is six a.m.
A sudden fleet of cars passes
drowning my breath for about the length
of a funeral. This has gone on ten years.

Paul Murray

b. 1947

RAIN

At the third hour always
the same dream,—suddenly
I am a child again. My eyes are opening
slowly. . . .
          At the entrance leading
to the cemetery of the dead
I am carrying a golden crucifix.
Above my head, invisible
among the trees, rain whispers endlessly.

At the fourth hour always
the same three Sisters
praying:
each with the same voice
saying the same prayers.
          Always
the same girl (golden-haired)
dead in her coffin.

At the fifth hour I am beside the grave.
Altar-boy.
I am made of stone (pink marble)
My thurible is black.
          If I close
my eyes, only two facts remain
unanswerable: why incense, sprinkled
over charcoal, smells so sweet;
and why, above my head, invisible
among the trees, rain whispers endlessly?

Ciaran Carson

b. 1948

THE INSULAR CELTS

Having left hard ground behind
in the hardness of their place-names,
they have sailed out for an island:

as along the top of a wood
their boats have crossed the green ridges,
so has the pale sky overhead

appeared as a milky surface,
a white plain where the speckled fish
drift in lamb-white clouds of fleece.

As their sails will be covering
for the first houses that they build,
so their boats will be hovering

in the smoke of their first fires,
like red blood falling will be
their landing on the first shores.

They will come back to the warm earth
and call it by possessive names:
mother, thorned rose, woman, love's birth;

to hard hills of stone they will give
the words for breast; to meadowland,
the soft gutturals of rivers,

tongues of water; to firm plains, flesh,
as one day we will discover
their way of living, in their death.

They entered their soft beds of soil
not as graves, for this was the land
that they had fought for, loved, and killed

each other for. They'd arrive again:
death could be no horizon
but the shoreline of their island,

a coming and going as flood
comes after ebb. In the spirals
of their brooches is seen the flight

of one thing into the other:
as the wheel-ruts on a battle-
plain have filled with silver water,

the confused circles of their wars,
their cattle-raids, have worked themselves
to a laced pattern of old scars.

In their speckled parchments we read
of word-play in the halls of kings,
of how these people loved to fight,

yet where are their fine houses now?
They are hammered into the ground,
they have been laid bare by the plough.

Yet their death, since it is no real
death, will happen over again
and again, their bones will seem still

to fall in the hail beneath hooves
of horses, their limbs will drift down
as the branches that trees have loosed.

We cannot yet say why or how
they could not take things as they were.
Some day we will learn of how

their bronze swords took the shape of leaves;
their gold spears are found in cornfields,
their arrows are found in trees.

Paul Muldoon

b. 1951

DANCERS AT THE MOY

This Italian square
And circling plain
Black once with mares
And their stallions,
The flat Blackwater
Turning its stones

Over hour after hour
As their hooves shone
And lifted together
Under the black rain,
One or other Greek war
Now coloured the town

Blacker than ever before
With hungry stallions
And their hungry mares
Like hammocks of skin,
The flat Blackwater
Unable to contain

Itself as horses poured
Over acres of grain
In a black and gold river.
No band of Athenians
Arrived at the Moy fair
To buy for their campaign,

Peace having been declared
And a treaty signed.
The black and gold river

Ended as a trickle of brown
Where these horses tore
At briars and whins,

Ate the flesh of each other
Like people in famine.
The flat Blackwater
Hobbled on its stones
With a wild stagger
And sag in its backbone,

The local people gathered
Up the white skeletons.
Horses buried for years
Under the foundations
Give their earthen floors
The ease of trampolines.

HEDGEHOG

The snail moves like a
Hovercraft, held up by a
Rubber cushion of itself,
Sharing its secret

With the hedgehog. The hedgehog
Shares its secret with no one.
We say, Hedgehog, come out
Of yourself and we will love you.

We mean no harm. We want
Only to listen to what
You have to say. We want
Your answers to our questions.

The hedgehog gives nothing
Away, keeping itself to itself.
We wonder what a hedgehog
Has to hide, why it so distrusts.

We forget the god
Under this crown of thorns.
We forget that never again
Will a god trust in the world.

Gregory O'Donoghue
b. 1951

THE WEB

Who wd. cope in this Quick
newmovingworld Brings
a tightfist to bear.
Chas. knows; the great coin in his head sings
And he, solid citizen, wd. dare
to refuse. (we kin
Chiefly murmur a surrogate Truth) Cait
brings gracefully in
Word of our safe unstrange world.

And a man, whose manners
Are perfect as god is good,
sits by the fire. Sits all crooked
& says, 'world . . . ee each know . . . do not imagine
mow tur cars changed it.'
And that old man, Fr. c. says,
Knows his onions . . . And this can go on
In any drawingroom (in civil i
                              zation) an incred
                                                    ib
                                                    ly
                                                    long time . . .

Acknowledgements

Permission to use copyright material is gratefully acknowledged to the following:

Diarmuid Russell and A. M. Heath & Co. for poems by A. E.; Calder & Boyars Ltd., Faber & Faber Ltd., and the author for poems by Samuel Beckett; Beatrice Behan and Hutchinson & Co. for a translation by Brendan Behan; Allen Figgis & Co. and the author for a poem and translation by Eavan Boland; Simon Campbell for poems by Joseph Campbell; the Dolmen Press and James Carney for his translation; Ciaran Carson for his poem; the Gallery Press and the author for poems and a translation by Eiléan Ní Chuilleanáin; the Dolmen Press and the author for poems and translations by Austin Clarke; the New Writers Press and the author for a poem by Brian Coffey; Oxford University Press for a poem and translations by Padraic Colum; Maurice James Craig for his song; the author and the New Writers Press for poems by Anthony Cronin; the Irish University Press and the author for a poem by Seamus Deane; the Dolmen Press for poems by Denis Devlin; Eilis Dillon for her translation; George Buchanan for poems by John Lyle Donaghy; Charles Donnelly's brother for a poem by Charles Donnelly; the Dolmen Press and the author for poems by Padraic Fallon; the Clarendon Press for translations by Robin Flower; for a song by Gogarty, to his executors; A. P. Watt & Son and the author for poems and a translation by Robert Graves; George Campbell Hay for his translation; the New Writers Press and the author for poems by Michael Hartnett; Faber & Faber Ltd. and the author for poems by Seamus Heaney; John Hewitt for his poems; May Higgins for poems by F. R. Higgins; the Gallery Press and the author for poems by Pearse Hutchinson; Mrs. Una Sealy and the Dr. Douglas Hyde Trust for translations by Douglas Hyde; the Dolmen Press and the author for poems and a translation by Valentin Iremonger; to Random House for a poem by Robinson Jeffers; the Society of Authors for poems by James Joyce; Katherine

Kavanagh and Martin Brian and O'Keeffe Ltd. for poems by Patrick Kavanagh; Joan Keefe for her translation; John V. Kelleher for his translations; Allen Figgis & Co. and the author for a poem by Brendan Kennelly; the Dolmen Press and the author for poems and translations by Thomas Kinsella; Victor Gollancz Ltd. and the author for poems by Michael Longley; Christine, Lady Longford for translations by the Sixth Earl of Longford; Sean Lucy for his translation; Faber & Faber Ltd. and the executors of Thomas and Donagh MacDonagh for poems and translations by Thomas and Donagh MacDonagh; A. P. Watt & Son and the estate of Patrick MacDonogh for poems by Patrick MacDonogh; the Dolmen Press and Maire MacEntee (Mrs. Cruise O'Brien) for her translations; the New Writers Press and Margaret Farrington for a poem by Thomas MacGreevy; the New Writers Press and Thomas MacIntyre for his translation; Faber & Faber Ltd. the estate of Louis MacNeice for poems by Louis MacNeice; Oxford University Press and the author for poems by Derek Mahon; the Dolmen Press and David Marcus for part of his translation of *The Midnight Court*; Vivian Mercier for his translation; Constable & Co. Ltd. for translations by Kuno Meyer; Ewart Milne for his poems; the Dolmen Press and the author for poems and translations by John Montague; Faber & Faber Ltd. and the author for poems by Paul Muldoon; Faber & Faber Ltd. and 'Poetry' (Chicago) for poems by Richard Murphy; A. D. Peters & Co. for translations by Frank O'Connor; Gregory O'Donoghue for his poem; Desmond O'Grady for his poem; the Dolmen Press for a translation by Desmond O'Grady; Evelyn O'Nolan for translations by Brian O'Nolan alias Flann O'Brien, and for passages from *At Swim Two Birds*, Hart-Davis, MacGibbon; Ruth Ó Riada for a translation by Seán Ó Riada; Dr. Michael Solomons for poems by Seamus O'Sullivan; George Reavey for his poems; Oxford University Press for poems by W. R. Rodgers; the Dolmen Press and the author for poems by Richard Ryan; the Bodley Head and the author for poems and translations by James Simmons; Robin Skelton and the Oxford University Press for poems by John Millington Synge; Mrs. I. Wise, the Macmillan Company of Canada and Macmillan, London and Basingstoke for a poem and a paragraph from *Irish Fairy Tales* by James Stephens; the Society of Authors for the version of *O'Bruadair* by James Stephens;

Arland Ussher for part of his translation of *The Midnight Court*; to Constable and Co., the Dolmen Press and the author for a poem by Richard Weber; Penguin Classics and J. F. Webb for a paragraph from his translation of *The Voyage of St. Brendan;* the Reverend Lawrence Wilson for a poem by R. N. D. Wilson; A. P. Watt & Son for poems by W. B. Yeats; the author and the New Writers Press for poems and a translation by Augustus Young.

While every effort has been made to secure permission, it has in a few cases proved impossible to trace the author or his executor. We apologize for our apparent negligence.

I would like to acknowledge the help I have received from the staff attached to the Irish Collection of the Central Department of the Dublin County Library in Pearse Street. Also many people who have made suggestions, particularly Valentin Iremonger whose idea this anthology originally was.

Index of Poets and Translators

Index of First Lines